Quiet Passion

Also by S. V. Dáte

S. V. DÁTE

Quiet Passion

A BIOGRAPHY OF
SENATOR BOB GRAHAM

Jeremy P. Tarcher/Penguin
a member of Penguin Group (USA) Inc. · New York

Most Tarcher/Penguin books are available at special quantity discounts for bulk purchase for sales promotions, premiums, fund-raising, and educational needs. Special books or book excerpts also can be created to fit specific needs. For details, write Penguin Group (USA) Inc. Special Markets, 375 Hudson Street, New York, NY 10014.

Jeremy P. Tarcher/Penguin
a member of
Penguin Group (USA) Inc.
375 Hudson Street
New York, NY 10014
www.penguin.com

Library of Congress Cataloging-in-Publication Data

Dáte, S. V. (Shirish V.)
    Quiet passion : a biography of Senator Bob Graham / S. V. Dáte.
        p.   cm.
    Includes bibliographical references and index.
    ISBN 1-58542-304-1
      1. Graham, Bob, 1936–   .   2. Legislators—United States—
    Biography.   3. United States. Congress. Senate—Biography.
    4. Presidential candidates—United States—Biography.
    5. Governors—Florida—Biography.   6. Florida—Politics and
    government—1951–   I. Title.
    E840.8.G665D38   2004   2003061398
    973.931'092—dc22
    [B]

Printed in the United States of America
10 9 8 7 6 5 4 3 2 1

This book is printed on acid-free paper. ∞

BOOK DESIGN BY MEIGHAN CAVANAUGH

For Mary Beth, Orion, and Rigel

Acknowledgments

Many thanks to the following for their insights and memories, for research assistance and access to files, for sharing photographs and arranging schedules, for their time and their patience:

BILL ADAIR	RICK FLAGG	BETTY PARKER
PAUL ANDERSON	ADELE GRAHAM	JOHN PROVENZANO
TYLER BRIDGES	PATRICIA GRAHAM	BECKY ROHR
FRANK CERABINO	WILLIAM A. GRAHAM	BILL ROSE
BILL COTTERELL	WILLIAM E. GRAHAM	DAVE ROYSE
BRIAN CROWLEY	CONNIE LAROSSA	KRISTINA SAUNDERS
RAJ DÁTE	LARRY LIPMAN	JAMAL SIMMONS
KRISTIAN DENNY	FRANK LOCONTO	GWYN SURFACE
MARTIN DYCKMAN	GWEN LOGAN	JOHN VAN GIESON
GARY FINEOUT	MARK LOGAN	MIKE VASILINDA

Special thanks to University of Florida oral historian extraordinaire, Professor Samuel Proctor, and the helpful staff at the Oral History Project. Dr. Proctor, over a period of a dozen years, compiled thirty hours of audiotaped interviews with Senator Graham, covering everything from his parents' childhood to the aftermath of the 2000 election. Simply put: This book would not have been anywhere near as comprehensive without Dr. Proctor's legwork. I, and I hope my readers, are forever grateful.

Thanks also to the Graham clan, particularly William A. Graham, for opening his home and sharing the details of an amazing American story. For this, he and his whole family have my deepest gratitude.

Finally, there are six individuals without whose assistance this book absolutely would not have happened.

First, Ken Siman, my editor at Tarcher, who thought of me for this project, guided it, provided much-appreciated assurances at difficult moments, and helped bring it in for a landing. I am in his debt.

Next, thanks to John Bartosek and Paul Blythe at the *Palm Beach Post*, for allowing me to serve two masters for a period of months. It made their lives harder, and they didn't have to do it. I appreciate their indulgence.

Most important, I must thank my wife, Mary Beth, and my sons, Orion and Rigel, whose patience and understanding over the past spring and summer have made this book possible—carrying on the semblance of normal family life while Daddy burrowed into his office for hours, even days, on end. I owe all three of them big time.

Contents

Author's Note

I have provided sources for all quotations that I did not personally collect. If quotations do not show a source, the reader may assume that they came either from an interview I conducted over the course of researching this book or of writing articles for the *Palm Beach Post*, or, in the alternative, from audiotape or videotape provided to me.

Quiet Passion

Senator
Graham Cracker

It is a breezy late Monday evening in November 1998 on the tarmac at Miami International Airport, and Florida's slate of Democratic candidates is putting on the bravest face possible.

They have spent all day flying around the state on a chartered American Airlines turboprop, from West Palm Beach to Jacksonville to Tallahassee . . . all the major television markets—one last chance to get out the message, encourage everyone to go vote.

They already know it's not much use. The next day, their internal polling has shown, the top of their ticket, Lieutenant Governor Buddy MacKay, as nice and as smart a guy as they come but a hapless campaigner, will go down in flames against Jeb Bush, more than likely starting a period of Republican domination lasting God only knows how long. It is the end of an era. Lawton Chiles is stepping down after two terms as governor, and it could be a long time before Democrats see anywhere near the kind of influence they are about to cede.

Yet over at the end of the row of grim faces is one pretty cheerful one. He looks much younger than his sixty-two years, with chipmunk cheeks, a friendly twinkle, and an odd necktie decorated with diagonal rows of little tiny Floridas. He's cheerful because *his* internal polling shows he will trounce the polite but callow hack the Republicans have sent up against him and will return to Washington for his third term in the United States Senate.

As the TV lights go down and the reporters scurry off to write their scripts for eleven o'clock, he finds one of them who's new to the state and hasn't yet heard his theme song. He needs no further prompting. In a proud, off-key baritone, he belts it out:

"Bob Graham is a cracker,
Be a Graham Cracker Backer!
Vote the man who will make Florida work again!"

His career has spanned the decades between Florida's most notorious women politicians—at the one end orange juice pitch lady Anita Bryant, saving Florida from homosexuals; at the other, the Cruella De Vil of the 2000 Election, Katherine Harris, saving the nation from Florida Democrats.

Through it all, Bob Graham not only survived, he thrived. Five times he stood for statewide election—over a stretch that saw Florida's population swell from 9 million to 15 million—and five times he won. His *average* margin of victory? Twenty-two points.

And through it all, political friend and foe alike found it impossible to pigeonhole him into any particular box:

He doesn't like to build prisons—but was the first governor to enforce capital punishment in the modern era of the death penalty.

He is at heart a shy man—who nonetheless will now jump up on stage with his pal Jimmy Buffett and sing his heart out.

He's as brainy as they come—but for a quarter century has been getting elected as the everyman next door.

He's one of the toughest foreign policy "hawks" from his party in a generation—but voted against President George W. Bush's Iraq war.

He is known as an even-tempered, moderate, never-seeks-the-credit, *boring*, consensus-builder in the Senate—but this is what he said to his colleagues on the floor of that chamber, arms waving, fingers pointing, when they refused to focus American attention on terrorist groups like al Qaeda and Hezbollah instead of Iraq's Saddam Hussein:

"We're not *talking* about a threat ninety days from now. We're not talking about a threat that may come *a year* from now if nuclear material is made available. *I'm* talking about a threat that can happen this *afternoon!*" Graham raged in a now famous eight-minute, fifty-three-second tirade. "If you reject that, and think that the American people are not going to be at additional threat, then, frankly, my friends—to use a blunt term—the blood's going to be on *your* hands."

With a new Holstein's valve in his heart, and the chubbiness back in his cheeks, Florida's favorite politician—a serious man with serious ideas who has managed somehow not to take *himself* too seriously—had, after decades of delayed expectations, finally made the jump onto the national stage.

Tracing Daniel Robert "Bob" Graham's life is like following a thread holding together various panels of Florida's and America's political tapestry over the past six decades.

His father, Ernest R Graham, was a state senator who came in third in the Democratic primary for governor in 1944 in a six-candidate field. A second-place finish would have put him in the runoff. Older brother Philip married the daughter of the publisher of the *Washington Post*, and turned a second-rate daily into a media empire while putting together the Kennedy–Johnson presidential ticket in 1960. When Philip's manic depression drove him to suicide in 1963, sister-in-law Katharine Graham took the *Post*'s helm, guided it through the Watergate crisis, and became a legend.

Philip met Katharine Meyer only because he went to Harvard Law School—which happened only because Florida legend and prominent alum Claude Pepper did Ernest Graham a favor and pulled strings to get the academically challenged Philip accepted.[1] And just to round things out with Claude Pepper and Philip Graham: Philip's college roommate at the University of Florida was none other than George Smathers, who, accord-

---

[1] Which means, when you think about it, that but for Claude Pepper, the *Washington Post* probably wouldn't have had the stature in 1973 to have broken the Watergate scandal. On the other hand, without Pepper, Philip Graham would not have been in a position to persuade Jack and Bobby Kennedy to put Lyndon Johnson on the 1960 presidential ticket, which probably would have meant that Richard Nixon would have become president that year, which would have meant there *wouldn't have been* a Watergate break-in in 1972. So never mind.

Bob and Adele Graham, 2003. *(Courtesy of the Graham for President Campaign.)*

ing to the urban legend, unseated Pepper from the Senate using accusations that he was known as a shameless extrovert and that his sister was a thespian in wicked New York.[2]

Bob Graham was a law school contemporary of Michael Dukakis, who later almost put him on a presidential ticket, and Janet Reno, whom Graham three decades later introduced to a president who was having a tough time finding a female attorney general who didn't have a nanny problem. That president, Bill Clinton, was a fellow Democratic governor in the class of 1978 and a close enough friend to call Graham to offer advice when Graham was dealing with the first execution in the United States following a dozen-year court-ordered hiatus.

And if all that weren't enough, Graham also had a tangential role in the undoing of Gary Hart in 1987. When the *Miami Herald* got its hot tip that a gorgeous blonde was on her way to Washington, D.C., for a tryst with Hart, the paper's reporters had a slight problem. They didn't know where Hart lived. Then one of them remembered that Graham's chief of staff,

---

[2]Smathers also supposedly told his backwoods North Florida audience that prior to his marriage, Pepper practiced celibacy. This is almost certainly apocryphal. But it makes a great story, doesn't it?

Buddy Shorstein, was renting an apartment in Hart's town house. A couple of phone calls provided the address. The rest is history.[3]

S o who is this guy?

For starters, D. Robert Graham, as he called himself when he first entered politics, is a policy wonk's policy wonk. Talk to him for any length of time, and details, names, places, and statistics come spewing forth in a torrent. He is a Harvard-trained lawyer and a multimillionaire, thanks to the pluck of his father and the financial acumen of older brother William, who thought to convert five square miles of scrub pastureland into one of the first planned communities in South Florida.

Notwithstanding all this, D. Robert Graham managed—through a brilliant string of campaign "workdays" during which he labored full, eight-hour shifts in a hundred different jobs, from bellboy to chicken plucker—to mold an image across Florida as plain old Bob. A common-sense guy who understood and worked for common Floridians.

"You never looked at him as a multimillionaire," said Republican congressman Mark Foley. "You looked at him as an average guy, and he always connected with people."

How did he connect? If you've ever chatted with Bob Graham, either governor or senator version, be it at a campaign rally or an airport or a restaurant, chances are pretty good that your name and address are listed in one of his much-maligned, color-coded, pocket-sized notebooks. More than likely, your entry in those annals has resulted in your receiving a personalized letter from him remarking upon the meeting and wishing you well. If you are like most people, that meeting, and the interest Graham showed you during it, will generate warm feelings toward him for years to come.

Foley said he remembered an Everglades meeting a decade ago with Graham, then-Governor Chiles, Lieutenant Governor MacKay, and himself in Chiles's office. As Foley spoke, Graham took notes. "I'm noticing: '9:45, Mark Foley said,'" Foley recalled. "That was the endearing part of

---

[3]Meaning, one can infer, that Gary Hart might have been president in 1988 had Bob Graham not been elected to the Senate two years earlier.

Bob Graham in the sense of he always acted so interested in you. . . . He'd write codes on the back of business cards. You always knew it went somewhere. It wasn't like, you know, a lot of people take your card, and you know that's probably going in the trash bucket."

Talk to politicos and journalists in Florida who have spent any time with Graham and they'll explain there is a simple reason why Graham is well liked: He is a likable guy. And he has been able to win Republican friends, and votes, because he's not a terribly partisan politician.

Tom Slade was Florida GOP chairman when Graham was running for reelection to the U.S. Senate in 1998. Right after the debate between Graham and Republican challenger Charlie Crist, Slade, the guy whose job it was to defeat Graham and get Crist elected, went out for dinner and drinks—with *Graham*.

"I consider him a buddy," said Slade, who knew him from his days in the Florida legislature in the late 1960s.

In 1983, over strong objections from Democratic leaders, then-Governor Graham appointed a Republican, former CIA analyst Porter Goss, to the Lee County Commission. Goss was later elected to Congress, and in 2002 chaired the House Intelligence Committee while Graham ran the Senate counterpart. The two worked together to investigate the September 11 attacks, and in late 2003, the political career that Graham started for him seemed as if it might culminate in Goss being named director of the CIA.

Even Foley, a Republican aiming for Graham's Senate seat, had only kind words:

"You can't help but like a man who's endured thirty years of Florida politics," Foley said. "He's a wonderful father, he's a great, great husband to Adele. They're a wonderful couple. You look at his whole family and they're just beautiful people, and they've lived in the limelight of Governor's Mansion, national politics, wealth, fame, and all of them are the most normal, nice people," Foley said. "None of them are troublemakers, none of them are thrill seekers, none of them are in the news for doing errant behavior. They're just beautiful people, and you respect him for that."

For his part, Graham said he has tried hard to keep separate the rancor inherent in political campaigns from every other part of his life.

"I have been able to maintain and generally enhance the positive friendship of all the people I have ever run against politically. That is, I do not have anybody that I carry any negative feelings about, and I do not believe they carry any negative feelings about me—which I consider to be a very positive part of a long political career."[4]

Spend any time with him and what becomes clear pretty quickly is that with Graham, what you see is what you get. He doesn't have fancy, television hair. He doesn't wear expensive suits. In a town where even lowly House members ride around in giant black SUVs, Graham drives a 1999 Mercury Sable station wagon. There are no airs about him. He is worth many millions, but the fact does not seem to have dawned on him.

"He was in a position to be spoiled rotten," said lifelong friend Robin Gibson. "Basically an only child in a wealthy family. But that was not the case."

He is notoriously frugal—his friends call him tight. He blames it on being a Scot. Older brother Bill is much the same way. He is even richer than Bob, having been the child who fell into the role of running the family business, but it doesn't show. His ranch in Albany, Georgia, has a modest, well, *ranch*-style house still decorated in 1970s-era dark paneling and wall-to-wall rugs—a Brady Bunch house without the second story.

"We're not palace people," daughter Gwen Logan says simply.

She and her husband of one year shared a condo with her dad for his first year in the U.S. Senate, while her mom, Adele, stayed in Tallahassee to let youngest daughter Kendall finish high school there. This was right after having lived eight years in Florida's Governor's Mansion, with its retinue of cooks and housekeepers and drivers. She remembers how easy the adjustment to doing everything for themselves again was because her dad was perfectly happy taking care of himself.

"He enjoyed doing his own laundry," she said. "He's pretty low-maintenance. He thinks spaghetti is gourmet."

He is the goofy but lovable father who would make race-car noises as he drove his children to school, or who would wake up his youngest daughter each morning singing *"It's Leon High School time, it's Leon High School*

---

[4]University of Florida Oral History Project, Tapes A–E, February 13, 1989.

time," to the tune of "It's Howdy Doody Time." At least that was slightly less annoying than what he sang to wake up eldest daughter Gwen: *"It's time to wake up / It's time to wake up / It's time to wake up in the morning."*

The singing—let's be clear here: very *bad* singing—is somewhat of a trademark. Anyone who has watched a three-year-old caught up in some activity, happy as a clam, singing to himself at the top of his lungs, never within half an octave of the correct key, can relate to this. Graham loves to sing and will do so at the drop of a hat. Sometimes even without the drop of a hat.

Explaining that he'd lost a bet with the governor of Oklahoma over the 1981 Orange Bowl football game, Graham told the Tallahassee press corps that he was on his way to Oklahoma to perform one of his celebrated "workdays" in an oil field there—and then quickly burst into Rodgers and Hammerstein: *"Ooooooooook-lahoma where the wind comes sweepin' down the plain...."* [5]

In the summer of 2000, arriving in Nashville for Tennessee's annual Jackson Day dinner for that state's Democratic Party, Graham spotted two guys with guitars on their backs at the airport and inquired as to their occupations. Upon learning they were, indeed, musicians, he asked whether they'd heard of "Tension on the Surface," a song he and a construction worker had written at a Daytona Beach workday four years earlier. They replied that, no sir, in fact they had not, which was all the excuse Graham needed: *"I got tension on the surface, but I'm boiling just below...."* [6]

And anybody who's seen Graham on the campaign trail—especially when he believes things are going his way—has heard his old standby, "We've Got a Friend in Bob Graham": *"We've got a friend in Bob Graham / That's what everybody's sayin' / All the way from Key West town to Tampa Bay."* [7]

In 1978, Graham actually released this as a 45 rpm single (remember those?).[8] The flip side was "The Farmer and Adele." [9]

A friend of Graham, South Florida songwriter/record producer Frank

---

[5]"People in the News," Associated Press, March 28, 1982.
[6]Brian E. Crowley, "Bob Graham as vice president? It's Now or Never," *Palm Beach Post,* August 4, 2000.
[7]Although Graham usually sings it: "*You've* got a friend...." See Appendix A for the official lyrics.
[8]Well, Franklin Delano Roosevelt had "Happy Days Are Here Again" and Harry Truman had "I'm Just Wild About Harry." Why shouldn't a politician in *this* century have a campaign song?
[9]Don't ask.

Loconto, wrote both of those twenty-five years ago. In 2003, he produced the presidential version of "We've Got a Friend" and seven other potential *Billboard* chart-toppers for the *Bob Graham Charisma Tour 2004* CD. Among the playlist: "Arriba Bob," "I've Done Every Job, Man," "My Adele," and the "G.W. Bushonomics, Supply Side Economics Blues."

No, Graham does not sing on the actual CD. That was left to professionals. Nevertheless, Graham will not concede his lack of singing ability. Of his detractors, he has this to say:

"Well, those are people who have no appreciation of music. They just want, you know, someone who is kind of a throwaway, as opposed to someone who understands the nuances of music and lyrics and the dynamic personality necessary to effectively communicate. All the qualities that I bring to my music."

B ob Graham is a funny guy. No—really. He is.[10]

For those whose knowledge of him consists of seeing his earnest and stiff performances on the Sunday-morning talk shows or listening to one of his formal campaign speeches, or reading the *Washington Post* magazine profile describing him as a modern-day Cassandra ("freakout candidate, a red-alert politician for a freakout nation"[11]), seeing the words "Bob Graham" and "funny" so close together in a sentence must seem patently absurd.

Anyone familiar with his long-winded, circuitous explanations of even the simplest questions might be similarly mystified. Ask Graham if he supports or opposes a particular program, and he is likely to go into a detailed dissertation on the pros and cons of both sides, along with brief corollary arguments that could also be relevant to the discussion, until finally eyes have glazed over and the original question forgotten.

Former Tallahassee journalist John Van Gieson said he remembered one press conference when a frustrated reporter finally demanded, over and over,

---

[10]See Appendix B for an essay Graham wrote about his relationship with the reporters covering him on the campaign.

[11]Michael Grunwald, "Running Scared; Bob Graham's Message to the Voters is Simple: However Frightened We Are, It Isn't Nearly Frightened Enough," *Washington Post*, May 4, 2003.

that Graham provide a simple yes or no. "He finally said, 'It was a yes,'" Van Gieson recalled. "Like it really pained him to say what he really meant."

Graham's University of Florida biographer, his old history professor from undergraduate days, occasionally encountered similar obfuscation. Samuel Proctor in a 1996 interview was trying to elicit details from Graham regarding disparaging remarks he made about Republican opponent Paula Hawkins in the 1986 Senate race—a contest that saw, by the end, its share of negative campaigning. Graham danced around the question for several minutes and then asked Proctor if that was sufficient response.

"That sounds just like the southern gentleman, a lot of mishmash without saying very much," Proctor said, and sighed, resigned to not getting an answer.[12]

Friend Robin Gibson explained that Graham believes that as an elected leader, his words will continue having meaning and consequence long after he's uttered them. "When he says things, that's part of the public record and the public domain and you can't take it back."

Balanced against that seriousness is a guy who, over the years, was able to emerge from his natural shyness into more or less a ham. Look, for example, at his participation in the annual press corps skits in Tallahassee during his years as governor. With each passing year, his productions became ever more extravagant.

One year, unlikely pal and Save the Manatee Club cofounder Jimmy Buffett came to the skits. Graham dressed like Buffett—flowered shirt, shorts, and flip-flops. Buffett dressed like Graham—dark suit and polyester necktie covered with the tiny Floridas. (Buffett, of course, had arrived in Tallahassee not even owning a suit. "How can you not have a suit?" Graham scolded. "Didn't your mother give you one?") Together they sang "Wastin' Away Again in Tallahasseeville."

Another year, Graham dressed like the artist formerly known as Prince, and had the Florida State University Golden Girls backing him up.[13] But he outdid himself his final year in the Governor's Mansion when he nar-

---

[12]University of Florida Oral History Project, Tapes Q–R, January 11, 1996.
[13]Yes, he was actually up on stage in a ridiculous getup, shakin' his groove *thang*. You know . . . he didn't do half bad for a guy in his mid-forties.

rated a video, offering snarky impersonations of the six candidates who hoped to succeed him. At the end of the tape he marched onstage dressed in a white Prussian Army uniform, complete with shoulder boards, campaign medals, and sword, and declared himself Governor for Life. "Ladies and gentlemen, I am here to bring the *dignity* back to *dictatorship*," he proclaimed, then motioned for the Florida A&M University Marching 100 band behind him to strike up "Hail to the Chief."

Graham humor has rarely since then found such a big canvas. It more typically has been much drier and much smaller.

When his biographer, Proctor, told Graham that, yes, he owned a copy of Graham's 1978 campaign book, *Workdays*, Graham deadpanned: "What I hope is that you have more than just one. It is the kind of thing that you need to have at your fingertips whether you are in the office or not."[14]

In 1994, former legislative antagonist Curt Kiser found himself running as a lieutenant governor candidate in the Republican primary, which meant placing phone calls begging for campaign money at every available opportunity. Kiser had once been the House Republican leader—that is to say: Whatever proposal Graham and his allies would offer, Kiser's job would be to jump up and make a speech about why it was a dumb idea. (This actually hurt Graham's feelings at first, and he called Kiser into his office to lecture him about it. Kiser told him not to take it personally.)

One July afternoon a decade and a half later in the Miami International Airport concourse, Graham saw an opportunity to even the score. Kiser was waiting for a flight, making some of his fund-raising calls. Graham had just walked off a plane, a bag over one shoulder, when he walked up to Kiser and snatched the phone away. "Listen, whoever you are, do not give this man any money. He will not use it for any proper purpose, I can assure you," Graham told the caller. Then he handed the phone back to Kiser, smiled, and was on his way.

Another time, Graham was explaining that his cameo in a 1985 Jimmy Buffett video made him the only governor to have appeared in a music video. When he was told that Louisiana governor Edwin Edwards had ap-

---

[14]University of Florida Oral History Project, Tape J, August 9, 1989.

peared in Fats Domino and Cajun fiddler Doug Kershaw's video of the song "My Toot Toot," Graham was quick to correct himself: "I guess that makes me the only *unindicted* governor to be in a music video."[15]

The rest of America finally got a taste of Graham humor later in the summer. The topic, of all things, was the September 11 hijackers and the assistance they may have received from a foreign government. Bob Schieffer, host of CBS News' *Face the Nation*, pressed Graham: Wasn't the foreign government Saudi Arabia?

Graham, whose tenure as chairman of the Senate Intelligence Committee in the year following those attacks informs his criticisms of the Bush administration policy, answered Schieffer: "Well, I do not want to take a detour to the federal penitentiary in my campaign for president, so I cannot confirm the foreign government."

Bob Graham talks like most people write. Correction: Bob Graham talks even more formally than most people write. Few contractions. Multiple, complex, dependent clauses. No sentences ending with prepositions.[16] Most people would say: "It's not gonna happen, is it?" Graham says it: "That seems rather unlikely, does it not?"

Here is what he told Proctor about why his father kept the nickname "Cap" long after his service in World War I: "I do not know what the basis of carrying that nickname was, but it was the most prevalent way by which he was addressed."[17]

Sometimes Graham-speak gets downright impenetrable. In his "blood on your hands" speech, instead of asking, "Why do you disagree?" Graham asked: "If you disagree with that premise, what is the basis upon which your disagreement is predicated?"[18]

Not long after he'd been in the Senate, Graham once said this, extemporaneously, about the possibility of a particular federal program taking ef-

---

[15]Frank Cerabino, "Graham Goes from Governor to Senator," *Palm Beach Post*, May 4, 2003.
[16]Sort of like the *Lost in Space* robot early on, back when he still possessed that vaguely menacing quality.
[17]University of Florida Oral History Project, Tapes A–E, February 13, 1989.
[18]See Appendix C for complete transcript of the "Blood on Your Hands" speech.

Jimmy Buffett with Adele and Bob Graham, 1987. *(Courtesy office of Senator Bob Graham.)*

fect: ". . . which I think will compound the already serious problems that we have with this legislation, in its inchoate form we have today."[19]

Inchoate. What kind of person uses *inchoate* in everyday speech? What kind of person even knows what *inchoate* means?

A walking dictionary/world almanac/encyclopedia, that's who. This is a senator who reads all the reports he's given, who understands subtle nuances of policy debates, who can recite historical facts and statistics off the top of his head.

In New Hampshire, asked about a Senate that blocks judicial appointments, Graham spun off on a history lesson, pointing out that the Founding Fathers gave the Senate and the president specific roles in the choosing of judges for a good reason: so that no one branch would have a dominant role over the independent judiciary. He referred those who wanted more

[19]*The Congressional Record—Senate*, November 19, 1989, p. S16199.

background on the matter to page 103 of *John Adams,* which was written by Pulitzer Prize–winning historian David McCullough, who just happens to be the father-in-law of his second daughter, Cissy.

"And by buying the book, you would also help put three of my grandchildren through college."

As governor, Graham took the time to master the subjects and digest the details of questions that came before him. Anyone who follows government knows how rare an animal this is—an elected official with both the brains and the work ethic to read and understand the guts of an issue, not just the executive summary. Typically, this function is relegated to a staff member with the particular expertise in that area, who in turn coaches the elected official through the problem.

Ed Montanaro, a tax policy expert within Graham's Office of Planning and Budget during his years as governor, still recalls with amazement Graham's ability to understand complex economic theories. In fact, Montanaro said, Graham understood in detail pretty much *all* the subject areas within his domain.

"He could have been his own staff, except for time," Montanaro said. "He could have been an economist, he could have done the budget, he could have done any job on his staff."

"He's a cerebral guy," said former House member Sam Bell. "He's smart. And he thinks. And that's not necessarily a good thing in public office."

Graham's thirty-seven-year public career has been remarkable for its longevity and its overarching rationality.

Few politicians have stayed in public life as long in Florida—Claude Pepper's name comes to mind—a state with an electorate with a notoriously short attention span. Prior to Graham's winning the Senate seat he holds, it had changed hands three times in three elections.

And over those decades, Graham has made his mark by adopting beliefs based on deliberate, rational analysis: a process that seems odd largely because so few politicians practice it. While most come to the stage with a prefabricated list of beliefs—"taxes are bad, regulation is bad, private sector is good," for example, has been an extremely popular platform in recent years in Florida—Graham comes to his positions on issues slowly, and only after intense research.

The practice has maddened reporters trying to get a straight answer and party legislative leaders trying to line up votes. Interestingly, it has not maddened Florida voters, who have returned him to office with margins other politicians, Democratic or Republican, would drool over.

Graham was a "deficit hawk," arguing for a balanced federal budget, long before that became cool among Democrats. Graham supported military action by Republican presidents Reagan and Bush in Nicaragua, Grenada, and Panama, irking Democratic congressional leaders.

At the same time, he has broken from Democrats in his vocal opposition to President George W. Bush both on tax cuts and, most famously, the second Iraq war.

And in thirty-seven years, only two of Graham's high-profile positions have the whiff of cynicism or political expediency: one, his energetic support of the death penalty during his eight years as governor, and two, his support during the 2000 Elián Gonzalez affair of putting the six-year-old in the care of the Miami Relatives rather than the boy's father.

In the Elián Gonzalez case, it seems more than a little incongruous that a man so deeply attached to his own children and grandchildren could oppose a father's right to his own son, even if he does live in a communist dictatorship. The position helped Graham maintain his high standing with the Cuban-American community, an influential swing vote in Florida. In Graham's defense, he has for decades sided firmly with the exile community in Miami—his hometown—in its insistence that Castro be isolated, if not overthrown outright.

And in the case of the death penalty, Graham signed death warrants at a furious pace that set the standard for governors to come, including at least three in which the condemned men appeared to be innocent of the crimes and ultimately were released. Graham, while stating that he was merely carrying out the law of the land, did so with startling enthusiasm. In 1986, the year he was running for the Senate, Graham signed three separate death warrants for the serial killer Ted Bundy, a new record.

Similarly, even if Graham's support of the death penalty is not *based* on politics, it is clear he appreciates the politics of the issue. In 1986, as he started his Senate campaign, Graham touted his death penalty record, boasting among his criminal justice accomplishments that he had, to that point, signed more than 130 death warrants. Yet in 2003, running for president in the Democratic primary, the Graham campaign's fact sheet on criminal justice issues was curiously silent on capital punishment.

B ob Graham doesn't talk much about God.[20]
This is a trait that flowed from his father. While his mother, Hilda, took young Bob to Sunday school, well, religiously, his father rarely attended. Dad was "a very ethical, moral person, but was not a formal religious person," Graham said during his oral history interviews, adding that his mother actually wanted him to enter the ministry. Graham's discomfort on the subject came through when biographer Proctor pursued the ministry question—allowing Graham to veer off on one of his favorite jokes:

"At one time, she felt that I would go into the ministry, and I have said that I hope there is reincarnation, because I am not going to be able to do all the things that I want to do this first time around. That is one of the things, as well as being an architect and a . . ."—here Proctor interjects: history professor?—"well, before the history professor, I would like to be a short reliever for the Los Angeles Dodgers."[21]

Graham, when pressed, concedes that his value structure[22] is not centered around organized religion. He described himself as an "ecumenical Protestant," a member of the United Church of Christ in the community he and his family built, Miami Lakes. That church was actually the first recruited for the town in the early 1960s, according to brother Bill, precisely because it was relatively nondenominational.

---

[20]Some voters may find this offensive; others will likely find it a blessed relief to be spared sanctimonious talk from politicians begging for their support.

[21]University of Florida Oral History Project, Tapes A–E, February 13, 1989.

[22]And, after almost four decades in elected office, it is obvious that he does have a strong one. He's come close to scandal only once, in his dealings with a crooked savings-and-loan operator named David Paul.

"I attend church sporadically," Graham said in 1989. "I probably go to church maybe an average of once a month and then attend at Easter and Christmas. Formal religion has not been a major part of my life. I think, like my father—about whom the same statement could be made—that religious values and an attempt to live a life that embodied ethical and moral principles has been an important part of my life. I am certain my religious training contributed to that."[23]

Graham *does* like to hold forth on the subject of his family.

Spend any time with him at all, and out will come the snapshots of the ten grandchildren and the explanation that their nickname for him is "Doodle"—except when he's done something exceptional, in which case it's "Super-Doodle." Graham attributes his attachment to his children's children to his inability to be around more during his own children's youth.

"I wish that I'd had more time to spend with my children as they were growing up. That occurred during the time that I was most active in politics, running for governor, then serving. Maybe I am particularly doting on my grandchildren because of that."

The job of raising his own daughters fell to Graham's wife, Adele, who since his first election to state office has been the classic political wife, knowing what to say to whom and, when necessary, pointing these things out to her husband. As Florida's first lady, she was the ever-gracious hostess and anchor of the family for the girls, with Bob so often absorbed in work. And on the presidential campaign trail, Adele—who at sixty-five retains the classical, high-cheekboned, trim-figured beauty that allowed her to work as a teen model—was part cheerleader, part political tactician, equally adept at organizing four daughters and ten grandchildren for a "family invasion" of Iowa as reminding Bob to mention his record as governor during his speeches.

Technically, Bob met the former Adele Khoury in the late 1930s when

---

[23]University of Florida Oral History Project, Tapes A–E, February 13, 1989.

both were in the same nursery "cradle-roll" at Trinity Methodist Church in Miami during the hours that their moms attended Sunday school there. The daughter of a Lebanese immigrant who settled in Miami Shores, she attended the rival high school before enrolling at the University of Florida. She was a new freshman, having trouble with science classes, when Bob, a sophomore who was both shorter and nowhere near as good-looking, bravely volunteered his tutoring services nonetheless. By spring semester that year, they were dating steadily. The following year they were engaged, and early in spring semester of his senior year, they were married and living in an apartment behind the Rexall drugstore in Gainesville.

As Bob moved on to Harvard Law School, Adele transferred to Boston University to finish her degree, then went on to teach seventh-grade history in Wellesley. After they moved back to Florida in 1962, they became two of the first residents of Miami Lakes, the Graham family's new planned community they were building on father Ernest Graham's old cow pasture.

Eldest daughter Gwen came along in January 1963, followed over the next six years by three more daughters—Glyn (known as Cissy, because of how similar her name was to Gwen's), Suzanne, and Kendall. When Gwen was born, Adele Graham gave up her teaching career to raise the children. "Each one of these children, while still in gestation, was known as Ernest Robert, who was going to be the name of our son. But Ernest Robert has become this string of girls."[24]

It's easy to love your children and have them love you back when they are very young. Perhaps more telling is that Graham seems to have held the affection of his daughters through their teens and into young adulthood. Daughter Gwen was twenty-four when she and her new husband shared a town house with her dad, the new United States senator. When youngest daughter Kendall took an internship in Washington a few years later, she found a rental across the street from her parents' Capitol Hill home.

That home, for a decade and a half, has been a white-painted brick town

---

[24]University of Florida Oral History Project, Tapes A–E, February 13, 1989.

house with green trim and a neatly tended front garden.[25] A dairy cow wind chime hangs on the wrought-iron gate next to a Japanese plum, and a palm-tree-and-alligator decorative Florida flag angles out from beside the front door. Four minutes away on foot is the Hart Senate Office Building, where Graham can catch the Senate subway to the Capitol.

And that had been the Graham family life these past years. Bob in the Senate. Adele involved in her volunteer organizations. The two of them spending as much time as possible with as many of the grandkids as possible.

Until that Thursday evening, January 9, 2003, as they were driving back to their Capitol Hill town house from dinner at daughter Suzanne's house across the river in Virginia. It was a moment that seemed to cement in Adele's mind that her husband was serious about an idea that was certain to throw their comfortable existence into turmoil. Bob was behind the wheel of the silver station wagon as they drove up Pennsylvania Avenue, then up past 1600 Pennsylvania Avenue.

"He said, 'Maybe we'll be living in that house over there in a couple of years,'" Adele recalled.

Graham's belated, heart-surgery-delayed 2003 entry into the presidential race culminated what no less a political expert than his late sister-in-law, Kay Graham, once called a "strange fulfillment" of both his father's and his brother's political ambitions. Kay Graham was not alone. So many others—friends, elected peers, the political press—have similarly seen in

---

[25]As it happens, Graham bought the town house from fellow senator John Kerry—a purchase that brought some grief to Kerry several years later. Kerry and his first wife had spent a good deal of money restoring the place, putting in new heating, air-conditioning, wiring, plumbing, as well as bringing in a Boston architect to redesign the interior.

"He really got it into first-class shape. During the course of all that and maybe contributing to it, his marriage fell apart. By late 1988 he had a nice place for a family to live, but no family to live in it," Graham told his University of Florida biographer in 1996.

Kerry decided to sell the place and Bob and Adele snapped it up immediately—before Kerry had lined up a new place to live. And that wound up providing fodder for Kerry's Republican opponent, William Weld, in 1996. "The allegation was that some lobbyists provided him with places to live while he was trying to find a new apartment. I felt we may have contributed to John's distress in his campaign by having evicted him from this nice house and putting him at the mercy of the lobbyists."

Graham presidential material. No sooner had Carter been ousted from the White House in 1980 than political writers casting about for possible Democratic candidates for the job in the coming years started tossing Graham's name into the mix.

In 1991, then–Senate Majority Leader George Mitchell said this about his still-new colleague: "I think he's going to be president someday. I mean that sincerely. I think he has all the qualities, and he comes from a large and growing state."[26]

Graham himself did little to discourage such thinking, telling the *St. Petersburg Times* when asked whether he ever thought about the White House: "I guess the honest answer is yes, since I recognize that a lot of things I'm interested in seeing accomplished will be accomplished when there's effective presidential leadership on that subject."[27]

Which, of course, begs the question: What took him so long to try?

Samuel "Buddy" Shorstein, a college pal who served as Graham's Senate chief of staff for a dozen years, said he expected a bid as early as 1988 and said he wouldn't have been surprised by one in 1992. "I always thought he would make a run. I wondered if time had passed him by."

Not only did Graham not run in 1988, 1992, or 2000, but in each year he was flirted with as a possible running mate by the eventual nominee but not chosen. Never the bride, never even the bridesmaid.

"Now, as people start examining that record, they're saying: What has he done, and why has he become this late starter, late bloomer into the political process?" said Republican congressman Foley.

Foley's theory—one that can be applied to any number of Democrats in 1992—is that Graham must have kicked himself when Bill Clinton so easily knocked George H. W. Bush out of the White House. "I think there's some degree of angst that he didn't run in '92," Foley said. "I'm sure to this day Bob Graham sits there and says: That would have been and could have been my year. And I let it slide."

But former Graham aide and current California State University chancellor Charlie Reed said Graham did not believe in previous elections that

---

[26]David Dahl, "Graham: Mr. Inside on the Outside," *St. Petersburg Times*, October 13, 1991.
[27]*Ibid.*

he knew enough to be president. "He didn't feel that he was prepared. He didn't feel that he was intellectually prepared."

Graham said that, in previous years, he also lacked the fire in the belly anyone needs to put up with the grueling schedule, the begging for money, the inane press questions, and all the rest of it.

"I think there are many ingredients to running for president. But this issue of passion, that you feel that you have something to bring to the American people—it's not just your own ego—is critical to being success-ful as a candidate, and certainly is critical to your success as a president," Graham said during a drive along a New Hampshire back road. "And I did not have that sense of passion in 1992, or in any other presidential cam-paign until this one."

Graham found that passion—anger, certainly, perhaps even rage—in the agenda pursued by George W. Bush from pretty much the earliest days of his administration: an agenda he saw as highlighted by an energy policy written by the big oil companies for the big oil companies, rollbacks of en-vironmental standards, a "disastrous" tax-cut plan that put the nation back in the red, and, following September 11, a foreign policy fixated on Saddam Hussein instead of those terrorists who actually attacked the United States.

"I saw all the hard work that had gone into strengthening the economy by balancing the federal books evaporate, almost overnight. We went from a $5 trillion projected surplus to a $2 to $3 trillion addition to the national debt."

Graham can talk about the deficit fairly dispassionately. When his re-marks turn to what he learned during his year as chairman of the Senate Intelligence Committee, his voice and his gaze grow intense:

"Then, in the months since September 11, I saw the pattern of decep-tion that has now become so publicly evident that this administration was engaged in, and I became further outraged. The American people were be-ing shut out of information upon which they could make better decisions, and which was not of a national security interest. And this administration was avoiding accountability on many fronts through the use of secrecy. So those were the two factors that inspired my belly to run for president."

What finally clinched it for Graham, he said, was Iraq.

"The whole debate over Iraq, and what I thought was a serious failure to present to the American people what the real options were there. Nobody from the administration told the American people that, incidentally, in order to go to war in Iraq, we're going to have to essentially abandon the war on terrorism," Graham said. "Nobody told the American people that we will win the military phase of Iraq convincingly, and probably very quickly—*but*, once we have won the war, then we're going to be faced with a country that has been battered by three wars in the last thirty years, whose economy is in disarray, where you don't have a sense of a unified nation, rather a series of almost tribal groups which have historically hated each other and have killed each other. And that's the country you're going to be taking over. None of that was shared with the American people. And I think, because of that, we didn't get the kind of open debate among the citizens that a decision of this importance justifies."

Graham's belly, by finding its fire so late in life, dropped him squarely into the middle of the Bush Brothers' sibling rivalry.

After President George H. W. Bush was wrongfully evicted from the palace in 1992 by, of *all* people, a womanizing Arkansas hick, the assumption in many Republican circles was that it would be brother Jeb who would avenge the humiliation and restore the family honor. Well-spoken, polished, smart, hardworking Jeb. But then, inexplicably, Jeb *lost* the election in Florida he was supposed to win against Lawton Chiles. Just as inexplicably, on the other side of the Gulf, older brother George *won* the race he was supposed to lose against Ann Richards in Texas, and Jeb's carefully laid life's plan went to hell.

Four years later, Jeb finally became governor of Florida—but George was *re-elected* governor of Texas—and within weeks became the Republican front-runner for the 2000 presidential race.[28]

Now the best, perhaps only, chance for Jeb to become president of the United States of America[29] is for brother George to win handily in 2004 and clear the way for Jeb in 2008.

---

[28]As H. Ross Perot might say: How 'bout them apples!

[29]As he was *born* to do.

So along comes Bob Graham to poke a stick into *that* anthill? As anyone who has crossed a Bush can tell Graham, there would be consequences.[30]

Jeb did not campaign with George as much as he could have in 2000. Some suggested it was because he was miffed that George was going to get to be president. Others said he didn't want to upstage his brother at campaign events.[31] If Graham were to wind up as the *vice*-presidential nominee, Jeb will not sit on the sidelines. It can be assumed that his assignment will be simple: to destroy Bob Graham in Florida.

For political junkies, such a thing would be pure theater: Jeb, the man who would be king, versus the last great icon of the Democratic Party in Florida. Jeb Bush makes no apologies for rough campaigning, calling politics a "contact sport." Graham, though, is no slouch when the going gets tough. In both 1986 and 1998, when his Republican opponent hit him with hard ads, Graham came back just as hard, if not harder.

As it stands, Graham's brief presidential campaign provided other Democratic candidates valuable political cover for attacking President Bush. Graham, in over eight years as Florida governor and seventeen years in the United States Senate, has consistently supported the use of force to further what he perceived to be American interests.

As governor, when other governors were objecting to President Reagan's sending National Guard troops to train in Honduras during the *contra* war in neighboring Nicaragua, Graham said he thought governors should retain that peacetime authority but supported the stated mission. Later, as a senator, Graham irked liberal Democrats by supporting Reagan's efforts to send arms to the *contra* rebels. Graham supported the invasions of Grenada and Panama and the first Iraq war under the first President Bush.

So when Graham opposed the latest Iraq war, particularly with his background as chairman of the Senate Intelligence Committee, other Democrats could make those same assertions with less risk of being labeled unpatriotic.

The importance of this fact cannot be overstated. In 2003, President

---

[30]Just ask Michael Dukakis about Willie Horton.

[31]Because, the theory went, if the two were compared side by side, the obvious conclusion would be that the wrong brother was running for president.

George W. Bush's greatest strength, according to polls, was his foreign policy. Americans already were unsure about his tax cuts and deficits. So if the public lost confidence in Bush's ability to manage the war on terrorism, he would be left with little political capital beyond his personal appeal.

And if, despite all the effort, things don't work out? Graham had, in years past, expressed a philosophy that suggested he would come to terms with that, too:

"One of the most important things to do before you go into politics is to be certain that you have an alternative to politics," Graham explained years earlier in one of a series of long interviews with oral historian Proctor. "That is important because this is a high-risk job. I was very lucky, for instance, to get elected to the state legislature in 1966. There were seven people running for the seat that I was running for, and if things had been a little different, one of the other candidates would have been elected in 1966 and that would have been the end of my political career.

"I was a very long-shot candidate to get elected to governor in 1978. If I had not gotten elected, that would have been the end of my career. I have been lucky, but this business is almost like being a professional athlete. There is going to come a time for almost all of us when the career is going to be over, and I have seen too many people in politics who were so traumatized by the prospect of losing office that they did unfortunate things, unethical things, or they shaded or they compromised themselves.

"There is no total antidote to that, but I think the best antidote is to know in your mind that there is something else you can do which will meet two tests: one, a financial test where you can support yourself, and second will be a psychological test that you will get the same gratification out of it that you get out of politics. I was always satisfied in my mind that if politics did not work out, I had some things [returning to Miami Lakes to the family business] that I could do that I knew I would be happy doing and that I knew I would be able to take care of my family."[32]

[32]University of Florida Oral History Project, Tapes F–I, May 24, 1989.

Even in the early, optimistic months of his presidential campaign, Graham knew the quest would be tough. The only Florida governor to become president was Andrew Jackson, and that was 175 years ago. The last one to try, Reubin Askew, spent months in New Hampshire in 1983 and 1984 but came in dead last in the primary, getting exactly 1,065 votes. He dropped out not long afterward.

"It is a daunting task. It's like running for governor in twenty states at the same time," Adele Graham said, as a new poll showed her husband at all of one percent in New Hampshire. But, as she pointed out, Bob was dead last among the half-dozen candidates for governor in 1978, too, before coming from nowhere to win.

"We're used to this," she said. "We've been here before."

I n the end, Graham's newfound passion, his fire in the belly, was not enough to overcome the late start, some questionable strategy decisions and, most important, a lack of cash. Graham had raised more money for U.S. Senate races in Florida than he was able to collect in his nine months on the presidential trail, and by late September that became the showstopper.

The run was also Graham's first serious campaign without the help of longtime friend and confidant Bob Squier, who died of colon cancer in 2000. Both Graham the person and Graham the candidate sorely missed him. Squier had been at Graham's side through two gubernatorial elections and three Senate runs over a quarter-century, and together they had always won by at least ten points. Graham's political operatives in 2003 didn't really know him. They had Graham the serious policy wonk and Harvard-trained lawyer sponsor a NASCAR truck. They had Graham, a funny guy who loves to banter and spar with reporters, limit his exposure to the journalists covering him. They never understood his passion for his "workdays," never understood that was the way he connected best with voters.

On October 6, 2003, exactly five months and nine hours after Graham climbed the stage in Miami Lakes to officially announce he was getting into the race, Graham went on CNN's *Larry King Live* show to announce he was getting out. It was sad but probably fitting that Graham was forced to wait nearly an hour until King could get done with the more pressing news: the mauling of Las Vegas entertainer Roy Horn by his trained tiger.[33]

The *New York Times,* which did not exactly give raves to his May 6 announcement, was quick to note in the third paragraph of its deep-inside-the-A-Section article that Graham's departure from the race had come only after a lengthy discussion of an animal act gone bad. After Penn Jillette, Wayne Newton, and Tippi Hedren had finished opining about the tragedy, Graham—who had made his first media appearance during his 1966 run for the Florida House on King's Miami radio show—came on at the fifty-two-minute mark to make what King had promised would be a "special announcement."

After a commercial break, Graham was introduced, and told King's viewers: "I have made the difficult decision to withdraw my candidacy for president of the United States of America."

Asked why, Graham said: "I'm leaving because I have made the judgment that I cannot be elected president of the United States. Primarily because of a late start, the result of completing my duties as chairman of the Senate Intelligence Committee, and the investigation of the events around 9/11, heart surgery, and then the delay caused by the war in Iraq. All of those things combined to make it difficult for us to have the time and to close the gap in organization and fund-raising, which have led to this difficult decision."

Graham did not endorse any other candidate, said he would work hard for whomever Democratic voters chose as their nominee, and hinted that he would accept the vice-presidential slot, should the eventual nominee want him.

The other shoe dropped four Mondays later, when Graham returned to Tallahassee to tell his constituents that he would not seek a fourth term to the United States Senate, that he would instead retire from that chamber in January 2005.

---

[33]Not unlike how the declining rock band in Rob Reiner's *Spinal Tap* winds up playing amusement parks and, even there, gets second billing to a puppet show.

Wearing a plaid maroon shirt, blue jeans, and work shoes, Graham spent the lunch hour at his 391st "workday" delivering a speech that he stayed up until midnight working over and had then gotten up early that morning to chew on some more. At seven minutes after twelve, Graham stepped before the microphone to evoke Winston Churchill: "This is not the end. This is not the beginning of the end. Perhaps it is the end of the beginning."

Political junkies quickly deconstructed the decision: Would it help him get the vice-presidential slot on the 2004 Democratic ticket? Or hurt?

On the one hand, retiring from the Senate would remove potential objections from national strategists that Graham *not* be chosen, for fear of losing his Senate seat in the closely divided chamber. On the other, what better way of proving your ability to win Florida as a running mate than to spend several months barnstorming the state on a reelection campaign? Countering that: What could be *worse* for a VP hopeful trying to show he can win Florida than to have a handful of overzealous GOP opponents barnstorming the state for several months telling everyone what a horrible, unpatriotic liberal he was?

Graham said the question simply was not a factor in his decision. He repeated, as many times as he was asked, that the vice-presidential spot was something beyond his control but that he was prepared to work in whatever capacity was most helpful to ensure a Democratic victory in 2004.

And with that, he escaped the press pack, climbed aboard a bulldozer and, his tutor beside him, eased the machine into gear and began tearing up Lincoln High School's running track so that it could be resurfaced.

And so it ended. Presidential aspirant to lame-duck bulldozer operator, in exactly twenty-eight days.

It is a June Sunday in 2003—when anything is still possible—in Mount Pleasant, Iowa, the site of a politics picnic served up by Governor Tom Vilsack. Graham is in attendance, along with fellow candidates Lieberman, Dean, and Kucinich. They are to mingle with some three hundred hardcore Democrats who will trudge out in the snow come January 2004 and through their various caucus meetings determine the first front-runner of the Democratic race for president.

Each candidate has ten minutes to speak. Graham uses his time to talk about education, which gets tepid applause, and about voting against the Iraq war, which gets a bit more, and about how President Bush kept the American people in the dark about everything from his energy policy to the true costs of the occupation of Iraq, which gets more still.

It is a measure of the voter who attends these sorts of things that Graham's biggest applause line is when he points to Howard Dean, now back in the audience, and says what a great job he has done in the campaign so far.

Then, his ten minutes almost up, Graham gets ready for the big finish:

"But friends, there is one final, but very important, reason why you should consider our candidacy for president of the United States, particularly on January the nineteenth," he says somberly. "And that is that we have a song. We not only have a song, we have a CD of songs, but I don't have time to share all of those with you. The man is giving me the cut sign, so I'm sorry that I'm reduced to giving you just one stanza of one song":

"You've—got—a—friend in Bob Gra-ham, that's what e-ver-ybody's sayin',
   All a-cross . . .

(Here there's stunned silence.)

   "the good ol' USA.

(The cheers begin.)

   "From the Atlantic (he points left) *to the Pacific* (he points right),
   We all say—He's terrific!"

(Wild applause and whoops now.)

   "That's why America needs Bob Graham, today!"

 Pennsuco

Part of the fun of history is playing the "what ifs."

What if King Philip's armada had not been devastated by a storm in the approaches to the English Channel? What if Giuseppe Zangara's bullet had, as intended, struck FDR three weeks prior to his inauguration? What if Michael Dukakis had told Bernard Shaw to stick the rapist question in his ear?

Here is a good "what if" from Bob Graham's life: What if the great hurricane of 1926 had not hit Florida where it did? What if, instead of Miami, the damage and flooding had been farther to the south or north?

Had that been the case, then the Pennsylvania Sugar Company might not have lost so much of its crop on its plantation northwest of Miami. Had it not done so, it might not have fallen into such ruin in the subsequent Great Depression. And absent such dire financial straits, it may not have signed over its holdings in Florida to its foreman for the value of the outstanding taxes—thereby giving him the leg up he was able to parlay into a family business of dairy, beef cattle, and, ultimately, land development.

As it was, the upper-atmosphere winds blew a certain way that day, and the continental air masses were so arranged, and the sea surface temperature was just so, and on September 18, 1926, a major, Category Four hurricane did hit Miami, killing 235 people and leaving another 25,000 homeless.

The Pennsylvania Sugar Company did suffer huge losses, and five years later it did divest itself of its holdings, selling 7,000 acres at rock-bottom price to Ernest "Cap" Graham. Graham's oldest son, Philip, eventually went to Harvard Law School, something he likely would not have done had his father still been a middle manager for a corporate farm. There he met the daughter of a newspaper publisher and went on to turn the small-time paper into a highly respected publishing empire. On the strength of that, Philip came to know the movers and shakers of Washington—and in 1960 did some moving and shaking of his own, persuading a young Massachusetts senator to choose as his running mate a savvy Texan. The decision won the pair the South, and the White House.

Seventy-seven years later, that equinoctial storm continued having consequences.

Because it was Cap Graham's youngest son, Daniel Robert, since become just plain old "Bob," who was able to use the family fortune made possible by that storm to fulfill the political ambitions of both father and older brother. He became governor as his father had tried to. And, in the summer of 2003, he dared aim for the office his father could not have even dreamed of and which his late brother had known only vicariously.

Ernest R Graham (the middle initial didn't stand for anything—it just was; kind of like Harry Truman's S) was born on February 10, 1885, in Croswell, Michigan, the son of Philip L. Graham and Mary Delilah Graham.

How his family came to be there is a story in itself. Graham's ancestors came to Massachusetts from Scotland after the American Revolution but before the War of 1812. They were, however, still somewhat loyal to Great Britain, so when Canada offered free land and an absolution from paying taxes to the Church of England, Graham's family was happy to head north. They settled in Ontario, where both of Graham's paternal grandparents were born in the 1840s. They moved back across Lake Huron into Michigan in the 1870s, opening a dairy and a general store.

Young Ernest was likely headed into the family business when events a thousand miles to the south—in Cuba, of all places—suddenly opened possibilities. The intensifying civil war there threatened the supply of Cuban sugar into the United States. Since Cuban sugar represented about half of the U.S. market, American sugar companies started scrambling. Not only did they need more sugar beets to be grown domestically, but they also needed mills to refine the sugar from these beets. One such mill came to Croswell.

"My dad, who was then a teenager—we are now into the late 1890s— and his older brother, Leslie Graham, both got jobs working on the construction of this sugar beet plant," Graham recalled in a 1989 interview for the oral history project at the University of Florida. "My dad came in contact with some of the engineers who had been working on the plant, and both he and his brother, Les, decided that they wanted to be engineers."[1]

Croswell was not exactly a hotbed of Michigan engineering schools— it did not even have a high school. Ernest and his brother set off for Lansing, where they enrolled in a high school preparatory program at what is now Michigan State University. But Ernest decided civil engineering wasn't for him and moved on to Houghton, on the south shore of Lake Superior, to attend the Michigan School of Mines, from which he graduated in 1907.

Ernest Graham wrestled and boxed at the Michigan College of Mines— reflecting his lifelong pride in physical strength and good health, and giving him a distinguishing physical characteristic he would keep for the remainder of his years: a misshapen nose from repeated boxing-related fractures.

At age twenty-two, he took his degree to his first job, a gold mine in Montana—a harsh place where, to pass the long winters, he would fill a luggage box full of books and hole up for two or three months, reading. He neither drank nor smoked, but he did learn to use his acumen for numbers to enhance his salary. At a bar in Butte was a bookmaker who took bets on baseball games. Ernest Graham had figured out the starting rotation of his favorite team, the Washington Senators, and realized that the .350 team

---

[1]University of Florida Oral History Project, Tapes A–E, February 13, 1989.

was instead a .750 or .800 team on those days that Walter Johnson was on the mound. On those days, and *only* those days, he would place his bets on the Senators.

"The bartender, not being able to figure out what system my dad was using, finally told Dad, 'Graham, I don't know what the hell you are doing, but you ain't gonna bet here anymore,'" Bob Graham remembered. "That was a great source of pride to my father—that he had beat the bookie."[2]

Ernest Graham's next job took him to Deadwood, South Dakota, where he was hired to run a gold mine. The place was as rugged as it sounds. A photo shows him in front of a rustic cabin on the side of a valley, mountains all around. He met and married his first wife, Florence, in Deadwood and started a family there. She was a schoolteacher from Lincoln, Nebraska, and they eloped in Sturgis, with a day-trip honeymoon to Rapid City.[3] Daughter Mary was born in 1914, Philip a year later.

"I gather from having gone back to Deadwood with my father as a boy that those were happy years for him. It was a very physically demanding kind of job, and the West almost of the fiction that we read about. It was the West of the *Lonesome Dove* type time in South Dakota in the early part of this century," Bob Graham said.[4]

That life of relative calm was interrupted in 1917 by World War I, when Graham enlisted as a private. He was trained in Kentucky and sent off with the 309th Engineers to serve in France, but got there as the war was ending. (The war's end, in fact, marked the only time Ernest Graham tasted alcohol. Someone poured a bottle of champagne over his head during the armistice celebration.)

Ernest Graham, now a captain—the nickname "Cap" would stick with him the rest of his life—returned home in 1919 to find that, with the war's end, the price of gold had plummeted. The Deadwood mine had closed, and he was out of a job.

He worked with the family businesses in Croswell for some time, the dairy and the store, when the folks who ran the sugar mill in town came call-

---

[2] *Ibid.*
[3] Katharine Graham, *Personal History,* Alfred A. Knopf, New York, 1997, p. 120.
[4] University of Florida Oral History Project, Tapes A–E, February 13, 1989.

ing. The owners, now known as the Pennsylvania Sugar Company, had an ambitious plan to raise sugarcane in Florida. Was Cap Graham interested?

The place was known as Pennsuco—short for Pennsylvania Sugar Company—and it was a collection of wood shanties and bunkhouses on the Miami River canal about 20 miles northwest of Miami. The remoteness, and the fact that Miami still was hardly worth mentioning, as urban centers went, was perfect for Cap Graham, who didn't much care for big cities.

A bit of background about the area: That it was habitable at all was thanks only to the vision (in retrospect, misguided vision) of turn-of-the-century governor Napoleon Bonaparte Broward, who decided that the only way to get anyone to live in South Florida was to drain the damned swamp. Prior to this, the Everglades stretched from Naples clear across to within three miles of Biscayne Bay. Water would run downhill, Broward realized quite logically, and set about cutting arrow-straight ditches from the Glades eastward to the sea. The land then dried to semimuck, rather than flooded muck, and was sold off.

The ditching and draining had the unintended consequence of disrupting the natural freshwater cycle for the entire South Florida watershed—but this little detail was not of concern in the early 1900s. Swamp was bad. Dry land was good. It was that simple.

And it was on some of this former swamp, this still-soggy patch of Everglades drained by a canal that ran southeast to the Miami River, that the Pennsylvania Sugar Company decided it would grow the crop that up until that point was largely imported from Cuba and elsewhere in the Caribbean.

Graham brought his brood south in late 1920 and took over the sugar operations the following spring. For the first four years, they all—Cap, Florence, seven-year-old Mary, six-year-old Phil—lived aboard a houseboat moored on the canal, about as perfect a symbol for rootless Florida as can be imagined. While afloat, second son William was born in February 1924. Six months later, they moved ashore into a two-story house built of coral rock about two hundred yards from the river.

Florence, whom Bob Graham describes as a "learned, literate person," tried her best to civilize the children in this watery frontier. "She subscribed to the *New Yorker* magazine," Bob Graham said. "I can imagine what it was like to have the *New Yorker* magazine arrive on his houseboat out in the middle of Pennsuco. She used to read to the children and encourage them to read. She was a great influence on the intellectual development of all her children."[5]

The *New Yorker* notwithstanding, the kids had a grand old time in one of America's last untamed wildernesses. Bill Graham remembered catching alligators, cottonmouth water moccasins, and raccoons, and putting them in a makeshift zoo he and his friends set up. "If you catch a 'coon as a baby, you can make it into a pretty good pet," he pointed out.

One time, he and a friend found an alligator nest just as the eggs were hatching. They swam across the canal to retrieve a feed sack, then swam back to collect the baby gators. Then they swam like hell getting back home—knowing that mama gator probably wasn't far.

"I think we set the record for the fifty-yard dash, swimming across that canal," Bill Graham recalled seventy years later. "Why we didn't get killed, I don't know."

Cap Graham's work, meanwhile, was not going well. For starters was the antiquated means of preparing the fields: men driving mules. He thought this ridiculous. He called north to Michigan and had tractors sent down, but the mule drivers couldn't keep them from getting stuck in the gooey muck. So he fired all the mule drivers and brought down the men trained to drive the tractors. That finally worked.

"My dad had great faith in machinery and in man's ability to innovate and develop ways to overcome what appeared to be insurmountable obstacles," Graham said. "I would imagine that my dad was very much impressed with and influenced by such things as the building of the Panama Canal, which occurred during the time that he would have been a young engineer."[6]

Some things, though, not even technology could solve. The Everglades

---

[5] *Ibid.*
[6] *Ibid.*

soil around Pennsuco simply was not proving particularly hospitable to the varieties of sugarcane seedlings being brought in from as far away as Bali.

The Pennsylvania Sugar Company quickly came to see that this whole sugar thing wasn't really working out. By 1925, they decided that other vegetables, like potatoes, might work better, and for a while it seemed that the different crop might do the trick. Then came the *Prins Valdemar* accident. On January 10, 1926, the 241-foot Danish barkentine overturned in Biscayne Bay, right at the mouth of the Miami River—thereby trapping the barges trying to move freight to port. One of those happened to be loaded with Pennsuco potatoes. Potatoes were fetching a nice price at market at the time, and the load may have been sufficient to inject enough cash into Pennsuco's bottom line to turn things around. But by the time the ship was cleared away seven weeks later, the potatoes had rotted and the company's cash situation had become even more dire.

The hurricane of 1926 rounded out that year as a financial disaster, and the start of the Great Depression pretty well institutionalized Pennsuco as a money pit. Pennsylvania Sugar had had enough of the Everglades, and in 1931 started virtually giving away its Florida holdings. About 7,000 acres went to Cap Graham as part of his severance agreement, and he settled back into his family's forte with his own business, using the dairy that had been operated for the benefit of the hired hands.

Cap Graham tried his luck at other forms of investments, but after he lost $2,000 in a Philadelphia subway company, he decided to stick with what he knew.

"He said that from that point forward, he was only going to buy stock that had four legs and a tail, so that if it went down, he could go pick it up," Bob Graham told his University of Florida biographer. "That was not meant to be a frivolous, offhand statement. He really believed that. When he died, the only stock he owned was stock in the family corporation. He did not invest in IBM or General Electric or any other stocks because of that bad experience that he had. So he concentrated whatever money he could get on buying land and buying the cows to pay off the mortgages on the land."[7]

---

[7] *Ibid.*

Cap Graham did diversify from milk cows to beef cattle in the mid-thirties—partly by bringing in cowboys from Oklahoma, at son Bill's suggestion, to round up and fence in some several dozen wild cattle roaming the lands he had bought. That herd was bred with registered Angus bulls, resulting in a herd that eventually numbered in the thousands.[8] Over the years, the black Angus herd came to rival the dairy operation in profitability, and it remains the principal element in the Graham family agricultural holdings today.

Bob Graham would joke years later that that part was an accident—that his father had attended a cattle auction only because he had been elected to run a local civic association. "Dad swears he just went because he was president, but they mistook a scratch on his nose for a bid," Graham recounted in 2002 at the fortieth-anniversary celebration of Miami Lakes's founding. "He always said there was nothing less profitable than Angus cattle."

The Graham brothers also would belittle the acreage their father received from his former employer. At the 1962 dedication, Phil declared: "We've been blessed with one of the ugliest pieces of ground anywhere. You don't have to worry about the developer screwing it up; we can only make it more attractive."

Ugly or not, the dairy farm became enormously profitable, and Cap Graham became known as "the Squire of Pennsuco." This is not to suggest that it happened easily or right away. Like most people, Graham and his family got through the Depression without many comforts.

"My mother used to say that we had two dollars a week that was our discretionary spending money. If we wanted to go to the movies on a Saturday or something, that had to come out of the two dollars," Bob Graham said years later. "We were, by the standards of the time, a lot better off than most people."[9]

Cap Graham never forgot where he came from, and he made sure to

---

[8]Explaining this to the IRS in the mid-1960s, when settling Cap Graham's estate—that it was possible in the 1930s in Dade County, Florida, to acquire cattle merely by rounding them up—made for interesting conversation.

[9]University of Florida Oral History Project, Tapes A–E, February 13, 1989.

drill that lesson into his children. He used the phrase "codfish aristocracy" to describe the newly rich and their ostentatious ways.

In any event, there was more pain to come before the good times. Not long after the dairy started making money came the diagnosis that Florence had breast cancer. She died in 1934 from complications during the surgery to try to save her. "They didn't really know what they were doing. She would have lived today," Bill Graham said.

Phil and Mary were basically grown, but raising a ten-year-old by yourself was not any easier in the 1930s than it is today. So when Cap Graham met a Fort Walton Beach schoolteacher at a common friend's home in St. Augustine in 1935, the romance was not an extended one.

Hilda Elizabeth Simmons was one of seven children of an Alabama country doctor who had settled as a young man in Walton County, Florida, halfway down the Panhandle from Pensacola to Tallahassee. Daniel Simmons—Daniel Robert's namesake—raised the sort of family that moved from Freeport, near the Gulf of Mexico, to DeFuniak Springs, the county seat, so the children would be closer to a good school. It was the sort of family in which the children each got an all-events pass for when the Florida Chautauqua geared up every year.

As might be expected in such environs, Hilda grew up to attend Florida State College for Women in Tallahassee and became an English teacher back in Walton County, only to have to return to school to learn business skills. The Depression had forced teachers in Walton County to take a pay cut, and Hilda was hoping to change professions.

Cap and Hilda were engaged that year and married early the next. There was an understanding that they would have no more children. Cap Graham was eyeing a run for the state senate, and three kids was plenty on top of the farm and the community obligations Graham already had.

Somewhere, one or two details regarding the "no more children" rule were perhaps not fully adhered to, and Hilda was quickly pregnant. Daniel Robert arrived on November 9, 1936, six days after Cap Graham was elected to the state senate (Graham jokes about being "afflicted" with politics in the womb). Two weeks later, baby Bobby was trundled up for the drive to Tallahassee for the swearing-in. Older brother Bill recalls stopping along the way to warm up bottles of milk.

That Cap Graham ever ran for senate in the first place was a result of that old standby in Florida, political corruption.

It is said that all politics is local. Cap Graham took that to an extreme—running for the state legislature because it was the only way he could think of to thwart the organized criminals in nearby Hialeah who were robbing from his new dairy business's bottom line.

Hialeah, it should be remembered, was corrupt from the word go. The celebration over the awarding of a city charter in 1925 was capped off with a shoot-out that left three people dead. There was, it seems, some disagreement over which gang would get control of what portion of the new government.

"Hialeah had a racetrack, dog track, and a jai alai fronton in open operation ten years before any of those were legal activities," Bob Graham explained, pointing out that "it would be pretty hard to hide a racetrack."[10]

This tradition has continued to the present day. In the mid-1990s, Hialeah gained the dubious distinction of re-electing a mayor who had actually been convicted of bribery (the conviction was eventually overturned, but voters did not know that at the time).

In any event, in the mid-1930s Cap Graham did not much care who ran the town, or what sort of gambling they did there. What bothered him was the protection racket that was being run by the notorious Hyde–Slayton gang.

"It was kind of a redneck hoodlum outfit, and one of the ways they made money was by imposing a toll on the roads to get through Hialeah, and if you did not pay up, they arrested you on some trumped-up traffic offense and would throw you in jail. Our milk truck drivers were a ready target," Bob Graham said. "In addition to putting the drivers in jail, they would park the milk truck out in the open sun so that the ice would melt and the milk would go sour. It made Dad mad as hell. So, in 1936, having put up with as much of this as he was going to, he came to the conclusion that the only way he was going to get rid of these guys was to run for office. So he ran for the Florida state senate."[11]

---

[10] *Ibid.*
[11] *Ibid.*

Cap Graham did more than get mad—he got even. One of the first bills he passed in the Florida senate was to abolish the city of Hialeah. His next bill reestablished the city and named a new mayor and an entirely new city commission—people Cap Graham was assured would clean up the place and prosecute the bad guys.

One of those guys, Bob Graham recalled, actually sent his dad a card years later, from the slammer: "It was dated from the state penitentiary at Raiford and it was from Red Slayton. It said, 'Mr. Graham, I wish I could vote for you for reelection, because you are the only honest politician I have ever known. When you ran in 1936, you said that if you were elected you were going to put us out of business, arrest us, and run us out of Hialeah. You did all three of them, but I can't vote for you because they have taken away my civil rights.'"[12]

Vanquishing the Hyde–Slayton gang was a personal triumph, but in the end inconsequential in the annals of Florida political corruption.[13] Cap Graham's first real mark in the Florida legislature was his effort to increase the state's pensions for the elderly. He successfully pushed a tax increase on the state's pari-mutuels, with the new money benefiting the elderly poor.

And it was that tax that led to Graham's historic effort to abolish the poll tax, a truly vile creation of Jim Crow–era Florida. Ending racism, though, was not Cap Graham's goal. Ensuring his reelection was.

The pari-mutuel tax was for some reason not producing the kind of revenues Graham had anticipated. When he delved into why, he discovered— big shock—that the racetracks were skimming off the top. The bulk of it was going on at a single track: Tropical Park, which was run by Chicago mobster Al Capone's gang. After Graham raised a stink, the good folks at Tropical decided that would be the end of Cap Graham's career. They would do this by bribing a bunch of poor people to vote against Graham and paying their poll tax to enable them to do so.

Graham saw that his best chance at retaining his senate seat was to get rid of the poll tax, period, and thereby let the elderly poor who were benefiting from his legislation come out and support him.

---

[12]*Ibid.*

[13]In fairness, dealing with political corruption in Florida is akin to keeping up the varnish on a sailboat. The work is tedious, frustrating, and, worst, never-ending. You're doing well just to avoid losing ground.

This being Florida, naturally, such a reform had to be snuck through under cover of darkness.

Graham used the one night in each legislative session set aside for each senator to get one and only one bill of his choosing directly to the floor—no committee references, no hassles. This was done in numerical order, according to district number, and Graham's district was number 13. For Cap Graham's purposes, it was not high enough.

"Dad thought that if he tried to bring up something as controversial as repealing the poll tax fairly early at night that people would vote him down," son Bob remembered. "They had a procedure [whereby] you could trade places, so he kept trading to go later and later on this special bill night and finally ended up being one, if not the last number, of all the members of the senate. . . . And he called up his poll tax repealer bill, and late at night or early the following morning, the bill passed the senate and got passed through the house."[14]

And so a fundamental right became easier for the poor and the dark-skinned, and Cap Graham's reelection became much more certain. "He got to the right place, but not necessarily for the motives that would drive Common Cause today," Bob Graham said.[15]

While his father was making a name for himself in Tallahassee, his youngest son was growing up, for all intents and purposes, an only child. By the time he came along, brothers Phil and Bill were twenty-one and twelve years old, respectively, and sister Mary was twenty-two.

The potential for growing up spoiled rotten was high, as sister-in-law Katharine Graham, whose father published the *Washington Post*, recounted in her Pulitzer Prize–winning autobiography, *Personal History*. Bob Graham's mention comes early on, in a description of her first visit to Pennsuco to meet husband Phil's family. (It was Katharine's first trip to the South, for that matter: "As we entered Florida, I saw a sign in front of an apartment

---

[14]University of Florida Oral History Project, Tapes A–E, February 13, 1989.
[15]*Ibid.*

house that read, 'No dogs or Jews allowed,' and was deeply shaken, never having seen or experienced anything so ugly."[16])

Her description of Bob, a toddler then, was limited to five words: "their somewhat spoiled only child." She recalls lying on their couch in the living room writing thank-you notes. "I was startled to be spat on by the three-year-old Bob. Phil's brother, Bill, later told me that this was, alas, Bob's habit at that point in his life. I thought, in my paranoid way, that there must be a message there."[17]

Two years later, with his dad serving in the state senate, Master Bob's young worldview manifested itself in expulsions from a string of preschools in just one year. The does-not-play-well-with-others deeds would ultimately lead to a frustrated teacher's phone call home.

"It was not the first or second day care center—in fact, it was the third, because I had behaved so badly that I had been asked to leave the first and the second. I was now on my third center. There were some little girls who were building a fortress out of wooden blocks, and I went over and kicked it in. The teacher came and said, 'Robert, we can't have little boys who behave like that in our home, and I am going to have to call your mother and ask her to take you and not bring you back,'" Graham said later. "I remember looking up at her . . . and thinking about what was going to happen to me when my mother came to pick me up. So I had a spotty record as a child."[18]

Whatever issues little Bobby may have had with his schoolmates, his grades were decidedly not a problem. He excelled from the start. It really was not an option, as he saw it. He recalled his first day in Lamar Louise Curry's eleventh-grade history class at Miami High School.

"The first day of class with Miss Curry, who always called me Robert, she said, 'Robert, do you see the desk over there?' She pointed at the desk on the side of the room and said, 'That is where your brother Phil sat. He was a very good student. Do you see the desk there? That is where your sis-

[16]Katharine Graham, *Personal History,* Alfred A. Knopf, New York, 1997, p. 123.
[17]*Ibid.*
[18]University of Florida Oral History Project, Tapes A–E, February 13, 1989.

ter, Mary, sat. She was a very good student. This desk is where your brother William sat. He was a very good student. Robert, I expect you to be a very good student.' In our family, doing well academically was not something that the parents talked about. You just knew that it was expected that you would do well."[19]

At age sixteen, Graham was named "Best All-'Round Teenage Boy" by the *Miami Herald*. In his final year at Miami High, Graham was senior class president. From there, it was on to the University of Florida, where, while his fraternity brothers had a great time, Graham studied.

Despite this, he managed to remain popular enough to eventually become the chapter president. "Bob was respected and well liked," recalled fellow Sigma Nu brother and lifelong friend Robin Gibson.

Graham looks back on those years with fondness—a definite Bob Graham–type fondness: "It was a very happy period in my life. It was a successful period. The things that I wanted to do academically, I accomplished. Probably the highlight of my life in terms of academic energy occurred during the spring semester of my freshman year when I was taking, I believe, eighteen hours of course work plus auditing another three hours, so I got a total of twenty-one credit hours in that semester with all A's. I was elected to the Honor Court and spent twelve weekends in Tallahassee with my girlfriend."[20]

How many other people recall college years in terms of "academic energy"? It was important to Graham, though—important enough that years afterward, he remembered clearly the one class that hurt an otherwise stellar grade point average: that perennial grade-buster, social dancing.

"I had a very good partner through most of the semester, but on the final exam day, she was sick or for some reason she was not there and I had a girl that I never had danced with before and who I did not think did very well in mathematics. She did not keep up with my smooth move. The consequence was, I got a D in social dancing. . . . For all time now, my curriculum and transcript here at the University of Florida is going to have me down as deficient in social dancing."[21]

---

[19] *Ibid.*
[20] *Ibid.*
[21] *Ibid.*

Decades later, putting her memories to paper, Katharine Graham pointed out that, the spitting episode notwithstanding, little Bob had evidently turned out okay—maybe even more okay, in fact, than the rest of his family. "Bob outgrew all this, of course, and developed into a highly successful, natural, and excellent politician, very different from the older three children but extremely able. He became governor of Florida and is now a senator, a strange fulfillment of both his father and Phil's ambitions. He has all the Graham family brains and charisma, and a great deal more stability than Phil had."[22]

Granted, Katharine Graham was not likely to say unflattering things about her living relatives, but it was an accurate observation nonetheless.

The "Graham family brains," as she put it, were on display when father Ernest Graham served in the Florida senate. In one dispatch, *Miami News* political writer Cecil Warren reverently described his abilities in floor debate: "To the observer, it appears that he has seized upon and mentally digested every scrap of available information on the particular subject—that his mind is a repository for facts, figures, incidents and even scraps of authoritative conversation relating to the matter debated."[23]

As to the fulfillment of family ambitions—well, that goes back to Cap Graham, who, after eight years in the senate, ran for the Democratic nomination for governor in 1944. He had been well liked by the newspapers, respected by his colleagues, lauded for his bills to take care of the elderly, and had generally been seen as a credible candidate. He finished third in a field of six, embittered by the failure of the man he'd helped get elected governor, Spessard Holland, to return the favor.

The loss hurt, and it made an impression on young Bob, Bill recalled. "He told my wife, when he was eight years old, that he was going to be governor someday."

Cap Graham made one final go at politics—four years later. But while running for governor had been a vision with a grand scale, the race for county commission in 1948 was a much smaller thing, born of his anger

[22]Katharine Graham, *Personal History*, Alfred A. Knopf, New York, 1997, p. 123.
[23]Cecil Warren, "'I'm no lawyer—but I'll push a pencil with you any day,'" *Miami Daily News*, August 23, 1941.

with the sitting commission for its failure to respond adequately to the hurricane of 1947 that had caused his dairy so much damage.

"He ran an emotional campaign based on his own bitterness rather than a smart campaign to get elected," Bob Graham remembered years later. "So he ended his political career with a defeat and it kind of tainted his view of politics. He was never as interested in or involved—[or] personally comfortable with politics after that experience."[24]

Perhaps, were it just his father's failed ambition, those two unsuccessful campaigns might have had a different effect on his youngest son. Perhaps he might have seen the heartbreak and bitterness political losses could bring and have decided it wasn't worth the effort. But it wasn't just his father. It was also Phil.

Eldest Graham son Philip was for several years in the late 1950s and early 1960s about as glamorous as glamorous gets. He was a close friend of President Kennedy and attended White House balls. He ran the *Washington Post* and *Newsweek*. His face was on the cover of *Time*. He and his wife hosted the most-talked-about social events in Washington and owned luxurious, expensive homes.

It was another world entirely from the one he was raised in—the wilderness of Deadwood, South Dakota, the equally stark landscape of the Florida Everglades. Younger brother Bob would recall stories about Phil catching alligators and playing with the children of Seminole Indians who canoed out of the Everglades to trade.

In school, he was a good student, but it was on raw brains, not necessarily hard work. At Miami High, he was senior class president and deemed "wittiest" boy by his graduating class.[25] Then came the University of Florida: party time. While the nation suffered through the Depression, Phil Graham and his new pals at the SAE fraternity enjoyed themselves.

---

[24]University of Florida Oral History Project, Tapes A–E, February 13, 1989.
[25]The presidency honor would have gone to George Smathers, later a United States senator, had he not stayed behind an extra semester so he could get another season of football in.

Ernest "Cap" Graham in the 1940s. *(Courtesy of The Graham Companies.)*

Brother Bob's theory was that they were patterning themselves after F. Scott Fitzgerald characters—putting their talents and intellects to much better use than mere grades.

"In fact, later in life, the university expressed some interest in giving him an honorary degree, and I think when they looked at his transcripts, they had some pause as [to] whether to do that," Bob Graham said. "In the depths of the Depression, dad was kind of teed off at Phil, who he did not think was working very hard at the university, and pulled him out of school for a semester or so and had him deliver milk so that he could learn what the real world was like."[26]

The "time-out" from school lasted a full year, brother Bill remembered. But Phil returned to Gainesville more or less chastened, and successfully graduated.

The leap from that point to the later successes in Phil's troubled life—

[26]University of Florida Oral History Project, Tapes A–E, February 13, 1989.

The Grahams at Earnest Graham's 70th birthday, 1955. From left to right: Ernest Graham, Bob Graham, Philip Graham, Mary Graham Crow, Lon Worth Crow, Jr., Ora McDuff, Bill Graham, Hilda Graham, Katharine Graham, Patricia Graham, and Cathy Crow. *(Courtesy of The Graham Companies.)*

he was eventually diagnosed a manic-depressive—came thanks to kind words at the right moment from a political friend, then–United States senator Claude Pepper. Phil wanted to attend Harvard Law, a dream of his mother who had passed away two years earlier.

"Phil's grades were not of the type that made him an early-admission candidate," Bob Graham recalled dryly. So their dad called on Pepper, who spoke to Harvard's admissions office on Phil's behalf, "essentially, I think saying, 'This is a young man from a good family who I think has potential, and consider taking a chance on him.'"[27]

Harvard gambled on Phil, and it paid off. In that more rigorous environment, Phil blossomed intellectually and academically. His grades improved. He made Law Review. And upon graduation, he won a clerkship with Justice Stanley Reed on the United States Supreme Court, followed by a second one with Justice Felix Frankfurter. And in that time in Washing-

---

[27] *Ibid.*

ton, Phil met the daughter of Eugene Meyer, the businessman and publisher of the *Washington Post.*

With war looming, Phil and Katharine Meyer married in 1940, despite Cap Graham's opposition.

"I came across a letter once which Phil wrote to Dad," Bob Graham recounted. "It was sort of a preemptive letter in the sense that it was identifying concern that Dad might have about Kay. . . . One of the concerns was wealth. I mentioned to you that my dad had a . . . disdain, that is a good word, for wealth, and so Phil was saying, 'Yes, these people are wealthy, but they earned it the right way. They worked for it and they are not showy or ostentatious.' The other was that the Meyers were Jewish. And he was saying that, 'Yes, she is Jewish, but we have worked out the religious thing.' "[28]

In fact, Eugene Meyer was Jewish, his wife was Christian, and Kay was raised with both traditions—but these finer points were not important. In any event, Cap Graham seemed far more concerned by Kay Graham's money than her religion.

There was little time, though, for lingering resentment. Phil went into the lend-lease program, America's backdoor effort against fascism. After Pearl Harbor, he signed up for real—as an enlisted man, just as his father had encouraged—but soon won his commission and was moved by the Army Air Corps into intelligence work. After a brief, unhappy stint in the Office of Strategic Services—Phil thought the place too political and full of "white-shoe" boys—he transferred back to the air force, and eventually was shipped to the Philippines to serve under General George Kenney, who was providing air support for General Douglas MacArthur's ground forces.[29]

When the war was over, Phil Graham was called by his father to help run the dairy farm at Pennsuco and by his father-in-law to help run the *Post,* which during the war had started its climb from the minor leagues of American journalism into one of the major players. Phil chose the *Post,* starting in 1946 as associate publisher. Six months later, when Eugene Meyer was tapped by President Truman to run the World Bank, Phil, barely thirty, became publisher. In the coming decade and a half, he remade the

---

[28]*Ibid.*
[29]Katharine Graham, *Personal History,* Alfred A. Knopf, New York, 1997, p. 146.

paper and put himself at the center of Washington politics—even if it meant bending the rules of what a newspaperman traditionally did.

In the summer of 1949, for example, a young reporter named Ben Bradlee had witnessed whites brutalizing black protesters attempting to use white-only city swimming pools. Bradlee and other reporters had seen pieces of wood with nails driven into them used as clubs. They'd seen people trampled by police horses. Bradlee was screaming for a front-page story.

Phil Graham had Bradlee repeat what he'd seen to a half-dozen top-ranking officials from Truman's White House who had been gathered in his office. Bradlee told his tale and then was sent out. Then Phil told the power structure that he would put the story on the front page—unless they agreed to integrate the pools. They agreed to his demand, shutting down the pools that summer but promising to reopen them the following year on an integrated basis, and Phil ran the story on page seven of the B section.[30]

And so it was in the summer of 1959, as head of the expanding *Post* empire, that Phil introduced Bob to the heady world of Washington politics. Philip had already persuaded Bob to forgo business school, which Bob had thought he should attend, and go to law school instead. Just like Phil. And just like Phil, Bob attended Harvard.[31] Bob was on his way to Boston with his new bride, Adele, stopping in Washington to intern for Miami congressman Dante Fascell.

As can be imagined, the relationship was not that of typical brothers. Their age difference alone made that quite unlikely. Phil, in fact, had told Bob that their age gap had been a subject of discussion in a Harvard Law School class on the Rule against Perpetuities—an English common law concept that forbade the passing down of inheritances beyond existing lives plus twenty-one years. (Twenty-one years was regarded as a good definition of a generation.) To illustrate, the professor had asked all the students who had a sibling who was either twenty-one years older or younger

---

[30] *Ibid.*, p. 186.
[31] Where he met, among many others, the son of Greek immigrants, Michael Dukakis, who later became the first in a string of presidential candidates not to ask Graham to run with him.

to raise their hands. Only Phil's hand went up. "He was the only one in his class who had to distinguish himself with having such a prolific father," Bob Graham said.[32]

Bob Graham described the nature of their relationship pretty simply: as one of "awe."

Four years earlier, during a summer vacation with their father, Bob had visited Phil and Katharine at their farm home. More than three decades later, Bob recalled meeting Justice Frankfurter at Phil's farm as a high point of the trip.

In the summer of 1959, Bob, through Phil, got to meet such people as Jack Kennedy, Joseph Alsop, and Adlai Stevenson at the famed Georgetown dinner parties.

"Here I was, a nervous young girl from South Florida," Adele Graham said years later. "And there's Bob, confident even with these people and willing to be part of these discussions about the most important events of the time."[33]

That, as it turned out, was only starters. The following summer, after working for Lyndon Johnson at Phil's advice (Phil thought that Kennedy, whom Bob wanted to support, was so well organized that any job Bob got in that campaign would be trivial, whereas Johnson was so disorganized that Bob might be able to score a meaningful position in that campaign), Bob went to the Democratic National Convention in Los Angeles, where he was able to watch firsthand as big brother helped arrange history.

Kennedy had the delegates for the nomination, but he faced a tough run against vice president Richard Nixon in November—unless he could lock up a big, conservative state like Texas as well as a couple of the southern states. For that he was going to need the help of the candidate he had bested, Phil decided. Phil labored for days to undo Jack and brother Bobby's suspicion of Texas senator Lyndon Johnson and convince them to choose him as Jack's running mate.[34]

The importance of this became clear in retrospect. Without Lyndon Johnson on the ticket, Kennedy likely would have lost Texas and at least

[32]University of Florida Oral History Project, Tapes A–E, February 13, 1989.
[33]Mike Ollove, "The Turning Point," *Miami Herald,* December 9, 1984.
[34]Katharine Graham, *Personal History,* Alfred A. Knopf, New York, 1997, p. 266.

two or three of the southern states. And without Texas plus Arkansas, Louisiana, Georgia, Alabama, South Carolina—pick any two—all the dead people voting in Illinois wouldn't have helped.[35]

So there it was. Philip Graham had made an American president, and Bob Graham was there to serve witness. The effect this had on Bob, a second-year law student, is hard to imagine. Your own brother, influencing the course of a national election!

Just as hard to imagine is what happened three summers later.

On August 3, 1963, Philip dramatically and painfully severed his association with brother Bob and everybody else. As Katharine napped upstairs in their Virginia farmhouse, Philip, checked out of a mental hospital for the weekend, climbed into a bathtub with his shotgun and ended his six-year fight with manic depression.

Bob was on a golf course in Miami Lakes, the "new town" his family had begun the previous year to branch out into the land development business. Polite as always, Graham thanked the club manager who brought him the bad news with little outward emotion. Inside, it devastated him.

"I think with sadness, from time to time, how positive it would have been if Phil had lived longer," Graham recalled twenty-six years later. "Because I was just in the years after his death starting my political career, and I think, had he lived, that would have been a time that we would have had an especially close relationship."[36]

Fortunately for Bob, there was another elder brother—one in many ways quite the opposite of Phil.

If Philip was the meteor streaking brilliantly and destructively across the sky, William, the youngest child of Cap Graham's first wife, Florence, was the steady, solid rock—the anchor for Bob's ambitions.

Bill, a mere dozen years older, would drive his kid brother to kindergarten on his way to Miami High during his senior year. Bill, a high school

---

[35]What if Nixon *had* won? He probably wouldn't have gotten all paranoid before the reelection and pulled a Watergate. Which means he wouldn't have been disgraced, and his vice president would have had a decent chance of winning in 1968, meaning . . .

[36]University of Florida Oral History Project, Tapes A–E, February 13, 1989.

basketball star, followed older brother Philip to Gainesville, but then he, too, was caught up by Pearl Harbor and the subsequent entry into the Second World War. Like Phil, Bill also joined the Army Air Corps, and was sent to the University of Minnesota for training as a B-29 navigator. It was there that he came to know the woman who would become his wife of nearly six decades, Patricia Culbertson, then an undergraduate.

They wanted to marry, but Cap Graham, predictably, objected to what he thought was a "wartime" marriage. They married anyway, in Minneapolis, on February 3, 1945, Bill knowing he would soon be shipped overseas. Pat wound up recruiting her college friends to be in the wedding party. Bill's family, including his father, did not attend.

Bill was on his way to Okinawa when the second atomic bomb was dropped and Japan surrendered. He returned briefly to the University of Minnesota until Pat graduated, then transferred back to Gainesville.

But whereas Phil left Pennsuco upon graduation pretty much forever, Bill went home to work in the dairy. He, too, had the family brains, and Cap Graham came to rely on his acumen. It was Bill who suggested in the early 1950s that the family either get out of the distribution side of the dairy business or become a major player. Cap Graham asked for Bill's recommendation. Bill said they should get out, and, a few phone calls later, they were out—becoming instead exclusively a milk producer.

It was Bill's idea to develop the Angus breeding that brought a new line of income. Most significantly, it was Bill's idea in the late 1950s not to sell off pieces of the family's extensive land holdings to developers, as all the other farmers were doing, but instead develop a big chunk in the fashion of the European "new towns"—self-contained cities with a mixture of residential and commercial construction.

It was a bold and risky proposal—looking for long-term, sustained income by forgoing instant wealth. More important, it meant learning a new business that the family knew nothing about. The Graham family launched Miami Lakes in the summer of 1962—just in time for the Cuban missile crisis to dry up demand for new housing in Miami.

"We had some troubles," Bill said of those years with characteristic understatement.

Even without the intrusion of foreign affairs, Bill Graham—with, by then, Bob's help—was not having an easy time selling prospective home buyers on the idea that there would eventually be a complete community where at the time they could see only cow pasture. "We put up a great big wooden fence around our models so they couldn't see that there wasn't anything else to see," Bill Graham recalled.

Over the years, the natural course of South Florida's expansion brought the Grahams a healthy stream of cash, and Miami Lakes quickly left behind its financial worries and growing pains and became one of Dade County's most lauded communities—development (insofar as development had to happen at all within what was once the Everglades) done right.

The Grahams, who had been hardscrabble farmers in the 1920s and '30s and dairymen of moderate means in the 1940s, had become, by the 1970s, plain, unequivocally rich.

The money made Bob Graham's political career possible. Bill Graham's success as a businessman and generosity as a brother allowed Bob to run for the statehouse in 1966 without feeling as if he was abandoning the family business. Four years later, it was even more of a time commitment in the state senate, and Bill had nothing but encouragement.

But in 1977 came the real gut check. Bob wanted to run for governor, and laid out a schedule that would see him spend a total of $750,000—between $25,000 and $50,000 a month—of his own money to let him be competitive. That inflates to about $2.3 million in 2003 dollars, and at the time represented fully a third of his entire net worth.

"The question was, did Bob really think he was going to get elected or not?" Bill Graham said.

Bill wasn't certain of the answer, but he helped arrange the finances so the company would buy back Bob's shares. What else could he do? "[Since childhood] I knew, in my heart, Bob was going to be in politics," he said.

Bob Graham understands well that as much of an influence Phil was in the romantic sense, when it came time for cold, hard reality, it was Bill who made his career happen:

"He is 12 years older than I am and was somewhere between being a brother and a second father when I was growing up. He is the person closest to me other than immediate family. We don't have to talk very much. We can understand each other," Graham said. Adele put things even more clearly: "We couldn't have done what we do in life if it had not been for Bill. I cannot tell you how wonderful the family has been."[37]

It could not have been the easiest thing, growing up the son of Cap Graham. He was distrustful of outsiders and could hold a grudge—sometimes a long grudge. It was years before he spoke to Spessard Holland again after Holland did not support Graham's candidacy for governor. After the *Miami Herald* wrongly accused him of using his influence on the State Road Board to bring U.S. Highway 27 to Pennsuco (the route had been planned before Cap Graham joined the board), Graham sued the paper, then framed the letter of apology it gave him and kept it on his office wall forever after.

Daughter Mary, who wanted to attend school up north to become a dress designer, was not allowed to do so. She was also not permitted to marry a much older suitor whom she loved. Ultimately, she drifted apart from her brothers, living in California after a bad divorce.

Cap Graham's later attempts to interfere with his elder sons' choice of life partners drove a wedge between him and them that perhaps never completely went away. Katharine Meyer's family was too wealthy for Phil and, a few years later, Patricia Culbertson's family was too poor for Bill. Consequently, both brothers got married outside their father's presence.

Bill Graham remembers the lengths to which his father went to stop his wedding. "I had to sign away my rights to everything. And I had not planned to come back," he said.

In the end, both sons reconciled with their father. There was never any question that he loved them dearly.

Daughter-in-law Kay Graham, in her autobiography, said she ultimately came to see all that was good in him—and forgave his initial attempts to steer his son clear of her. "I came to know and admire and, finally, to love Ernie Graham, Phil's two-fisted, rough-hewn, upright father."[38] Kay Graham, of course, was a truly forgiving woman. She also forgave the girlfriend

---

[37]Anne Groer, "Teflon Bob," *Orlando Sentinel,* January 8, 1995.
[38]Katharine Graham, *Personal History,* Alfred A. Knopf, New York, 1997, p. 124.

for whom Phil, up until a few months before his suicide, was planning a divorce from Kay.

Still, she seems to have appraised Cap Graham fairly.

Youngest son Bob might have the fondest memories of his youth among the Graham brothers. Part of it may be that, unlike his older siblings, he did not grow up in poverty. While he did his farm chores and later, in school, participated in 4-H, such activities were not critical to the survival of the family business, as Phil's and Bill's work at the dairy had been in the 1930s.

Bob recalls politicking with his father, passing out chocolate milk at campaign events, and attending baseball games. Every summer, there would be a road trip planned around the major league baseball schedule, and Bob and Cap saw games in Detroit, Cincinnati, and New York as well as any number of minor league games in Miami and Miami Beach, where Cap held season tickets in the 1950s.

Even Bob, though, seemed to sense the trouble his father had expressing what he felt for his family. He described Cap Graham as "a hard charger" and "gruff."

"It was not easy for Dad to show emotion," Bob Graham recalled. "I cannot think of very many times when he and Mother would hold hands or hug or do other things demonstrating emotion. Not that he did not feel that way, but it was just difficult in his character to do that. I remember one time when I was a boy, five or six years old, dad became ill. At the time it appeared as if it were a more serious illness than apparently it was. Maybe it was a false heart attack. He was getting in the car to be driven to the hospital with very great concern as to whether he would ever come back again. I remember his having me come in the back of the car, and he held me and he said, 'Robert, I do not know what is going to happen to me, but I want you to take good care of your mother.' And he cried."[39]

There is more than a little irony in Bob Graham describing his father's unwillingness to show emotion—the same has been said of Graham. Even friends and aides who have known him for years say that talk about

[39]University of Florida Oral History Project, Tapes A–E, February 13, 1989.

feelings and fears and dreams is not something that often comes up in conversations with him. Apart from Adele and brother Bill, there are not many who profess to have a particularly close relationship with him.

Nature or nurture? Probably some of both. It's not the typical life, to be the only child of the second wife of a hard-charging patriarch old enough to be a grandfather. Add to that an upbringing in the isolation of a true American wilderness, and you have the ingredients of Bob Graham—and at least a basis for understanding the political story that emerged.

A Brief Guide to
Bob Graham's Florida

To understand Graham—or, more accurately, to *appreciate* Graham—it is important to remember the place he comes from.

Politically, it's easiest to think of Florida as if it were the Balkans, albeit with somewhat less violence. North Florida is the South, South Florida is like New Jersey with palm trees, the Panhandle may as well be lower Alabama, while the Southwest coast is Ohio with better golfing.

Candidates who run for statewide office find that these geographical distinctions are far more important than traditional party labels. For example, Republicans dominate in both Naples and Leesburg, but the similarities end there. The latter is located squarely in the Bible Belt, and the local version of the Christian Coalition and similar groups exert tremendous power in primary politics. The midwestern retirees of Naples up through Sarasota are also Republicans, but aren't fanatics about it, often electing pro-choice, anti–school voucher candidates to county and state offices.

Democrats, meanwhile, have similar chasms of sensibility separating the retired northeastern union workers of Broward County's many condominiums and the remaining "Yellow Dog" Democrats of the state's Panhandle. The former will reliably vote for the most liberal candidate running; the latter believe in school prayer, guns, and the flag.

When all the factions' various jealousies have been thrown together, the result has been a state that has tended toward Republicans in recent presidential elections. Florida went for Nixon in 1968 and 1972, Carter in 1976, Reagan in 1980 and 1984, Bush in 1988, Bush, barely, in 1992, Clinton in 1996, and, depending on where you stand, Bush by 537 votes or Gore by 2,500 to 25,000 votes in 2000.

The above, of course, is old hat to political pros and utter gibberish to the tens of millions of Americans each year for whom Florida remains the location of sanitized and safe Walt Disney World, and little else.

From airport to theme park to hotel to theme park to airport are visible the remnants of pine forest and semitropical scrub, congested roads, and—depending on whether the visitor is staying on Disney property or off—miles upon miles of garish tackiness.

The more adventuresome might day-trip over to Universal Studios or Sea World or even the Kennedy Space Center on the east coast or Busch Gardens on the west. Few bother with natural wonders like the Everglades or historical sites such as St. Augustine.

So it is small wonder that much of what makes the national television news from the Sunshine State bewilders the rest of the nation—from Anita Bryant's antigay crusade to Ted Bundy to the fad of murdering European tourists to Elián Gonzalez and his Miami Relatives to the butterfly ballot that changed an election to the preferred flight training locale for Islamic terrorists.

This is a state where entire quorums of the Hillsborough County commission, the Lee County Commission, and the Escambia County Commission have been arrested and hauled off to court; where five sitting and recently retired state legislators have, in a seven-year span, been convicted of felonies. One Miami state senator went down for Medicare fraud after inventing patients out of whole cloth for the purpose of bilking millions from the federal government. Another was a former senate president, a wily old coot who used to sell loose diamonds and various other trinkets to lobbyists who would then appear before him in committee. The man was convicted—only after his departure from the legislature because of term limits—of bribing a fellow Escambia County Commissioner with a cook pot filled with $200,000 in cash.[1]

This is the state where a single state legislator cast a single floor vote that spelled the beginning of the end of the tobacco industry's stranglehold on American politics—only to resurface seven years later as the congresswoman who suggested exhuming the bodies of the American soldiers buried in France and bringing them home to protest French foreign policy regarding Iraq.

This is the state whose top election official, twenty months after helping deliver the presidential election to the candidate she supported, was automatically removed from office because she failed to understand the state's election laws when she ran for Congress.[2]

This is the state whose house speaker recently gave a former Hooters waitress one of the top jobs in his office—notwithstanding her lack of requisite qualifications, like college degree and experience.[3] The voters in his district were so indignant about this that they promoted him to Congress.

This is the state whose central ingress point, Interstate 75 at the Georgia border, has as its first attraction a Confederate flag. A huge Confederate flag. An enormous, parking-lot-sized Confederate flag. The biggest Confederate flag, in fact, in the whole world. Among the speakers at its dedication in 2002 was a sitting Democratic member of the state house of representatives as well as the only lawmaker to preside over both the state house and the senate. The first Union flag of comparable size does not show up along the highway for nearly a hundred miles. Naturally, it marks an all-nude eatery.

And, speaking of which, this is the state where a U.S. Attorney, after losing a big drug case, bought a $900 magnum of champagne at a strip club and reportedly bit one of the dancers. He resigned not long afterward. Naturally, he later wound up on the Miami Relatives' legal team.

---

[1] As this went to press, his appeal was pending. It's not clear why a cook pot.

[2] Yes, that would be Katherine Harris.

[3] Admittedly, one way of looking at this is: If as house speaker you can't put a Hooters waitress on staff at public expense, then what the heck point is there to being house speaker?

How, the rest of the nation must wonder, can a state with a place as nice and clean as Disney World be so . . . well, so weird?

It should be noted, in fairness to Florida's current citizenry, that this weirdness is nothing new.

Students of history will recall that recounts and vote disputes affecting the presidency were not invented in the year 2000. No, pretty much the same thing happened 124 years earlier. Allegations of voter intimidation and fraud were rampant in three southern states: Louisiana, South Carolina, and—where else?—Florida.

Politicians and the national press thronged to Tallahassee until, in 1877, the congressionally appointed Electoral Commission awarded, by a one-vote margin, the three states to Republican Rutherford B. Hayes, who thereby defeated Democrat Samuel Tilden by a single vote in the Electoral College despite having lost the popular vote. The deal with the devil then was that federal troops would be withdrawn from those three states, thereby appeasing white segregationists and opening the door for the Jim Crow era that followed.

Florida has pretty much been the red-haired stepchild of the rest of the nation since it was acquired as a territory from Spain in 1821. In 1824, Congress gave Frenchman Marquis de Lafayette $200,000 and a township to settle the nation's debt to him from the Revolutionary War. Of course, the land we gave him was in Florida, the moral equivalent of recycling an unwanted wedding gift. LaFayette was given thirty-six square miles, centered around what is now the northeast quadrant of Tallahassee. He never came to Florida, but sent over several dozen Norman peasants to set up a plantation of vineyards, olive groves, and mulberry trees in a quixotic attempt to prove that free labor could outperform slave labor. The idea went bust and his land was eventually sold for $103,000. A city park and its surrounding neighborhood in the middle of the original grant now bear his name.[4]

In 1827, Ralph Waldo Emerson visited the territorial capital city—a

[4]Allen Morris, *The Florida Handbook, 1971–1972*, Peninsular Publishing Co., Tallahassee, 1971, p. 5.

town chosen because it was halfway between the two original settlements, Pensacola and St. Augustine. He wasn't impressed, writing in his diary that the place had been "rapidly settled by public officers, land speculators and desperadoes."[5]

Old Ralph pretty much nailed it. As to the land speculators and desperadoes, he could have been talking about any part of Florida going forward the better part of two centuries. The land, and how to get rich off of it, and the characters who've been drawn to the nation's southern frontier have been and continue to be central threads in the state's storyline, even from before official statehood in 1845.[6] Then, the population lived in the Panhandle town of Pensacola, the eastern port of Jacksonville, and lesser towns scattered across the forests, flats, and rolling hills of Florida north of Orlando.

For all intents and purposes, there was no South Florida. There were a few military garrisons stretched along both coasts, and some cattle ranches set up by the more daring adventurers and marauders who were willing to make a home on land only recently stolen from the natives. But that was pretty much it, and that was pretty much how things stayed through the early decades of the twentieth century.

The state—run as it was by agricultural interests who profited from slave labor—joined the rest of the South during the Civil War. Sparsely populated, it was never the scene of the major battles, nor did it suffer the damage sustained by more important parts of the Confederacy.

Yet the aftermath of the war brought fundamental changes to institutions that have shaped and continue to shape Florida and its politics to this day. Like the other southern states, Florida was run by the Union army immediately after the war, gradually replaced by a locally elected government that chafed under the conditions imposed upon it by the North (like having to let former slaves vote). To minimize the power a carpetbagger governor could have, lawmakers wrote a constitution that made him[7] share executive power

---

[5] *Ibid.*, p. 7.

[6] English explorer and privateer (that would be a euphemism for state-sanctioned pirate) Sir Francis Drake, for instance, sacked and burned the Spanish settlement of St. Augustine in 1586. Why? Well . . . why not?

[7] To this day, Florida has not had a woman governor. The first female lieutenant governor was appointed to that post in 2003 by Governor Jeb Bush.

with six others: an attorney general, a secretary of state, a commissioner of agriculture, a treasurer, a comptroller, and a commissioner of education.

Like the governor, the six cabinet members were elected by voters statewide every four years. They did not answer to the governor. They did not have to do what he told them. He could not fire them. As submitter of the state budget and holder of the veto pen, the governor was more powerful than any of the cabinet members, to be sure, but as governors go, Florida's was a weak one.[8]

The net effect of this has been to enhance the power of the legislature and diminish that of the titular head of state. The ramifications of this on Florida's body politic have been awesome—as significant as Henry Flagler's railway and the invention of air-conditioning were to the explosive growth that moved Florida from the thirty-first most populous state in 1930 to the fourth in 1990.

All cabinet officers had good reason to get it into their heads that they, too, could be governor because they had won statewide races. And in 1978, two of the six cabinet officers decided to run for governor. So did the sitting lieutenant governor. Each held a loyal constituency but could not win a majority in the primary election—thus letting a virtually unknown state senator with a great gimmick and a brilliant TV adman sneak in out of nowhere, come in second in the primary, and then, with the momentum behind him, roll to victory in the primary runoff and general election.

Bob Graham has never looked back.

[8]The Cabinet was shrunk by voter approval in the 1998 constitutional revision. The treasurer and comptroller were merged into the "chief financial officer," and the commissioner of education and the secretary of state were eliminated, with the responsibilities shifting to the governor. The changes took effect in January 2003.

Workdays

Wherever you live, whatever you do, there's a good chance Bob Graham has done your job.

Over the past twenty-six years, on an average of once a month, Graham has spent the day doing somebody else's chores. He has driven a truck, cleaned fish, and unloaded freighters. He has picked tomatoes, picked oranges, and picked up garbage. He has fixed roofs, paved roads, and worked the high steel. He has, on separate occasions, sold shoes, sold life insurance, and sold tires. He has been an elf, a stable boy, a sports photojournalist, and a railway track inspector. He has been an actor, twice—once playing the role of a dead body. He had to lie still nearly the entire production, before his surprise speaking role at the end.[1]

He has taught school. A lot of school. Twenty-two times he has spent the day in a classroom, his most popular gig. Next has been construction worker, sixteen times, followed by assembly line worker, seven times.

Over those two decades, he has spent a "workday," as he calls them, in 109 different Florida cities, from Key West (dive boat operator, lobster fish-

---

[1] October 26, 1977. The Broward Community College production of *The Real Inspector Hound.*

erman, intelligence watch officer) to Pensacola (bricklayer, social worker, Coast Guard crewman).

Workdays, of course, began as a gimmick, invented purely to get Graham, then a no-name state senator, into the Governor's Mansion. To that end, they were a phenomenal success, both in that initial race as well as subsequent elections to the United States Senate.

But why, after twenty-six years, does the gimmick continue to resonate with Floridians?

For one thing, a gimmick stretched over a quarter-century earns a measure of respect, for its own sake. But even more important, the workdays have produced a fundamental change in the man—a truly remarkable transformation when you consider Graham's pre-workday persona.

Once upon a time, Graham was a shy introvert who had trouble walking up to people he didn't know and speaking to them in a way that seemed remotely human. This is not, obviously, a desirable trait for someone who wants to get complete strangers to vote for him or, even more important for a new candidate, give him a check for $500.

"When we started campaigning, he'd get in a room full of people and he'd just look down at his shoes," recalled Tom Lewis, who wound up serving eight years for Governor Graham in various jobs. That demeanor changed only as the workdays got started. With those under his belt, instead of being able to speak only about himself, Graham immediately had two areas of common ground—hometown and occupation. "That made him a conversationalist."

John Van Gieson, who over the years covered Graham for the Associated Press, the *Miami Herald,* and the *Orlando Sentinel,* decades later remained impressed with the transformation.

"He sort of reinvented himself," said Van Gieson, now a Tallahassee publicist. "He made himself into this interesting, outgoing guy, when actually he was boring and ponderous. You've got to give him credit."

Prior to 1977, Bob Graham actually called himself D. Robert Graham. That's what his nameplate said in the Florida legislature. He worked hard to learn all he could about the issues, especially education, and he pushed big, idealistic proposals to fix Florida's woes and believed other law-makers would support his bills because it was the right thing to do.

He was, obviously, somewhat naive.

That he was in the legislature at all was a result of fortuitous timing. For decades, political power in the state had been jealously guarded in North Florida—*real* Florida, according to denizens of the rural counties who regarded all the transplanted Yankees, Jews, and, later, Cubans of South Florida as both politically and morally suspect. Every decade, the U.S. Census would show that more and more of Florida's populace resided in the growing cities along the coasts. And every decade, the Florida legislature would reapportion the state legislative districts so that the northern, rural counties continued to dominate.

While most of the country abided by the maxim "one man, one vote," Florida lived more by "one pine tree, one vote." In 1955, a mere 18 percent of the population elected a majority of both the state house and the state senate.

The group that did the apportionment—or, according to southern Florid-ians, malapportionment—naturally used this power to send much of the state's largesse to their own constituents. This was the Pork Chop Gang, which held sway right through the 1960s, when the courts finally forced the Florida legislature to do what even legendary governor LeRoy Collins had failed to do in the 1950s.

In 1966, as Graham worked with brother Bill building Miami Lakes, it was determined that a new apportionment plan would, overnight, increase Dade County's representation in the state house sevenfold. Instead of just three members, Dade would get twenty-two. (It also went from one state senator to nine.)

And here, fate intervened in the form of a family friend, who asked young Bob Graham to lunch at the Minerva Restaurant—a hangout for politicos in downtown Miami—and asked if he had any interest in the state legislature. By all accounts, Graham knew as a child that he would pursue politics as his father had done. Back when he was eight years old, he had told his big brother Bill's wife, Patricia, that he would be governor someday. He repeated the boast a dozen years later, on a double date with

Adele, at Joe's Spaghetti House in Tallahassee.[2] At the Minerva Restaurant, Graham told Jesse Yarborough that, yes, he was planning on running for the legislature at some point but didn't think he was ready. Yarborough reminded him that Dade would have nineteen open seats in the coming election—something that would not happen again for who knew how long. If he wanted to run, now was the time.

The argument made sense to Graham, who, along with a couple hundred others, filed papers to run for one of the twenty-two house seats, all of them countywide (single-member districts didn't come until later). His particular seat had seven candidates, including Graham. He spent $20,000, total, and worked for as many endorsements as possible, on the theory that since everyone was a relative unknown, voters would probably pay more attention to the advice of community groups and newspapers than they might otherwise.

The strategy worked. Graham, thanks to his command of the issues, impressed editorial writers and won the endorsement of both the *Miami Herald* and the *Miami News*. He won a clear majority in the primary, beating six opponents without needing a runoff.

The result in 1966 was that among the eighty-five freshmen of the 119 members in the Florida House of Representatives, one was D. Robert Graham, Harvard Law, 1962, full of brilliant ideas about education and social welfare and ready to change the world.

Ordinarily, a freshman lawmaker in a new chamber does little but sit quietly and bide his time. Not so in 1966 in the Florida house—because not only were there eighty-five newcomers, their opinion actually wound up mattering when it came time to picking a speaker. Normally this was preordained several years earlier, but in this case, speaker-designate George Stone had died in a car accident earlier that summer. Graham cast his lot with Ralph Turlington, a progressive supporter of education from Gainesville, and when Turlington won, Graham was rewarded with the chairmanship

---

[2]At the time, Graham was actually dating the other girl at the dinner, his freshman sweetheart. Adele asked her afterward if Bob was serious about the governor thing, and was told that, yes, he was.

of the subcommittee in charge of education spending—an incredible responsibility for a freshman.

"It was a very heady experience," Graham recalled.[3]

Graham had always been a quick study, and his intellect served him well in the house. He was voted second most effective by his peers. Fellow Miamian Talbot "Sandy" D'Alemberte, who later became the president of the American Bar Association and then (thanks to his friendship with Graham) president of Florida State University, was rated most effective.

Graham recalls those years with fondness, calling them "the most joyful" of his time in the legislature. "We sort of saw everything that happened before as being the old days, the old Florida, and we were there when the new Florida was going to begin."[4]

After four years in the house, Graham took advantage of an open seat and moved to the state senate, where his career quickly stalled. The house, filled with freshman members, was big, chaotic, loud—fertile ground for a new legislator willing to work. The senate had little resemblance to it. With only forty-eight members (in the reapportionment of 1972, that figure was reduced to forty), the senate was a club, with its clique of leaders and wanna-be leaders.

The election of 1970, as it happened, saw two senators who, because of their similar philosophies, might have placed D. Robert in high-powered roles. Instead, they left the chamber for bigger and better things. Lawton Chiles, of Lakeland, walked the length of Florida and into the United States Senate. Reubin Askew, of Pensacola, defeated the sitting attorney general in the Democratic primary and then oddball Republican incumbent Claude Kirk to become governor.[5]

Instead, the senate was left with Dempsey Barron, of Panama City, who ran the chamber through a series of minions for the better part of two decades. Barron's way was backslapping and dirty jokes and you-scratch-

---

[3]University of Florida Oral History Project, Tapes F–I, May 24, 1989.
[4]*Ibid.*
[5]Actually, "oddball" is being gentle. Kirk brought a "mystery date," who was dubbed "Madame X" in press accounts, to his inaugural ball (he later married her) and had such a hostile relationship with the legislature that, to spite him, it once passed without alteration the disastrously flawed budget he submitted to them, forcing him to veto it and start all over.

my-back-and-I'll-scratch-yours horse trading. This, as can be imagined, was not D. Robert Graham's forte.

Pretty quickly, D. Robert found himself giving long, impassioned speeches to a virtually empty chamber in support of this bill or that amendment. When he was finished, his idea would get the "thumbs-down" from leadership and be killed on a voice vote, and he would sit back down.

His friends saw this banishment as a career killer. How can you possibly run for statewide office if you can't even get a bill heard, let alone passed? One close adviser told him: " 'Bob, I think you ought maybe to reconsider whether you are going to make this campaign for governor. You already are way behind Bob Shevin.' His analogy was that I was already fifty yards behind in a hundred-yard-dash race, and that somebody had just hit me over the knees with a two-by-four."[6]

Graham's exile actually turned out to be a blessing. If you are the chairman of an important committee and are at all conscientious, you have to spend extra days and weeks in Tallahassee. This is time that you cannot spend out in the rest of Florida where real voters live and work. What's more, being part of a leadership team limits the severity of the criticism you can unload. Graham, on the outs, had no such limits.

"I could be a mad dog. I could pick out whatever issues I was interested in and attack with no sense that I was being disloyal, because they certainly had shown that my loyalty did not count." Besides, Graham had already determined it was time to move on. "I decided by 1975–1976 that I was not going to spend twenty years in the legislature, so my ostracization—if that is the right word—coincided with my personal decision as to where my future was going to be."[7]

Actually, Graham was already thinking about a run for governor in early 1974, when an opportunity came along to lift himself out of the legislative doldrums.

[6]University of Florida Oral History Project, Tapes F–I, May 24, 1989.
[7] Ibid.

The sitting education commissioner, Floyd Christian, was under indictment for bribery and conspiracy charges and had been accused of taking
$70,000 in kickbacks. That spring, he decided to resign rather than be im-
peached by the state house. Governor Askew announced that he would be
appointing someone to fill the remaining months of Christian's term. Whoever got it would have a tremendous advantage in the November 1974
election—essentially running as an incumbent.

The Tallahassee establishment saw it as a no-brainer. Askew would
choose Graham. One, Askew liked Graham. The two shared a passion for
preserving Florida's environment, and Graham would often sponsor Askew's
bills for him. Two, everyone knew that Graham loved education policy and
had made himself a wonk in the field. And three, Graham wasn't getting
much done in the senate anyway.

In the minds of pretty much everyone in Tallahassee, it was a done deal.
Well, maybe in the minds of everyone in Tallahassee *except* Bob Graham.

He didn't want the job. He had bigger plans, and sidetracking over to
run the Department of Education bureaucracy was not part of them. You
see, he told reporters in early 1974, he was going to run for governor in
1978, to succeed Askew after his second term.

It seemed outlandish at the time, but three decades of hindsight make
things much clearer. His father had been a Florida senator, and now Graham was a Florida senator. His father had run for governor, and now he was
going to run for governor. Why would he shoot for some third-rate cabinet
post instead? "Taking a detour as commissioner of education wasn't going
to get him there," said longtime aide Charlie Reed.

Naturally, everyone made fun of his decision. How did someone like
Graham think he could possibly compete against the popular attorney general in a Democratic primary?

Actually, in 1974, Graham himself had no idea how that might happen, either.

And like so many things in life, Graham's selection of the campaign
strategy that put him in the Governor's Mansion was based in large mea-

sure on a number of chance occurrences—the first of which was his attendance in the spring of 1975 at the Education Commission of the States meeting in Denver.

For it was there that Graham ran into law school classmate Dick Freese, who, over dinner one night, suggested to Graham that if he was looking for a political consultant for the gubernatorial run he was considering, he ought to take a look at a guy he knew named Bob Squier. Graham took his advice and wound up meeting Squier at his Washington, D.C., office in the autumn of 1975.

Which is when chance occurrence number two came into play: Over the next two years, Squier was going to be working for the president of Venezuela. And to get to Caracas from Washington, one had to then (as one pretty much has to now) fly through Miami.

And so it was that the Ionosphere Lounge at the Eastern Airlines terminal at Miami International Airport became the war room for Graham's long-shot run for governor. Squier later became one of the top-shelf political consultants in Washington—handling television advertising campaigns for candidates Michael Dukakis in 1988 and Bill Clinton in 1992 and 1996.[8] At the time, though, he was still an up-and-comer, working on Jimmy Carter's long-shot 1976 campaign.

Squier loved an underdog, so he was well paired with Graham, a candidate who had "zero name recognition and zero vote."[9]

So how could an unknown from the Florida senate get elected governor against a heavily favored opponent who had won statewide election previously? For inspiration, Squier and Graham turned to 1970—when State Senator Lawton Chiles, from tiny Lakeland, had beaten former governor Farris Bryant. The two analyzed Chiles's now-legendary walk from Pensacola to the Keys, studying its structure, and came up with the following:

First, it made great television. Every night, there was a strong visual image for the nightly news—a candidate walking past the city limits or into a downtown, surrounded by increasing numbers of supporters.

[8]Squier reportedly told Clinton after he picked his friend Al Gore for running mate in 1992: "He'll never stab you in the back, even though you may deserve it."
[9]Bill Peterson, "The Kingmaker of the 30-Second Spot: Robert Squier, Political Image-maker on a Winning Streak," *Washington Post*, November 27, 1979.

Second, it was something ordinary enough that regular people could identify with. Chiles was walking, not riding in a chauffeured limousine.

Third, the candidate would learn something from the experience—by the time he reached Key Largo, Chiles was a fount of anecdotes and adventures about everyday Floridians.

And last, it had a beginning and an end. Few voters or even journalists paid Chiles much mind when he started at the Alabama line in the western Panhandle. By the time he neared the end, there was enormous media interest to see him finish.

"The way, I believe, you have to conduct a modern political campaign in Florida is by going directly to the voters with a message, and one that is presented in a way that will attract their attention. They must first accept you as a person; then they will accept your ideas."[10]

All that would be Graham-speak for: "We needed a gimmick like Chiles's."

Merely repeating Chiles's gimmick, of course, was out of the question. "We understood that we couldn't emulate his walk without being accused of plagiarism," Graham explained a quarter-century later. They considered qualifying for the ballot through the petition method—holding a series of open houses to gather signatures—and having *that* be the gimmick, but that was rejected.

And then came the happy confluence of two more chance occurrences, both of which had already taken place.

It was the summer of 1974, and Graham, then chairman of Florida's Senate Education Committee, was giving a speech in Dade County and discussing the shortcomings of the social studies curriculum. High school graduates, he complained, seemed to know so little about basic civics. Afterward, a teacher named Sue Reilly came up to him and suggested that seeing as how he had all the answers, would he like to come give it a try himself?

"I have a rule of life, which is that if someone asks you to do something that, by accepting, will cause you to be ingratiated to them and that has almost no prospect that you will actually be required to do anything, accept—quickly," Graham said years later. "So I did, and forgot about it. Ten days later, Sue called and said, 'I have worked it out.' I asked, 'What is it that you have worked out?' 'You are to come to Carol City High School on the day after Labor Day. You are to report to Room 207, where I have arranged for you to teach a twelfth-grade civics class, which will meet at eight in the morning for the next eighteen weeks.' Well, that was a little more than I had contemplated, but I felt I was committed."

Carol City is a poor, high-minority neighbor of Graham's own Miami Lakes.

"It was really a life-changing experience for me. I learned more about kids, parents, and the reality of education than I had in the eight years sitting on education committees in the legislature," Graham said.[11]

Graham mentioned that experience to Squier—and found out that Squier had dreamed up similar workday gigs for Tom Harkin's congressional campaign. Harkin lost his first race in 1972, in part because many in his rural Iowa district saw him as a city boy. So for Harkin's second campaign in 1974, Squier designed ads that featured Harkin laboring at a series of farm-related jobs. This time, Harkin won.

Graham's "Workdays" campaign was born. Now the question was how to pay for the TV ads.

That television would play a pivotal role in the campaign was a given. Graham was enough of a realist to understand that in a state as large and as diverse as Florida, it was simply impossible to win the necessary support going door-to-door. The vast majority of voters would learn about the candidates primarily by what they saw on television.

Big corporations know this well. They understand that it takes an average of seven exposures to the name of a particular brand before a consumer is likely to give that brand a try. So it is with politics. To rate even a second look by potential voters, they have to have heard your name. (This is why politicians will perhaps cynically but probably correctly tell reporters: I don't care what you say about me so long as you spell my name right.)

---

[11] *Ibid.*

Television was, of course, expensive—especially in Florida, where a statewide "buy" means going to stations in a half-dozen separate markets from Miami clear to Mobile, Alabama. Graham in 1978 was a state senator, elected solely by Dade County voters in three elections in which he faced no strong opposition. Given that anonymity, and given his legislative exile, raising money at first was going to be virtually impossible, particularly with fellow Miamian Bob Shevin in the race. And that meant opening up his own wallet.

In all he spent $750,000—about $2.2 million in 2003 dollars—by cashing in some of his stock in the family business. At the time, that was about a third of his entire net worth. "As a Scot, it was a tough thing to do, but every month I would put in between $25,000 and $50,000," said Graham.[12]

There came a point, in fact, when Squier made it clear he needed a $250,000 commitment to keep the campaign going. Graham agreed, and it was his kid brother's willingness to part with that kind of cash that convinced Bill Graham there was a real possibility that Bob would win.

"It was really a lot of money to him," Bill Graham said two and a half decades later.

No campaign of this scale, however, can be pulled off by just a candidate and his paid staff. Before they could go any further, they needed a core group of Graham's longtime friends to sign on—to get behind Bob and lay the organizational groundwork for him if and when the campaign took off.

The first big sales pitch took place at a friend's law firm conference room in Tallahassee in the autumn of 1976. It was scheduled for the morning of the Florida–Florida State game that year—Saturday, October 16. Most of those present had attended Florida, as had Graham. All were political junkies and public policy wonks, as was Graham. Still, he stunned many of them when he told them he planned to run for governor and wanted their input.

Put simply: They thought he was nuts, and tried to tell him so as gently as they could. Who outside his senate district in Miami even knew who he was?

---

[12]University of Florida Oral History Project, Tape K, May 3, 1991.

But Graham had made up his mind. This was something he had wanted since childhood. He had even turned down an appointment to the vacant commissioner of education job two years earlier. His friends at the Saturday war council tried to fathom why Graham was doing this. He told them he was running for two reasons: one, his father had run in 1944 and had failed; and two, in a few weeks, he would turn forty, and he had to do *something*.

Fine reasons, his cohorts thought, but neither of them compelling enough to persuade voters to back some guy they didn't know. He had the right makings of a legislator, they told him, but perhaps was missing some of the characteristics that make for a good statewide candidate . . . like, say, charisma. He was too intellectual, they said. Too aloof. He had a tendency to go off onto long-winded policy explanations on the simplest of questions—a trait hardly conducive to the all-important television sound bite.

Leesburg lawyer Walter "Buddy" McLin told him: "When people ask you the time, you tell them how to build a clock."[13]

McLin was being kind. Graham is more apt to tell you how to build a clock, the importance of clocks, the history of clock-making, and go off on side tangents about the lives of some illustrious clock makers and the distinction between sidereal and solar time.

And so the discussion came around to the consensus that if Graham was serious about this, he needed a gimmick—something to help him connect better with average Floridians. The talk turned to Chiles's walk across Florida. Graham's friends started getting excited. What if Graham could invent such a stunt? By now, Graham and Squier pretty much had planned the workdays gimmick, but Graham let his friends brainstorm down the same path.

Years later, many of those friends now take credit for the workday concept. "It was one of those ideas that had a lot of parents," Graham said, looking back on it. "As Jack Kennedy said, if it hadn't worked out, it would have been an orphan. But because it did, lots of people are claiming part of the parentage."

The friends who would in coming months play an ever-larger role in

---

[13]Tyler Bridges, "Strategy Changed Him from Shy Policy Wonk to Popular Politician," *Miami Herald*, April 27, 2003.

spreading the gospel and passing the plate for Graham's campaign had bought into the plan. Now it was time to get a primer from the master.

Squier, Graham, and Graham's campaign manager, Garry Smith, met with Congressman Tom Harkin in Washington in early 1977 at Harkin's congressional office, two and a half years after Squier's workday campaign had put him in office.

Two things were critical for successful workdays, Harkin counseled: First, work the whole shift. However many hours the workers put in, you do it too, or they won't respect you. He had seen one candidate work while the reporters were there and then leave after an hour or so.

"You need to go when the workers go to work and leave when their shift ends," Harkin told Graham and his team. "Don't cut it short. You have to do the whole thing, whatever that shift is. That is the single most important element of this."[14]

The second piece of advice: Set a time for press availability, and then cut them off. "That way when you do a workday, the workers feel that you were there to work and that you weren't there just for the press."

Graham took Harkin's advice, then sent up his plan for him to review. It called for a hundred workdays by the time of the primary election. Harkin told him to forget it. "That's too many," Harkin remembered telling him. "That's all you'll be doing."[15]

But by now Graham had his mind set on one hundred, and one hundred it would be—or, actually, ninety-nine, if you don't count the semester he spent teaching civics at Carol City High School in 1974. Graham counts that as Workday One, even though it took place nearly three years before his campaign for governor.

Before they unveiled the plan for public consumption, a couple of other details were resolved—like making sure Graham would actually be able to do the work. Raised on a farm, Graham was no stranger to manual labor. But that had been as a child. In early 1977, he was going on forty-one. A

---

[14]*Ibid.*
[15]*Ibid.*

Michigan candidate for governor had tried a stunt like this, only to injure himself so severely in front of reporters that he had to drop out of the race.

There was also the issue of being able to do this without looking like a dork—to make sure "that the people on the job would react positively and would not see me as being a buffoon interloper."[16]

S ure, it was a gimmick. But like everything else, Graham took it seriously.

As any newspaper feature writer can tell you, there's an easy way and a hard way to shadow people on their jobs. The easy way is to show up at a comfortable hour—say, ten or eleven in the morning—fill up a notebook with quotes and wry observations, then retire to the office by early afternoon to spin the yarn. The hard way is to show up when the regular employees show up, often before even the sun is up, and then hang in there for a full eight or ten or twelve hours of whatever it is being done. Usually this winds up being a lot more painful on the newbie than on the regulars, who have built up the necessary muscles and calluses over months and years.

Graham did it the hard way—as he was advised by Tom Harkin. At least once, Graham's enthusiasm for keeping up with coworkers for the day nearly got him laid up. At a fertilizer plant in Frostproof, Graham and his mates were wrestling fifty-pound bags of iron sulfate. "I don't know whether to blame my clumsiness, or a seam between the sheets of plywood that had been laid down over the metal on the floor, but the handcart with eight bags on it tipped over, knocking me down and bringing the bags with it," Graham wrote. "The curved right handle of the cart grazed my right ankle, bruising it but not causing any serious damage. I learned a lesson here: I want to work hard and be as productive as I can, but if I try to outdo the men who work on the job every day I'll end up battered or maimed. As I lay there somewhat dazed on the floor, the first question that passed through my mind was how I could do next Wednesday's shrimp boat job with a broken ankle."[17]

---

[16]University of Florida Oral History Project, Tape J, August 9, 1989.
[17]Bob Graham, *Workdays*, Banyan Books, Miami, 1978, pp. 88–89.

On September 3, 1977, Graham's eighteenth campaign workday, the would-be governor spent a night with the Tallahassee Police Department.

Not a day, but a night. The distinction is an important one.

Lots of politicians go for "ride-alongs" with police. Typically this is done in the mornings, when there is very little crime. Street thugs as a rule don't wake up until late morning or early afternoon, so mornings are best for made-for-the-noon-news adventures in police cruisers, smiling and waving at law-abiding citizens, glad-handing with patrol officers, and generally spreading campaign good cheer.

Not Graham. As he recounted in his 1978 campaign book, *Workdays: Finding Florida on the Job*, Graham showed up at police headquarters at 10 P.M., as officers were getting orders for the night shift. After listening with the officers to the series of bulletins about "suspicious persons or circumstances and stolen cars," he accompanied Officer Charles Garner onto the dark streets.

And as tends to happen in even medium-sized cities, what crime occurs generally does so at night. Alfred Dennis was a young black officer and a recent graduate from Florida State University with a degree in criminology. A quarter-century later, Dennis is the public information officer at the Florida Department of Law Enforcement. That Graham showed up for the night shift made a huge impression on Dennis.

"Cats and dogs and criminals are roaming that time of night. . . . I thought that was very impressive," Dennis said. "We all said to ourselves when we got off that shift: This is somebody to vote for."

At 10:39 P.M. (praise here to Graham's notebooks), Graham and Officer Garner, his partner for the night, hit the streets. By 11:19 P.M., they were responding to a shooting. They found a Ford Torino parked in a run-down neighborhood. A man stood beside the car. A woman lay slumped over the steering wheel, bleeding.

It's important to note here that, up until this point, Graham was not terribly keen on blood.

According to medical records that became public during his 1986 run for the United States Senate, Graham had never even been comfortable in a doctor's office for a routine visit. As a fifth-grader, he had fainted in class when the teacher started talking about "blue babies"—babies born with heart defects. As an adult, he told his doctor he couldn't bear watching hospital scenes in movies.

When Graham's longtime doctor, Franz Stewart, first examined him in 1963, Stewart wrote: "He is quite anxious over the examination, not because of any specific defect. . . . He is sweating profusely under the arms. He is ticklish, and he hesitates to have a blood count even though he realizes this is foolish."[18]

Graham even sought counseling in 1969 to rid himself of the phobia. Those sessions helped, Graham said, but what finally did the trick was that workday with the Tallahassee police and finding Hattie Hayes, fifty-four years old and bleeding to death from a gunshot wound to her belly from her drunken, possibly deranged, boyfriend.

"A lady had four or five shots fired into her. You are so involved with what you are trying to do—take care of the lady and secure the crime scene," Graham said. "A visit to the doctor is a lot less traumatic than that."[19]

Hayes died at the hospital, and Graham and Garner spent two hours gathering evidence. One photo shows Graham, a young millionaire running for the state's highest office, rooting through garbage cans at the scene.

"That experience," Graham recalled recently, "was a sad tragedy for that lady, but it has had a permanent benefit for me."

After the obligatory paperwork, the night shift continued, and so did Graham's education into the lives of the underclass. Not three hours after the shooting, Garner and Graham were at the scene of a domestic violence call, where a distraught young woman was accusing her drunken, now-sleeping husband of having beaten her.

The husband didn't put up much of a fight as they led him into the patrol car—but the wife did. As frequently happens in domestic violence cases, the complaining party, usually the woman, had a change of heart

---

[18]"Graham's Medical Records Show He Conquered Phobia of Doctors," Associated Press, March 30, 1986.
[19]*Ibid.*

upon seeing her loved one trussed up and on his way to jail. She told Garner to release her husband. When Garner would not, she began flailing at him with her arms, earning her a pair of handcuffs, too.

The couple continued to fight, then reconcile, then fight again. Graham and Garner left them at 5:12 A.M., after the jailer told the couple they could make one phone call between them. "The couple began to argue over to whom the call should be made," Graham wrote.[20]

One thing that clearly registered with Graham during his workday campaign was how little money most Floridians got by on.

Florida, it's important to note, was a poor state. It still is. Although the state's per capita income in the 2000 Census was $21,557, ranking it nineteenth among the 50 states and the District of Columbia, the figures are skewed because of the huge proportion of elderly residents with high to moderate retirement incomes. A more telling figure is the percentage of children who live in poverty: 17.2 percent. That puts Florida sixteenth from the bottom among the states and the District of Columbia.

In 1977 and 1978, it was even worse. In 1977, per capita annual income in Florida was $6,950—which works out to about $18,992 in 2000 dollars. Most families scraped along on a few hundred dollars a week—which must have come as something of an eye-opener to a politician who, thanks to his brother's management of the family fortune, never really *had* to earn a living.

Most chapters in *Workdays* include the salary of the people with whom Graham had spent the day.

Officer Garner earned $1,250 a month, including overtime. He also worked twenty-five hours a week as a security officer at Lewis State Bank. "Now that I have a family, I wish it weren't necessary to hold down two jobs to support my wife and children," Garner told Graham.[21]

Garner's $15,000-a-year police salary meant he was making more than twice what the average Florida worker earned, not to mention the medical

---

[20]Bob Graham, *Workdays*, Banyan Books, Miami, 1978, p. 25.
[21]*Ibid.*, p. 26.

and retirement benefits he enjoyed. Most of the state's workforce muddled through on considerably less, as Graham reported.

The average mechanic at Ken Roberts Toyota in Homestead could count on taking home $200 to $300 per week, although one of the men Graham worked with was living on $40 a week, largely because personal problems at home were making it hard to get the piecework at the shop done.

Graham's fellow bellhops at the Orlando Sheraton Twin Towers made do with two dollars an hour and about $20 in tips per day, or a total of $9,360 a year, assuming no vacation or sick days. His fellow busboys at the Versailles Restaurant in Little Havana averaged $15 a day, including salary plus a share of the tips.

Johnny Denton, an orderly at a Deland nursing home, took home $17 a day, or about $4,400 a year.

The importance for Graham to have met people like these and learned to see the world through their eyes, so to speak, cannot be overstated. One of the biggest knocks against Graham then and now is that he's a Harvard-educated millionaire.

All a political opponent has to do, particularly when addressing a middle- or lower-class crowd, is toss out that phrase. Harvard-educated millionaire. If once isn't enough, maybe a couple of times in the course of a speech. Harvard-educated millionaire. Harvard-educated millionaire.

It's not precisely clear whether would-be voters are to be more offended by the university or the wealth—whether the presumption is supposed to be that he went to Harvard *because* he was a millionaire, or whether the fact that he went to Harvard gave him the expensive résumé and unfair connections that allowed him to become a millionaire. It doesn't really matter. As a bit of populist rhetoric, particularly in a Democratic primary, when all the other candidates are bragging about their blue-collar roots ("My father worked in the coal mines"; "My mother slaved away in the mills"; "My father got up at four every morning so he could work in the mill, and *then* worked *evenings* in the coal mine"...), the moniker sticks, and it can sting, with a clear implication that D. Robert Graham is a spoiled rich kid who has absolutely no clue what it's like to sweat ten hours a day for a paycheck.

The workdays gave Graham loads of ammunition to fight back. Sure,

State senator and candidate for governor Bob Graham refills water glasses as he spends a day as a busboy at Little Havana's Versailles Restaurant, 1977. (Photo by Joe Rimkus/*Miami News/ Palm Beach Post.*)

the other candidates could talk about the experiences of their own parents' grunt-work jobs. After the workdays, Graham could speak with authority about his personal forays into the salt mines.

"These work experiences are going to give me an appreciation of the conditions under which many Floridians live," Graham wrote in *Workdays*. "My own family is one person smaller than Johnny's, and I thought about how we could support ourselves on seventeen dollars per day."[22]

Graham reported that mullet gutter James Bishop's salary was $2.35 an hour, working about forty or forty-five hours a week, but that about $40 a week of that went directly to pay his wife's medical bills.

"Thinking about that made me remember something Mickey Rivers of

[22] *Ibid.,* p. 38.

the New York Yankees said when a sportswriter asked him about the pressure of playing in the World Series. Rivers said that what he did in the Series was *fun*. He said that *pressure* is a guy with a wife and three kids, a $200 bill to pay, and no job."[23]

As bad as Johnny and James and the others had it, it could at least be said that they *had* jobs. This was not the case for the folks Graham mixed with in the last section of *Workdays*, when he hit the streets of Tampa Bay with fifteen dollars in his pockets and a change of clothes in a brown paper sack. He would spend two days looking for temporary work—an even more desperate, albeit more brief, foray into the lives of lower-class America than the one writer Barbara Ehrenreich took a quarter-century later in *Nickel and Dimed: On (Not) Getting By in America*.

The results push Graham's prosaic narrative style into something almost poignant. Readers can see that what started out as yet another workday—or, as Graham puts it, a "nonworkday"—draws up in him frustration and anger at the indignities foisted upon the working poor.

"Let it be said that I am no fan of the Florida State Employment Service," Graham begins, and it goes from there. "Two particular instances of bureaucratic crudeness stick in my mind. In a Tampa office of the state employment service I found the men's room posted with the sign 'For Employees Only.' I tried the door, but it was locked. Imagine being unemployed, waiting on some indifferent state worker, and having to keep your legs tightly crossed."[24]

Later, trying to get food stamps at a different office in a city largely built by Spaniards and Cubans, Graham notices a sign: *Todos los aplicantes que no hablan ingles, necesitan traer un interprete*. Graham translates for us: "This means that all food stamp applicants who do not speak English must bring a translator with them."[25]

The outrages come fast and furious. Like all the other job-seekers, Graham must wait in an "ugly, Mussolini-style state building" without rest

---

[23]*Ibid.*, p. 102.
[24]*Ibid.*, p. 123.
[25]*Ibid.*

rooms "for the people they supposedly serve," as state workers glare at him angrily, presumably for being poor and unemployed. He encounters not-so-subtle racism in the one job he manages to get, delivering office furniture, when his black coworker, a forty-two-year-old born-again Christian, makes the mistake of checking in with the receptionist at a customer's office.

"She looked at him with a mixture of fear and disgust and rained questions on him. 'Where'd you get a key to this office? You're not supposed to be in this building!' Then she saw me, as grimy as Fred and dressed just as poorly, but my face calmed her down. Fred lost none of his dignity. Perhaps his religion helps him stomach it."[26]

The $12.50 Graham earns from that job at least allows him to spring for a bunk at the YMCA in St. Petersburg for the night: "A cut above the Salvation Army or the John 3:16 Mission on Third Avenue where the derelicts and winos stay."

The second day doesn't go nearly as well. The counselor at the state job office tells him that, as it is Friday, she doesn't expect any work. Graham turns to the *Tampa Tribune* classifieds. "When I called for a telephone operator job, the man just laughed at me. A sandwich shop downtown was advertising for help, but the man on the phone said they were looking for waitresses. I'd been foiled by a combination of sexism and an ad deficient in essential information. I even called an encyclopedia salesman number, but the people wanted a full-time commitment. A diner dishwasher job looked promising, but bus service is so poor in Tampa that the diner took hours to reach, and upon arrival I discovered that the kindly proprietor was looking for full-time dishwashers. I paid his waitress thirty-two cents for my single cup of coffee.

"With no prospects for a job, I started walking toward the warehouse district on Hillsborough Avenue. It began to rain. Nobody in the sloweddown stream of automobiles on Dale Mabry Highway seemed to look once at me and my brown paper sack as I trudged through the overgrown grass of the median littered with Ronald McDonald cups, beer and Coke cans, filter tips, and pop-tops. Puddles sloshed into my farm boots. I passed the

---

[26] *Ibid.*, p. 126.

King Arthur Motel, early 1960s with fake bridges, moats, and castle battle-ments. About every other block there seemed to be a neon sign advertising 'Live Girls.' Tampa must be the nude-bar capital of the hemisphere. They were going full tilt, and it wasn't even noon.

"Soaked, and lucky that the rain was a warm one, I finally reached a Tupperware warehouse. A job had been advertised in the *Tribune* for two days, and forty people had applied for it on the first day alone. What do you do?"[27]

Graham suffers through his final humiliation applying for food stamps late in the afternoon. "A food stamp worker, not missing a chew of her Juicy Fruit or a word of her conversation with her bored coworker, gave me a form to fill out. Figuring that I had been living more or less between Tampa and St. Petersburg, I asked her if it mattered which place I put down for residence. 'You gotta choose one,' she smacked. When I filled out the form, I learned that I would have to return for an interview. Naturally, not on the weekend. Nor on Monday. But twelve or thirteen days later. So it goes being down and out in Tampa—St. Petersburg."[28]

Which is not to say that it was all hard-luck stories and gritty, there-but-for-the-grace-of-God-go-I insights. Graham clearly had fun on his campaign workdays, and recounted much of it in his particular brand of arid humor.

In October 1977, nearly a year before the primary election, Graham fi-nagled his way into working for a day as an electrician in the still-under-construction, twenty-two-story Capitol Building in Tallahassee. Photos show Graham and his coworkers wearing safety goggles and wielding wire cutters.

"While we may look like latter-day versions of the Watergate burglars (who, as I recall, were Floridians of a sort), this is only an ordinary Muzak sound system crew," Graham wrote.[29] "The locale of our job, however, isn't

---

[27] *Ibid.*, p. 128.
[28] *Ibid.*, p. 130.
[29] *Ibid.*, p. 115.

exactly ordinary. These are the offices of the governor . . . and Florida's press found it interesting that my workdays campaign actually landed me in the governor's office almost a year before the primary and election. Our job for the day was to wire several offices to enable them to monitor the legislature."[30]

In the middle of his day clearing tables at the Versailles, Graham reported that his efforts to pass himself off as a Miami Cuban had failed.

"I noticed that a matronly woman kept staring at me. Finally, Señora Suarez came over and confronted me. I told her who I was and why I was wiping the black beans off the otherwise immaculate counter. 'I knew there was something funny going on around here,' she said. 'You don't even look Cuban, and your Spanish isn't good. What I thought was that the Equal Employment Opportunities people had come to Versailles and told them to hire an Anglo. I thought you were it.'"[31]

In the section devoted to his stint making Cuban sandwiches at La Tropicana in Tampa, Graham enumerated the woes of making a meatball sub: "The meatball sandwich is the bane of the counterman, since it entails an operation involving a piece of bread and three meatballs slightly larger than golf balls and covered with a heavy spaghetti sauce. These take four sheets of wax paper to wrap and special attention to tucking corners— otherwise, a messy sandwich will turn into an unacceptably sloppy one. The really demanding challenge is sticking the toothpick through the four layers of wax paper, a task I never mastered. One of the television stations did what seemed like five minutes of film on me trying to put a toothpick in a meatball sandwich. Thank God they didn't use it."[32]

Later, still at La Tropicana, Graham got a little insight into the free-market competition among the nude clubs for which Tampa is renowned, when one of the owners came in for a sandwich and Graham got a job offer other men might have killed for. "One club had gone so far as to introduce kissing between the live girls and the live patrons. The owner of a

---

[30]After twelve years in the legislature, Graham should have known that wiring the local bars would have been a more effective way of accomplishing that goal.

[31]Bob Graham, *Workdays*, Banyan Books, Miami, 1978, p. 99.

[32]*Ibid.*, p. 94.

competitive club was agonizing over whether to meet the challenge—he even offered me a job as wardrobe assistant. This was not quite the experience that the workdays were intended to provide, and could have put a spectacular end to my political career."[33]

It was a theme that surfaced repeatedly in *Workdays*—and, for that matter, through the subsequent years of workdays: Bob Graham, notorious straight-arrow, encountering the cultural values of Joe Lunchbucket.

"Freddie and I struck up a quick friendship during brief intervals when the forklift truck was gone. I knew I had made progress when he broke out his Skoal snuff and offered me a dip. I told him I had given up all forms of tobacco, which was slightly untrue since I had never really started and wasn't about to do so with Freddie's snuff."[34]

The most fun campaign workday for Graham was probably his stint at the Sheraton Twin Towers, carrying luggage for women activists on both sides of the ERA debate, helping the leering veterans of the Fourth Armored Division of World War II gathered for their convention and—could it have been better scripted?—humping bags for his main opponent in the Democratic primary, the guy everybody thought would win and win easily, Attorney General Bob Shevin.

Graham showed up at 6:55 A.M., five minutes early, and learned the ropes from a 20-year-old who had been working there three years. At 7:41 A.M. (thank God for the little notebooks, huh?) he had his first bellhopping call, to room 1546. After a quick introduction to the coding behind room numbers—rooms whose last two digits are between 1 and 23 are in Tower A, those between 24 and 46 are in Tower B—we are introduced to one of the 8 A.M. bellhops, Richey Tribue, "a tall, young black man," whom Graham deemed "the most politically aware and interested of the bellhops," and with whom Graham spent much of his slack time.

Tribue opposed any more sales tax increases—Florida's tax had gone from three cents to four in 1968, under Governor Claude Kirk—as well as

---

[33]*Ibid.*, p. 96.
[34]*Ibid.*, p. 84.

any more taxes on cigarettes. He did opine that the horrendous traffic on Interstate 4 would be one local program for which he would support a tax increase. Then came Tribue's thoughts on the drug problem.

"Richey said that he is very interested in the possibility of legalizing marijuana and that a gubernatorial candidate who comes out for repeal of criminal penalties for the possession of marijuana will get 90 percent of the youth vote."[35]

Tribue then asked about Graham's position on black issues:

"I told him of my general positions: the importance of state government being representative of the diversity in the state and the specific importance to blacks of quality public services; economic development; and tax reform, since the negative side of all these hits blacks and other low-income people particularly hard," Graham wrote. "He seemed satisfied."[36]

Or maybe diverted.

"Richey then left politics to give us expert evaluations of the female guests as they came by the bell station. One time he was so descriptive that he had to apologize to the other bellhops for his language, an apology that didn't seem necessary. Richey said he had to discipline himself not to go near the hotel pool because the bikinis would distract him for the rest of the day."[37]

"At 2:40 I encountered a leering fellow too young to have been in World War II but old enough to know where the action was. He said that his father-in-law was there for the Bulge memories and that he and his wife were taking part of their vacation. He asked me if I worked at the hotel, and I told him I did in a limited way. 'How do you pick up something free? I don't believe in this paying stuff—I am a free enterprise man. In most conventions, though, it's a monopoly.' I wondered if his wife knew of her husband's special interest in economics."[38]

But what made the Sheraton workday memorable was Graham's encounter with the guy who was supposed to clean his clock fourteen months later, his front-running opponent for the Democratic nomination, Attorney

---

[35] *Ibid.*, p. 53.
[36] *Ibid.*
[37] *Ibid.*
[38] *Ibid.*, p. 57.

General Bob Shevin. Shevin was an invited speaker at the International Women's Year Conference while Graham schlepped bags.

"At 10:03 a lady whom I vaguely remembered came to the bell station, pointed out a large red bag, and asked me to deliver it to the Cypress Penthouse. As we were walking to the elevator for Tower B she asked if I were not Bob Graham. I told her I was and explained what I was doing. She seemed amused and as we entered the elevator asked me if I knew who was in the Cypress Penthouse. I told her I did not, and she informed me that it was Bob Shevin's suite. When the doors opened on the nineteenth floor I told her that I did not want to embarrass anyone and suggested that I leave the bag outside the room to the suite. She insisted that I carry it inside and opened the door to Myrna Shevin, the wife of the attorney general, who was wearing a green and white dress with a half-inch green and white sash around her neck proclaiming 'Shevin for Governor.' Myrna, whom I have known more than ten years and whom I genuinely like and admire, was not particularly happy about the situation, and I tried to explain why I was there and that it was coincidence that I had been asked to deliver the bag. Myrna motioned toward the far side of the living room of what appeared to be a two- or three-bedroom suite at the top of Tower B.

"As I was putting down the bag, a female voice came from one of the rooms asking us to be quiet because 'The General is still sleeping!' I left on tiptoe. There was no tip."[39]

Twenty-six years of hindsight later, it is clear that Graham's workdays did, in fact, make a huge difference—just as they had been designed to do.

"When we first saw them, we thought they were hokey," said former Democratic House member Sam Bell. "The press couldn't resist covering them, as hokey as they were."

Graham went from 1 percent in the polls in mid-1977—the sixth candidate in a six-man field[40]—to 8 percent in the spring of 1978, thanks in

---

[39]*Ibid.*, p. 54.
[40]Technically there was a seventh candidate: LeRoy Eden, a Miami real-estate salesman who two weeks before the primary married his campaign manager and dropped out. He received 13,864 votes—or 1.34 percent.

large part to increasing press attention to the workdays combined with a quarter-million dollars of television advertising Squier had produced and placed for him, featuring Graham at work in various of his workday occupations. "Working for governor" was the tag line for each spot, and they were good—fast, punchy, with great visuals: Graham emptying trash cans, wearing a hard hat, talking earnestly to high-school students.

Until those commercials went up, most political pros in Florida had pretty much dismissed Graham. When they started seeing those ads, they realized he was onto something. Eventually, even the press came around.

Bill Rose began covering Graham for the *Miami Herald* in the spring of 1978. At the time, he was still viewed by politicians and pundits as one of the "also-rans" in the race against Shevin.

Rose said he began to question that assessment on the very first workday that he covered—an overnight shift on a shrimp boat during the final days of that year's legislative session. He, Graham, and some other reporters drove out that night to Port St. Joe, a paper mill and fishing community southwest of Tallahassee on the Gulf of Mexico.

That night, he saw Graham like he'd never seen him before. Where just hours earlier Graham had been in the Florida senate chamber, delivering the pedantic lectures that passed for his version of floor debate, now here was Graham on a working trawler, dressed like a crewman and talking with the other crewmen as though he genuinely belonged.

One of the chores on the boat when it came time to lower the nets and actually catch shrimp was for someone to walk out to the end of a long boom and release the mechanism. Rose watched in amazement when Graham scampered up and out along the boom—no harness, no life vest, at night on the Gulf of Mexico.

"That was the point he was making: I'm going to do the hard things, not just the easy ones," Rose recalled.

In the subsequent two weeks, Graham spent days as a crab fisherman in St. Petersburg, a deliveryman and a stock clerk in Miami, and a short-order cook in Fort Walton Beach.

Everyone had started out, not unreasonably, thinking of the workdays as gimmickry, but Rose came around to seeing that spending that much time with real Floridians was having an actual effect on Graham. The everyday problems of everyday people were starting to creep into Graham's campaign remarks. Graham was growing more folksy, more at ease with people with whom he had, until then, very little in common. "I talked to a whole bunch of people and they said: This man is really learning," Rose said.

Graham was a teacher's aide in Homestead, a maintenance man at a public housing project in Pompano Beach, a clerk at the Shell Factory in Fort Myers, a book salesman in Tallahassee, and a factory worker at a paper mill in Palatka.

Rose periodically broke off from Graham to cover Hans Tanzler, mayor of Jacksonville and a candidate many thought would give Shevin the most trouble in the primary. The contrast between the two camps was clear. Tanzler's supporters seemed to know they had missed whatever zeitgeist a successful candidacy is supposed to have. Graham's camp knew they had it.

In the month of July, Graham was a boat maintenance man for Miami Outboard Yacht Company, a plumber's assistant in Tampa, an electric supply assistant in Lakeland, a maintenance man at Great Lake Dredge back in Miami, a busboy in Orlando, a ticket taker in Tampa, a busboy again, this time in Titusville, and a park restoration worker in St. Petersburg.

Polls started to reflect what Rose already sensed: Graham's candidacy was taking off.

"When I was doing job number seven or eight, people could be skeptical and sort of ho-hum, and thinking it was a funny gimmick," Graham said. "But when I was doing job number seventy-three, people were starting to take it seriously, thinking, 'My God, he is really going to do this.'"[41]

Without a doubt, so many candidates running for the Democratic nomination worked to Graham's advantage. Had he been running against only Shevin, Graham likely would not have beaten him in the September 12 primary and Shevin would have been the nominee.

But it was not just Shevin. It was Shevin, Tanzler, sitting lieutenant governor Jim Williams, sitting secretary of state (and son of a former U.S. sen-

[41]University of Florida Oral History Project, Tape J, August 9, 1989.

ator) Bruce Smathers, and former Republican governor (now running as a Democrat) Claude Kirk.

Graham was lucky to have them all. Because each had a small but committed core of support, Graham could almost certainly count on Shevin not cracking 50 percent—which pretty much guaranteed a runoff.

And that, given Florida's history, would give whoever finished second the clear momentum. Florida's "second primary" system was created originally to prevent black candidates from getting elected—the thought being that all the white voters would rally around whichever white candidate made the runoff, should a black candidate be the other option. The system accomplished that goal pretty well until courts started insisting on single-member districts to increase minority representation.

An unintended consequence was the creation of a dynamic that, almost counterintuitively, favored the number-two finisher in a multicandidate primary. It worked like this: The favorite candidate would, by definition, do worse than expected by failing to win outright in the primary, while an unknown underdog was exceeding expectations merely by finishing second. Unless the spread was huge—say, 48 percent to 21 percent—the conventional wisdom said that the runner-up in the primary became the person to beat in the runoff.

Certainly it had worked out this way for some of Florida's most notable leaders. LeRoy Collins, Reubin Askew, and Lawton Chiles had all gone from relative unknowns in the primary to winner in the runoff to start distinguished careers.

It turned out that way yet again on September 12, 1978: Shevin came in first, but with only 35 percent. Graham ran second, with 25 percent. A Shevin-Graham runoff was now twenty-three days away.

Shevin came out swinging. He accused Bob Graham of being D. Robert Graham, for eight years a senate liberal, now passing himself off as a moderate, middle-of-the-road, man of the people. He came out with a television spot featuring an adding machine ringing up the costs of the programs Graham had supported in the legislature and concluding that Florida could not afford a Graham governorship. Shevin's newfound allies in the senate, Dempsey Barron and W. D. Childers, produced a talk-show-like tape in which they told viewers how terrible it would be if a liberal like

Graham were to win and be beholden—God forbid!—to the *Washington Post* because of his family connections.

It sounded shrill, and Graham was able to shrug it off, almost as if it were beneath him to respond.

Certainly it didn't help Shevin any that he was Jewish. Florida had not had a Jewish governor, and it has not had one to this day. True, Shevin had been twice elected statewide to the attorney general position on his tough-on-crime stance, but more than a few Florida bigots draw a distinction between what can be tolerated in a mere cabinet officer and what can be tolerated in a governor.[42]

The issue actually came to a head at a candidates' forum held in the Panhandle—then, and now, a bastion of bigotry—when a man got up and asked Graham and Shevin of their positions on some issues, their military service, and the name of the church they attended.

Graham got up to answer first, telling the crowd that both he and Shevin, as well as their wives, shared a strong faith in God. The crowd got the message: Graham thought the question was out of line.

Shevin got up and said that he believed his faith in his Creator was as firm as anyone's in that room. It was a strong and classy answer. "It didn't matter, because Graham had beaten him to the punch," reporter Rose recalled. "Afterward, they mobbed him like a rock star."

Graham, who had pumped three-quarters of a million dollars of his own money into the race prior to the primary, found that he didn't need to spend any more of the family fortune. All the big-money boys had sensed which way the wind was blowing and started investing in the guy they had a hunch would be the next governor.

The final blow came just before the runoff—a debate to be televised statewide from a Jacksonville television studio. Unfortunately for Shevin, he had recently been quoted as scoffing at one of Graham's last workdays, a shift at the Drapers Poultry chicken-processing plant in Jacksonville. Shevin told reporters that the people were never going to elect a chicken plucker as governor. So, the night of the debate, Shevin arrived after a long

---

[42]Richard Stone, elected one of Florida's U.S. senators in 1974, was defeated in the Democratic primary of 1980. His Jewish faith was a perceptible undercurrent in that race.

day campaigning and was confronted outside the studio by two dozen chicken pluckers from Drapers.

They carried signs: "Chicken Pluckers for Graham" and "We Want a Chicken Plucker as Governor." One even threw a rubber chicken at Shevin, hitting him as he walked into the studio. Shevin was left dazed, Graham felt, and had a consequently poor showing in the debate.

On October 5, 1978, Graham finished a two-year campaign by coming from behind and winning, 54 percent–46 percent. He had lost the primary by 103,000 votes but won the runoff by 64,000.

At that point, the general election became largely a formality. "Once we won the nomination, we felt we were going to be elected. We moved from being the guerilla campaign, the underdog, to all of a sudden being the heir apparent," he said later.[43] Graham handled it without breaking a sweat, winning by twelve points.

On November 8, 1978, the *Miami Herald*'s headline proclaimed: "Graham Lands 101st Job."

That could have been the end of the workdays. Chiles, after all, did not walk the state a second time after his election to the Senate. And Harkin didn't bother much with workdays after reaching Congress.

Here was Graham's genius regarding the workdays: He realized their inestimable value—on both his standing with the electorate and, perhaps just as important, his relationship with the press corps outside Tallahassee.

This has to do with the natural dynamic between any elected official and the reporters assigned to cover him. After a brief honeymoon, reporters get bored with the everyday and begin looking for something out of the ordinary to write about—out of the ordinary usually meaning a scandal of some sort. This is not the case with reporters outside the state capital, who rarely get to see a governor, let alone see one in a situation as naturally fun to write about as a workday.

In that regard, the workdays have been an unqualified success. As they do with most politicians who give them good access and treat them collegially,

---

[43]University of Florida Oral History Project, Tapes F–I, May 24, 1989.

Adele Graham straightens husband Bob's hair on election night, 1978. (Photo by Bob Mack/ *Miami News/Palm Beach Post.*)

reporters who have covered Graham typically like him personally, which has translated into coverage with a generally positive tone. Articles and television news pieces about the workdays have been almost uniformly positive.

On Graham's final workday prior to the September primary—it, like Harkin's final workday, was in a private home, as a housewife—the state's newspapers carried a photo of him cleaning a toilet bowl. The *Miami Herald* called him "a rich man who doesn't mind working his tail off under a broiling sun 'to better understand the problems of Florida's working men and women.'"

Two months into his first term as governor, Graham "worked" as a political reporter at the *Florida Times-Union* newspaper in Jacksonville. He was assigned the task of interviewing himself. Graham told the Associated Press reporter covering the event that he had worked hard "to make sure the governor didn't evade my questions." His lead paragraph—or "lede," in newspaper lingo—was also carried in its entirety by the wire service:

"In a wide-ranging interview, Governor Bob Graham emphatically reiterated that he has no intention of recommending that driving in Florida be restricted by age."[44]

In the ensuing years, Graham continued to get extensive coverage for his workdays, and won national notice for a stint with the Brothers of the Good Shepherd homeless shelter in Miami. Graham helped prepare and serve meals at Christmas for four hundred former mental patients, refugees, winos, and drug addicts. Graham spent the night at the shelter with the monks, awakening at 4:30 A.M. to get breakfast ready.

"I never had a governor wake me up before," one of the residents told the *Washington Post.*

Graham was visibly moved by the experience of "looking into hundreds of faces of the down and out." He asked Brother Paul Johnson, director of the Camillus House shelter: "Brother, how do you handle this emotionally?"[45]

By reminding Graham on a monthly basis how most of his constituents live and work, the workdays have also had a public policy benefit. In some cases, they have even provided Graham with a nontraditional network of experts in dealing with problems. In 1979, Graham called the over-the-road truck driver with whom he had delivered tangerines during his campaign to serve as a special adviser on the truckers' strike.

Naturally, not everyone is a big fan of the workdays, particularly some Republicans who see the media's extensive coverage of Graham at "work" as yet more proof of their liberal bias.

Others, like former House Republican leader Curt Kiser, are still amazed that living proof of Graham's privileged life somehow worked in his favor.

"Well, good God, if he'd grown up like everybody else, he'd have known what it was like to wait tables and dig ditches," said Kiser, who recalled doing exactly those jobs as a teenager in Iowa. "He's going out there doing these jobs that most of us did as kids paying our way through high school and college."

[44]F. T. MacFeeley, Associated Press, March 10, 1979.
[45]David Bird and Paul L. Montgomery, "Florida's governor helps serve the hungry," *New York Times,* December 27, 1980.

Still, some of the criticism rings a bit hollow, particularly considering that Graham has been consistent with his workdays through the years, even in years he has not faced reelection.

No question, politics has frequently played a prominent role. A hastily scheduled workday at the end of 2002 was to work the sidelines at the Orange Bowl game on January 2, 2003. Graham had just announced he was considering a run for president, and the game featured the University of Iowa versus the University of Southern California. (Graham promised he would not try to help Iowa win.) And it is certainly no coincidence that the first three workdays outside Florida since a 1982 stint in Oklahoma[46] were in New Hampshire, Iowa, and New Hampshire, respectively, in the spring and summer of 2003.

In a 1981 *Washington Post* column, Richard Cohen made fun of Chicago mayor Jane Byrne's very temporary move into public housing and also took a side dig at Graham: "Bob Graham is governor of Florida today because during the campaign he worked at as many jobs as he could. Of course, he never knew what it felt like to be stuck in one of those jobs, to see nothing in the future but what you saw that day, to work, as lots of people do, day after day at jobs they hate."[47]

Well, taking a literal view of things, that's true. Bob Graham always knew, even in his forty-eight-hour stint as a homeless job seeker, that the experience would come to an end and he could return to his comfortable existence. On the other hand, is true empathy for those with dead-end jobs or, worse, *no* jobs impossible except by those who have actually experienced it for themselves? Is there no value, then, for a politician (or a writer like Ehrenreich, for that matter) to delve into the lives of their hardest-luck constituents? Is Florida actually *worse* off that Graham took the trouble to pursue this gimmick rather than, say, dip even deeper into his family fortune to fill the airwaves with television ads?

---

[46]Graham was paying off a bowl game bet. Had the Florida State Seminoles beaten the Oklahoma Sooners, Oklahoma governor George Nigh would have had to pick oranges in Florida for a day.

[47]Richard Cohen, "Slumming Won't Teach What Slum Life Is Like," *Washington Post*, April 9, 1981.

Governor Jello

There is Florida, and there is Miami. For nearly a hundred years, or pretty much since there's been a Miami, the two haven't gotten along so well.[1]

Even before Miami became the cosmopolitan bazaar it is today, as much a Latin American outpost as it is a *norteamericano* megalopolis, the ranchers and farmers and lumbermen and paper mill workers of central and north Florida had little use for the city slickers down at the end of U.S. Highway 1.

So when Bob Graham's father ran for governor in 1944, he was immediately at a geography-based disadvantage. It didn't matter that he was a dairy farmer from a tiny settlement twenty miles outside of the urban center, or that he himself intensely disliked big cities. In the shorthand of politics, Cap Graham was from Miami, and it would be a cold day in hell before a Miami man became governor of Florida.

Thirty-four years later, the Florida governor's security team had to rus-

---

[1] Even Graham repeats the joke that the nice thing about visiting Miami is that it's so close to the United States.

tle up a space heater for the dais on the front steps of the new, twenty-two-story capitol as Bob Graham took the oath of office and became the state's thirty-eighth governor.

"It even snowed," recalls Adele Graham.

Bob Graham reveled in the irony. He had done it. What his father had not been able to do, what older brother Bill had worried might break Bob's heart if he failed to do, Graham had somehow managed to pull off.

Not that he reveled too long. No, there was too much work to be done.

Some politicians want to win a particular office so badly that, once they get there, they have no idea what to do next. This was not a problem for Graham, who from his first days knew exactly what he was going to do—a whole long laundry list of things. So many things, in fact, that it became his biggest problem.

In retrospect, Graham realized clearly what went wrong: "I succumbed too often to the temptation of drifting off into other fields and dissipating effort."[2]

It is a testament to his energy and intellect that even without focusing laser beam–like on a small number of priorities, Graham was still, by the end of his second term, able to bring sweeping changes to Florida, some lasting, others less so.

From an increased use of community-based care for the elderly to rolling back property taxes to increasing teacher salaries to putting some 125,000 acres of environmentally sensitive land under state ownership to—possibly the most lasting achievement—starting a program to restore the Everglades, without question Graham left his mark.

That he managed even half of that is amazing, given the disorganized chaos that marked much of his first term.

Probably the most instructive thing about Graham's first years in the Governor's Mansion was his nickname: Governor Jello.

It came from an editorial writer at the *St. Petersburg Times*—a paper, it

---

[2]University of Florida Oral History Project, Tapes L–M, April 6, 1994.

should be remembered, that *liked* Graham. It was first used to describe his handling of, of all things, the issue of whether convicted prison inmates who were new mothers should be able to keep their babies in a special prison nursery.

Graham had originally supported the idea, but after much complaining from his Department of Corrections about implementing it, he reversed himself and adopted his prison secretary's recommendation to scrap the program. That was it. The *Times* had seen enough of Graham's tepid leadership and blasted him for the way he quavered anytime the legislature crossed him. Graham, the *Times* had determined, had all the courage of a bowl of Jell-O when it came to dealing with legislative leaders.

Much to Graham's horror, the moniker "Governor Jello" soon spread around the legislature and the press corps, not just on that particular issue but as a comment on his whole administration.

Years later, Graham still smarted over the name. He told his University of Florida biographer: "(A) I thought it was not an accurate description of our administration; (B) it certainly was not kind; and (C) of all of the issues that a governor has to deal with, the one of dealing with pregnant women in prison is an issue of highly specific and relatively infrequent application by the nature of the circumstances."[3]

In fairness, "Jello" implies that Graham had no core beliefs and would therefore change his positions based on shifting public opinions. That really wasn't the case. Graham wasn't waffling on issues so much as he was failing utterly in advancing his agenda.

There were a number of reasons. First and most obvious: Graham was new to this. He'd never been a mayor or a county chairman or held any similar type of executive post. Second, Graham made a common mistake made by many newly elected executives—he brought his campaign staff with him to the Governor's Office.

This is understandable. Candidates come to like and trust those who have put them into office and, naturally, want their top aides to be people they like and trust. But running a campaign is much different from run-

---

[3] *Ibid.*

ning a government. In a campaign, the aides' job is to present the candidates' record and statements in the best possible light for consumption by a general audience. Good government administrators need different skills. They need to be experts in their area, they need to be quick studies, and they need to convey this information accurately and honestly to their boss. "Spinning" the facts, rather than being useful—as it was in the campaign—becomes detrimental to good governance.

The third, and biggest, problem for Graham was the legislature he had just left—specifically, the de facto strongman of the Florida senate, Dempsey Barron, who was determined to punish the man who'd had the moxie to somehow jump from neutered lawmaker to chief executive.

First and foremost, the Florida senate is a club. There are members, and there is everybody else. Members are expected to feel, more than anything else, that it is an honor and a privilege to be able to consort and pass time with other senators within the hallowed chamber, where mere mortals are not allowed. Freshman senators are supposed to shut up and quietly accept the scraps that fall to them when the leaders are done gorging.

Why the institution is this way is somewhat of a mystery. It is, at the end of the day, just one of two coequal chambers of the Florida legislature, an institution that has had more than its share of nincompoops and rogues through the decades.

Perhaps it's because the Tallahassee lobbying corps fawns on them so obsequiously that the title *Senator* goes to their heads. After all, the *senators* of ancient Rome killed the mighty Caesar! Surely the honorific ought to convey at least a *little* of that.

Whatever it is, the chamber has always been this way—conservative in the truest sense of the word, which is to say, not necessarily pro-business or anti-feminist or any of those labels, but institutionally conservative. Pro-*Senate*, at all times, and at all cost.

When Graham arrived there in 1970, he had no use for the sucking up that is expected of newcomers and quickly found himself on the outs. To be an effective senator, you were expected to pal around with the leaders, tell them how smart they were, go hunting and drinking with them.

One of the traditions of legislative life in Tallahassee, for example, were meals of fresh shrimp or filet mignon or lobster tail, downed with fine wine and liquor, while in the company of attractive young ladies—all catered by the various interest groups. Led by the mobile home industry, Tallahassee lobbyists for years maintained three trailers on the outskirts of town. One was used to prepare thick steaks for legislators, any way they wanted them. The second was a full bar to attend to their thirsts. And the third was a "hospitality" trailer, where lawmakers could, uh, converse with a young lady on a wide variety of topics.

Graham, on those rare occasions when he attended legislative social outings, was not exactly the party animal.

"Graham wouldn't even have known where the trailers were," said longtime aide Charlie Reed, now the California State University system chancellor. Reed said he recalled one cocktail hour Graham attended with some other senators, alcohol and nubile young ladies everywhere, and Graham was still trying to win votes for his amendment. "He's in the room, and he's still negotiating the budget, and they're just wanting to drink and raise hell."

Graham thought he could succeed by learning the issues before him in great detail, so as to make informed decisions and persuade his colleagues to do the same. Buddy Shorstein, a college friend who at the time was an accountant in Jacksonville, said Graham definitely succeeded in learning the issues. Whenever a friend or a client had a question about what was happening with a particular bill, Shorstein would call Graham. "He was one of the few people who actually knew what the hell was going on in the legislature," Shorstein said.

Of course, knowing what was going on didn't necessarily mean being able to do anything about it. Graham operated under the theory that legislators should support an idea because they believe it is a good idea and oppose an idea because they think it is a bad idea. Who was whose friend, and who supported whom in the last leadership election, and who gave your district a little hometown goody, should have nothing to do with it.

This, naturally, did not cut it with the senate power structure, for whom these personal friendships and loyalties meant the world.

Jerry Thomas was president of the senate in 1970 and put Graham "on the shelf," according to Graham's former colleagues in the house, and "gen-erally thwarted [him] at every turn," in the words of one political writer. The writer theorized that a new senate president in 1973 would turn Gra-ham's fortunes. He even produced a quote from that man, Tallahassee Democrat Mallory Horne, to back it up: "Bob Graham is one of the hardest-working people I've ever known. I'm going to rely on him heavily."[4]

Unfortunately for Graham, one of the things for which Horne would rely on him heavily was to lard up the state budget with money for Horne's alma mater, Florida State University. When the budget was printed and few of the items Horne had demanded were in there, Horne blew a gasket. He ordered Graham and his fellow lieutenants into his office and railed at them for failing to protect his interests.

Graham took umbrage at that. The interests to be protected were those of all Floridians, not just the senate president's.

That was the beginning of the end of Graham's legislative prospects. Sure, he had a safe senate seat for as long as he wanted it. But he had crossed the ruling junta, and for that there would be consequences.

Sam Bell, a Democratic house member from Ormond Beach, remem-bers one of them: Graham's attempts to modify his own education bill on the senate floor. One after another, he would stand up and explain an amendment and why it would improve his bill. And one after another, the members, acting on instructions from leadership, would kill each amend-ment on a voice vote.

This expulsion became institutionalized two years later. Graham and a group of like-minded troublemakers decided that Horne and perennial senate power broker Dempsey Barron ought not to be able, virtually by themselves, to install Barron as the next senate president. They got it in their heads that there should be some sort of democratic process involved in the selection.

They lost, of course, and were duly punished when Barron took over. They were stripped of their committee chairmanships and given seats in the back rows, a spot normally reserved for the party out of power, even

---

[4]Robert Hooker, "Kindergarten Teachers of Tallahassee, Beware," *Miami Herald,* August 13, 1972.

though Graham and his pals were all Democrats—"Doghouse Democrats," they were soon tagged.

In a way, this fall from grace wasn't so bad. It let Graham be Graham,
proposing his idealistic schemes to fix this or improve that without the
burden of horse-trading and back slapping, which he didn't enjoy doing
anyway.

And so there sat Graham in the back rows, fighting in vain to revamp
the school funding formula. There sat Graham—and this one really ticked
off the wine and spirit lobby—waving a bottle of rotgut and a bottle of
top-shelf whiskey, to point out the absurdity of taxing liquor based on vol-
ume instead of price.

"He was not very effective as a legislator," recalled Republican Curt
Kiser, who in those years represented St. Petersburg across the rotunda in
the house.

Not effective, sure, but not ignorant, either, about the workings of
statehouse politics. He had spent a full dozen years in the legislature—long enough to understand how bluster and attitude were often
more important than actual facts.

Years later, Graham recalled his first hard lesson in this area at the
hands of someone who was usually an ally in the house, Alachua County
representative Ralph Turlington. The debate was over a constitutional
amendment that would put the budget-writing authority in the hands of
the governor—which, Graham pointed out, was how it was done in forty-
three other states. Turlington quickly asked: What about South Carolina?
How was it done there?

"Well, the answer was that I did not know what the hell North and
South Carolina did and neither did Ralph, and it was totally irrelevant to
the issue, but I stumbled and said, 'I don't know.' . . . And he sort of used
that to take off on one of his famous speeches.

"I learned a good lesson then, and that was in parliamentary debate, the
prize goes to the person who appears to know what they are saying,
whether that is the case or not, and four years later I was debating a bill

that I had introduced for a joint acquisition of the Big Cypress, a large land area north of Everglades National Park.

"This was being opposed by sort of anti-environmentalist Republicans, one of whom . . . got up and he said, 'Senator Graham, you want to buy 300,000 acres of this swamp out there and spend all this money. Do you know how many counties in Florida are smaller than this land that you want to spend all this money on?' And I said, 'Yes, thirty-seven.' He was just completely taken aback. Just like the discussion of South Carolina's budget, neither he nor I knew the answer to the question, but by answering as if you knew, that stopped the line of discussion."[5]

Still, a rough idea of how to finagle what you wanted through a legislative chamber of which you are a member doesn't automatically confer the knowledge of how to get something through that same chamber when you are the executive. At least it didn't in the case of Graham.

Former Tallahassee journalist John Van Gieson said that while it was true that Graham had been in the legislature, he had not been part of the cliques that mattered. "Although he'd been in the process a long time, he'd been an outsider in that process," Van Gieson said.

Graham the ineffective state senator also didn't have to deal with the various and sundry state crises. Graham the governor had more than his share.

He had been in office barely five months when the state's independent truck drivers went out on strike. This was a national issue, but Graham saw what a disaster it could mean for Florida, which depends so much on its tourism industry for its sales tax collections, which in turn depends so much on the heavy summer months. Even more critical: Gasoline could not get from Fort Lauderdale's Port Everglades to South Florida gas stations without trucks, threatening to shut down the economy of the most populous region of the state.

Graham quickly called out the National Guard to provide armed escorts for gasoline trucks. He designated special fueling stations along major highways that visiting tourists could rely on to buy gas to get them to the

---

[5]University of Florida Oral History Project, Tapes F–I, May 24, 1989.

various vacation destinations and then enough to get them started on their way home.

He took steps to mediate the strike, too, and even called up his "work-day" colleague, Leon Felix, with whom he had delivered tangerines during his campaign, to serve as a special adviser. The strike was settled within two weeks, and Graham got high marks for acting decisively to solve what could have been a major problem.

Later that year, two hurricanes struck Florida within ten days of each other. Hurricane David skirted the Space Coast, causing $95 million worth of damage before heading north to hit Savannah, Georgia, and Hurricane Frederic came up the Gulf Coast, finally hitting the cities of Mobile, Alabama, and Pensacola, Florida.

"No one gives you any training before you're governor in how to deal with these types of situations," Graham said a couple of years later. "In this business, you don't have time to sit in a Hamlet-like pose questioning the decision you've just made because it's already time to make another one."[6]

The following year, 1980, provided even more headaches.

In April began what would eventually become a 125,000-refugee exodus from Cuba in the Mariel boatlift, giving Graham problems for years to come. Crime and the demand for social services in Miami increased manyfold, and the federal government was not exactly eager to help pay for any of it.

Then, on May 9, a harbor pilot guided a freighter into one of the support piers for the Sunshine Skyway bridge across the entrance to Tampa Bay. Eight vehicles plunged 140 feet into the water, including a Greyhound bus carrying twenty-six. In all, thirty-five people died and traffic in the area was disrupted for years to come.

And just nine days later, blacks in Miami's Liberty City slum, already angry at what they saw as preferential treatment for the Hispanic refugees, exploded in rage when an all-white jury acquitted four white former police officers in the beating death of a black insurance executive. Graham had to call in more than 5,000 National Guard troops to quell the violence, which ended up claiming eighteen lives and causing $100 million in damage.

[6]Mike Ollove, "The Turning Point," *Miami Herald,* December 9, 1984.

Dealing with the curveballs thrown at him was one thing, and Graham handled them well. Dealing with the things expected of a governor was quite another. To put it mildly, he flopped.

Graham had come into office having made a number of promises he intended to keep. Tax reform, for starters. Graham wanted to rejigger the funding scheme for public schools, increasing the share from the state and decreasing the share from local property taxes.

To achieve that goal, Graham called a special session toward the end of his first year. Apparently no one told him that calling a special session without having some sort of deal in place to accomplish whatever it is you want to achieve is a recipe for disaster. Graham had no plan for getting his package through. The legislature convened and, after a few days, adjourned and went home without doing anything. It was a disaster.

"Just an abomination," said Kiser, by then the Republican leader in the house. "Just terrible. We prevented any of his reforms from passing. *Zero*."

The root cause was Graham's naïveté. Just because he had a good idea did not mean the legislature—particularly *this* legislature, run by the likes of Dempsey Barron—was going to study the proposal in a rational, grown-up way and offer constructive criticism and so on.[7] Heck no, these people were going to mess with the new governor as much as they could, teach him a few things about who really ran Tallahassee.

It didn't help that he had around him a team of aides who weren't exactly seasoned Tallahassee pros. For instance, his first budget director put together a proposed budget that didn't quite balance, as proposed budgets are supposed to do in Florida. Naturally, this gave the press and the veteran lawmakers a field day. Governor Smarty-pants can't even draft a budget that adds up. On top of that, simple, basic things weren't getting done. Mail to the Governor's Office was going unanswered. Appointments were missed or never made, the result of plain old disorganization.

---

[7]Much as you might imagine the Founding Fathers talking things out in Philadelphia, one hand in the air in grand gesture, the other tucked into the opening of their jackets.

To make things worse, Graham's liaison to the legislature was a trio of campaign aides, none of whom had much Tallahassee experience.

Tom Lewis, who prior to signing on with Graham's campaign had been an Orlando architect, puts it like this: "We didn't know shit about the legislative process."

Team Graham was so disorganized about how to go about getting what it wanted that former house member Sam Bell recalls one occasion when Graham's staff, watching the house proceedings on television in the governor's suite, sent an aide up to the fourth-floor chamber to deliver the governor's position to house leadership. "Before the guy could get up to the fourth floor, they called and said, 'We just sent this guy up there to tell you something, but we've changed our minds,'" Bell said.

Graham wanted to do too many things, and therefore wasn't getting any of them done.[8] "He didn't recognize you couldn't heal the world in sixty days," Buddy Shorstein recalls.

"We had the biggest fights to try to get him to narrow his agenda down," said eventual budget director Tom Herndon. "He just would not hear of it."

Graham was the idea guy[9]—constantly taking notes, constantly giving his aides instructions, never really slowing down to set his priorities. One maddening thing to his staff was Graham's tendency to give the same assignment to several of his aides. He was therefore more certain to see that it was accomplished, but also certain to irritate and demoralize his aides.

By the end of his first term, Graham had brought in competent, experienced staff: Dick Burroughs, who had run the Department of Business Regulation and had been one of the "white hats" in Jacksonville when much of city government was getting hauled off to court; Charlie Reed, a professional educator whom Graham had brought in from the Department of Education; Tom Herndon, a social worker by training who had been budget director for the house.

---

[8]Except for one populist bill he managed to push through: the elimination of the state safety inspection for all cars. Having seen "what a joke" the inspections were during a workday, Graham vowed during his campaign to get rid of them.

[9]Not unlike the Michael Keaton character in *Night Shift*.

Getting Reed, particularly, was seen in hindsight as a major coup. He'd had years of experience finagling things from the legislature—just the sort of expertise Graham's office was missing. Getting him, though, took characteristic Graham persistence.

Reed—a former George Washington University halfback who resembles in both appearance and manner Ed Asner's character, Lou Grant, from the *Mary Tyler Moore Show*—liked Graham, but he knew from experience that he could either have a life or work for Graham but not both.

"Because he worked all the time," Reed said, recalling all the assignments he'd get from Graham the state senator when he wasn't even Reed's boss. "I didn't work for him, and he made me work all the time."

Tax policy analyst Ed Montanaro remembers meetings at odd hours to discuss some issue Graham wanted to understand better. "We're meeting in the small conference room at 10 o'clock at night. Or we're meeting at the Mansion at 9:30 on a Saturday morning."

Reed declined the offer when Graham asked him to join his team. Graham asked again. Reed declined again. Finally, Graham called Reed's home one afternoon and asked his twelve-year-old son, Chip, to tell his father that Graham wanted him to work for him and to tell him to go to the Mansion for breakfast to talk about it.

Reed remembers his son asking him: "Dad, why don't you want to go work for the governor?"

Reed went to the breakfast, and finally relented—an accomplishment for which Graham was, in the years to come, almost universally hailed. Reed started out in the Office of Planning and Budget as education policy director, before rising to chief legislative lobbyist and, eventually, chief of staff during Graham's second term in office. Like Graham, Reed was as smart as they come. Unlike Graham, he was also good at the political deal, and brought the bear-hugging, backslapping, "we-can-work-together" skills that Graham eschewed.

Which is not to say that smart and politically savvy staff like Reed, his immediate predecessor as chief of staff Burroughs, budget chief Herndon, perennial friend and aide Buddy Shorstein, and architect-cum-technocrat Tom Lewis were able to channel Graham into two or three priorities. That would have been impossible.

"He had too many priorities," Reed still says. How many? "It was like a thousand."

Reed said Graham was constantly coming up with new priorities. A favorite time to do this seemed to be Sunday nights.

"He had to call me every Sunday night at 11:30," Reed said. "I started keeping a notebook next to the bed. Finally, my wife said to him: 'Why do you always call him at 11:30?'"

Graham explained that he usually came up with lots of "to do" things for the coming week as he watched the 11 o'clock news. When it was over, he called Reed to share his list.

Reed's wife wondered why it couldn't wait until morning.

"But I want him to start thinking about it," Graham told her.

"Well, I don't want him to be thinking about it," she replied.

Eventually, Graham learned to focus. Kind of.

"In the end, instead of sixty things on his agenda, he had eighteen, when he should have had six," said Lewis, who wound up running the Department of Transportation and then the Department of Community Affairs over Graham's two terms in office.

Another problem for Graham, particularly when combined with his tendency to attempt too much, was his need to know *everything* about an issue before deciding and announcing his position. It drove his staff nuts. It drove reporters nuts. It drove editorial writers absolutely bonkers. It kept some meetings of the independently elected cabinet going into the wee hours, as Graham pressed for more details on some educational issue or another.

But it was pure Graham.

Montanaro, who worked in Graham's Office of Planning and Budget for the better part of both terms, said Graham would typically ask for briefings on a topic from as many staffers as there were sides to the issue. Each aide would argue, as passionately as possible, his or her assigned side.

"It was something very much like jousting, in the medieval sense," said Montanaro. "What he was trying to do was tune out the noise."

Graham would listen patiently, taking notes furiously—a judge in an adversarial proceeding of his own creation. After everyone was finished, he would thank them and send them on their way. A decision would come in hours, or days, or weeks. Sometimes the advocates would be called back in to explain a new wrinkle Graham had thought of.

"He is at heart a student," said Bill Rose, who as a young reporter for the *Miami Herald* covered Graham's first campaign, and is now the deputy managing editor of the *Palm Beach Post*. "This is his biggest strength, as well as his biggest weakness."

It was a weakness that made a lot of extra work for his staff, as Graham insisted on making sure every detail was perfect. Charlie Reed, who worked for Graham for six years, said his staff had to invest in bottles of vodka with which to co-opt a little old lady who worked in the Secretary of State's Office. She was the keeper of the official time clock, meaning the Governor's Office needed her as an ally when it was pushing deadline on particular documents—like veto messages.

"He would edit every veto message," Reed remembers. Every word, every comma. To the point where his aides were forced to get their friend to unplug the time clock until Graham had finished. "And then we'd plug it back in at 11:58 and we'd get them all punched in."

Even with better organization and more focus, there remained the problem of Dempsey Barron, the man behind the curtains in the Florida senate, who had famously declared Graham "the worst governor in the history of the world."[10]

Part of that opinion, no doubt, derived from Barron's difficulty in coping with Graham as governor after having so thoroughly emasculated him in the senate two years earlier. "He must have thought: Here's this little pipsqueak who tried to keep me from getting my job, and now he gets to be governor?" recalled Rose.

It's a view Graham himself shared. First there was Pensacola's Reubin Askew, not really a Dempsey favorite, going from the state senate right to

---

[10]This was nothing. Barron had walked into Graham predecessor Reubin Askew's office, sat on his desk, turned his back to the governor, and told him: "Stay the fuck out of my senate."

the Governor's Mansion. Eight years later, here was Miami's D. Robert Graham, doing the exact same thing.

"I think Dempsey Barron always felt that he ought to have been governor and never felt very comfortable either with Reubin or myself being governor."[11]

How to deal with the imperious Barron became a consuming issue for Graham's office. Barron, it should be noted, was not the simpleminded buffoon he was sometimes made out to be. On some issues, Barron had stood tall for his principles, risking potentially grave consequences from his not-so-enlightened constituency in Panama City.

In Florida's great fight over desegregation, Barron stood against those who wanted to dismantle the state system of education funding and thereby allow local counties to shortchange schools in black neighborhoods if they wished.

That said, Barron was a power broker out of central casting, with a folksy manner and deep drawl and, when halfway provoked, a quick temper.[12] "He'd just as soon fistfight you as have a drink with you," remembered Tom Slade, a former state senator from Jacksonville and later the chairman of the state Republican Party.

Barron was also among that breed of politicians who crave power—not because he wanted anything for himself or even his district, but for its own sake.

"He never wanted anything," Charlie Reed said. "That's what made him so powerful."

"It was more the game for the game's sake," agreed Buddy Shorstein.

It was a game Graham did not particularly care for. Never one to seek out the smoke-filled back rooms to engage in the deal-making, neither did Graham like one-on-one, eyeball-to-eyeball, see-who-blinks-first showdowns.

---

[11]University of Florida Oral History Project, Tapes L–M, April 6, 1994.

[12]Here's a Dempsey Barron observation of a medical malpractice bill from 1987, according to the *St. Petersburg Times*: "It's like mixing sugar with manure. It doesn't improve the manure, and it ruins the sugar."

And then there's this quip from a 1990 *St. Petersburg Times* interview: "I sure as hell feel sorry for people who don't drink, because when they get up in the morning, it's the best they are going to feel all day."

And here is what Barron, who died in 2001, said in 1982 when he announced that he would not run against Graham: "I might not have the tact to be governor. I would want to get rid of too many bureaucrats who don't do a damn thing but live off the taxpayers. And besides, I'm not very good at hosting teas and having my picture taken with strangers."

"Graham was not big on confrontation," Tom Herndon said. "That was not his strong suit."

Still, the day came when Graham's aides determined that he had to get right in Barron's face to set the record straight over who was governor and who was not and so forth. A half dozen of them got together, helping Graham rehearse what he was going to say and how he was going to say it. Dempsey was going to support the governor on this one particular bill, and that's the way it was going to be.

"Three or four of us were firing questions at him in a mean, snarling Dempsey Barron kind of way," said Tom Lewis, who was in the legislative affairs office then.

Finally, they were ready. Graham was prepped. They had even taught him a few choice cusswords (Graham is not ordinarily a cussing man) to help drive the point home. Then they called Dempsey down to talk. Reed and Lewis ushered Barron in and then waited in the outer office. From the inner office, there was no noise at first, and after a while there was laughing, and carrying on, and more laughing, but no throwing of glassware, anything like that. After a half hour, Barron came out, all smiles, and went his way. Reed and Lewis scurried in. How did it go?

Oh, it went fine, Graham reported. He's really not a bad guy. Graham went on to regale them with the stories Barron had told. Reed and Lewis listened impatiently. Finally they had to ask: What about the *bill?*

Graham dropped his eyes. "Well, that didn't come up."

"I'll always remember those words: 'Well, that didn't come up,'" Lewis recalled. "What the fuck do you mean it didn't come up? That was the whole point of the meeting!"

Say this for Graham: Despite his failures, he was persistent. If he thought he was right, he kept at it and kept at it and kept at it, until he could persuade enough people of the wisdom of his ways or at least wear them down into submission.

Take the state's school financing formula. Graham campaigned on the idea that schools should get more state money and be forced to raise less local property tax money, as a way to even out the inequities between rich and poor counties. At first he tried to cut the tax rate the state required counties to impose in order to participate in the state program. When the legislature refused, he tried a different tack: increasing the property tax "homestead" exemption—the value of a homeowner's own dwelling that goes untaxed—from $5,000 to $25,000.

"Florida had had a $5,000 homestead exemption since the 1930s," Graham explained. "It had dwindled in value as inflation was functioning. Essentially, the $25,000 number was designed to bring the exemption back to the same relative position that it had when it was originally adopted."

In 1979 and 1980, local property appraisers howled long and hard that, should Graham succeed in raising the exemption, so much taxable value would fall off the rolls that local governments would go broke. Graham countered by insisting that these same appraisers value their property at fair market value, as the law required, instead of a small fraction of that amount, as appraisers had been doing to curry favor with powerful property owners.

"I do not know if we ever actually had to remove a property appraiser, but we scared the hell out of several of them to get their rolls up to meet the standard of fair market value. And that substantially benefited the school systems in terms of increasing their property tax base."[13]

By the end of his first term, the homestead exemption was $25,000 instead of $5,000—meaning most households were paying considerably less property tax than they were when he was elected. More subtly, the change shifted the burden from homeowners to businesses, who were not eligible for the homestead exemption but whose properties were similarly subjected to the valuations. At the same time, Graham had forced the legislature to come up with massive spending increases for education—most notably in 1983, when he vetoed the entire education budget with the new school year just weeks away.

Graham's stubbornness on that point, in fact, created what became perhaps the biggest fight during his second term as governor. To generate the kind of money Graham wanted for schools, he and the legislature had to come up with an additional $100 million. The sales tax had just been increased a full penny the previous year, so that was out of the question. After some discussion, the legislature and Graham settled on something

[13]University of Florida Oral History Project, Tapes F–I, May 24, 1989.

called a "unitary tax"—a controversial levy already in use in California and some other states. Essentially, the unitary tax forced multistate and multinational corporations to calculate their total worldwide profits and then apportion an appropriate percentage to Florida for taxation purposes. That meant a company could not have a factory or a distribution center in Florida while avoiding the state corporate income tax by showing all its profits in a lower-tax nation or state.

Graham was convinced the tax made sense. It generated the needed amount of money. It passed the legislature and everyone was happy. Then the multinationals figured out what had happened, and all hell broke loose. The corporate home offices had realized that if tax-resistant Florida could pass such a law, then so could pretty much any other state.

The tax had to be repealed, a mob of their lobbyists began demanding, or Florida would lose all its major businesses. Graham hung tough.[14] The lobbyists' din grew louder, and the multinationals managed to get Florida businesses on board by predicting economic disaster.

In the Governor's Office, Graham brought back his economists and had them once again present the pros and cons of the tax. Again he came to the original conclusion: the tax made sense. What's more, it affected less than 10 percent of all corporations in Florida, as most businesses operated entirely within the state. As the lobbyists ratcheted up their screaming, Graham again brought in his economists and once again determined that he had been right all along. In October 1983, Graham told London's *Financial Times* of the tax: "It looks at economic reality as opposed to the alternative, which would say we will accept your corporate tax structure and accounting methods which have encouraged, not illegal or unethical, but creative accounting in corporate organization structures to try to shelter income in low-tax areas and restrict income in high-tax areas."[15]

"What really impressed me was how much the merits of the policy mattered to him," tax policy aide Ed Montanaro remembers.

---

[14]At one point, however, his lieutenant governor did not. It was at the start of Graham's vacation to Hong Kong, with Graham on an airplane over the Pacific, when Wayne Mixson (who was chosen as a running mate primarily because he was a Panhandle conservative) announced that Graham had agreed to repeal the unitary tax. Graham had agreed to no such thing. Intensive discussions were had upon Graham's return to Florida.

[15]William Hall, "Rebellion in the camp," *Financial Times*, October 27, 1983.

The drumbeat of phone calls, public threats of closing factories, and so on was starting to have an effect, though, and Graham started to sense that the legislature could well repeal the unitary tax with veto-proof majorities in both chambers—leaving the schools short once again. Most state lawmakers then, like now, did not do their own research on most issues, relying instead on the lobbying corps' instructions.

Sam Bell, who was a ranking house member on his way toward the speakership,[16] is a perfect example: "I don't understand it," he said of the tax recently. "I didn't understand it then. I don't understand it now."

Graham told the business community: Fine, have it your way. He told them he would not oppose a repeal as long as the business community agreed upon a different tax to replace what was lost. A consensus emerged to increase the corporate income tax from 5 percent to 5.5 percent, and in December 1984, nearly a year and a half after the tax was originally passed, Graham reluctantly signed the repeal into law. "It really pained him," Montanaro said.

Two decades later, Graham remains baffled by smaller Florida businesses going along with something that increased their own tax while lowering that of the giant multinationals.

"I think that that is a fundamentally fairer way to assess tax responsibility in an economy that is becoming increasingly global," Graham said, adding that he had foreseen how hard the multinationals would push to undo the tax. "I guess what I didn't anticipate was that there wouldn't be a counter-response from Florida businesses which today are paying a disproportionately larger share of the corporate tax under our current system."

The bottom line, unitary tax or no unitary tax: The proportion of education spending coming from the state versus that coming from property taxes had dramatically shifted toward the state. Graham had gotten what he came into office promising.

It was Reed, finally, who put together Graham's first victory in a Dempsey Barron showdown. It was over a bill making it easier for people to drive around with loaded guns. Graham thought it was a stupid idea

[16]He did not get it, though; he lost reelection in 1988.

and decided to veto it. Barron came to tell him that he better not veto it, or Barron would override him.

Graham vetoed it anyway, and Barron set to work to round up the twenty-seven votes he needed in his forty-member chamber. Graham's people scrambled to hold fourteen "no" votes. Reed was able to do it, but only by promising Jacksonville senator Mattox Hair funding for some bridge repairs.

"We won by one vote," Reed said. "We were so happy. Adele brought a chocolate cake."

Then Graham asked how Reed had done it, and blanched when Reed told him about the bridge money. "Oh, we don't do that," Graham told him.

"Well, would you rather lose?" Reed asked.

"Don't ever do that again," Graham replied.

It was a pure power play, and Barron respected it. But it was only later that Barron came to respect Graham personally. It was during a hunting trip at Barron's ranch—designed principally to get Graham doing some outdoorsy things in which he would, being a nerd, look foolish, thereby reinforcing Barron's upper hand.

They got to the ranch, and Barron brought forward a horse for Graham to ride. "A wild-ass, big horse," Reed recalled.

Barron was an expert rider—his official portrait in the Senate chamber, in fact, is of him in the saddle. The idea was that Graham would be too afraid to mount the horse, or perhaps even fall off. Instead, Graham climbed on and rode off, leaving Barron openmouthed.

"Having grown up on a farm, I knew how to put one stirrup before the other on a horse," Graham recounted. "So that gave us an additional bond. Helped smooth things out."

How Graham dealt with Dempsey Barron, the legislature as a whole, his own lack of focus—none of it registered even the slightest with political observers outside of Florida. To them, Graham was the first governor to kill a man.

It was all perfectly legal. The man was John Spenkelink, a condemned murderer, and Graham was the newly elected governor of a state so devoted to its executions that it called a special legislative session for the express purpose of passing a new death-penalty statute after the U.S. Supreme Court decision in 1972 invalidating every such law in the nation. The wheels of justice grinding as they do, it took six additional years for all the courts along the line to give the necessary green light for the first electrocution to occur.

So here he was, the round-eyed, chubby-cheeked young governor whose passion was fixing Florida's dismal education system, who had not cared much at all about the death penalty until he was on the campaign trail running for governor. True, he had *said* that he would enforce it . . . but no one believed that. He was a liberal, everyone thought, who, when confronted with an actual, honest-to-God death warrant, would blanch and trip over himself in his attempts to backtrack on his campaign pledge. For this reason, even death-row inmates like Spenkelink had rooted for Graham to win. "They shared the belief that Bob Graham's election would be good for them, that he was 'a wimp' who would not pursue the death penalty with any vigor," according to journalist David Von Drehle's seminal work on the subject, *Among the Lowest of the Dead*.[17]

On May 18, 1979, with the U.S. Supreme Court recently having given Florida's new death-penalty law the final go-ahead, Graham was confronted with his very first black-bordered death warrant, for the aforementioned John Spenkelink. He did not hesitate. He signed it, and then gave Attorney General Jim Smith the keys to the state jet to fly from courthouse to courthouse around Florida, the Southeast, and finally Washington, D.C., to help him argue against delaying the execution.

Critics point to the fundamental problem with Spenkelink: Here was a guy whose murder was so pedestrian by Florida standards that prosecutors were willing to let him off with a second-degree conviction and seven years behind bars.

He was an escaped con from California, touring the country and committing crimes. He hooked up with a parole violator from Detroit, one Joseph Szymankiewicz. In a Tallahassee motel room on February 4, 1973, Spenkelink and another small-time crook named Frank Brumm blud-

---

[17]David Von Drehle, *Among the Lowest of the Dead*, Times Books, New York, 1995, p. 49.

geoned and shot to death Spenkelink's erstwhile partner in crime. Spenkelink was arrested and helpfully offered his "yes, but" confession. Yes, I killed him, but it was because he made me have sex with him. On another occasion: Yes, but it was because I was afraid he was going to kill me.

In the not-so-sensitive lingo of cops and crime reporters, it was "misdemeanor murder." One crook kills another crook. No big, hairy deal. Let him take a plea to murder two, stick him in maximum security Raiford for maybe a dozen years, then extradite him back to wherever he busted out of to face charges there, and that would be the end of it.

Except Spenkelink, young and stupid, turned down the plea deal and decided to roll the dice at trial. He lost. The jury heard his tale of bad childhood, poor peer group, and so on, and recommended nonetheless that he die in Old Sparky for the crime. And then, after the U.S. Supreme Court validated Florida's death penalty through its decision in another inmate's case, Spenkelink had the misfortune of having confessed to the crime and of having been an escaped convict at the time of its commission—elements that would serve to eliminate possible questions of actual guilt as well as diminish possible public compassion.

In 1979, there were plenty of killers—even child-murderers—on death row more loathsome than Spenkelink. Unfortunately for Spenkelink, former governor Reubin Askew had signed his warrant in 1977, largely on the strength of his confession.

But to execute any of those nastier killers would have taken time. Many of their convictions were still under the so-called "direct appeal"—the very first review of the case by the Florida Supreme Court, as it automatically does for each death-penalty case. That first appeal looked at questions of guilt and innocence. Subsequent appeals looked at secondary issues, with many of the reviews later repeated in federal courts. All these took time—many months, or even years.

If any inmate was to be killed within any reasonable period of time, it was going to be Spenkelink. So in May 1979, Graham decided: Spenkelink it would be.

"My general policy was to try to implement the death penalty in as fair and nonpersonalized a way that I could. Part of that was . . . [Spenkelink] was the most advanced in terms of the judicial process, so he was the one I signed first," Graham later said.

Working on Graham's behalf was Attorney General Jim Smith, a fellow Democrat but one whose North Florida sensibilities made him a lot more conservative than Graham (eight years later, he, along with seemingly half the Democrats in Florida, became a Republican). It was Smith and his lawyers who would fly to New Orleans and Atlanta and Washington, D.C., to personally deliver briefs opposing the stays of execution sought by Spenkelink's advocates. Most of the arguments were highly technical in nature—capital cases have always been the most arcane in criminal law.

But while Smith was handling the legal technicalities, Graham turned to another lawyer to get him through the mechanics of the event—college fraternity brother and fellow Miamian Robin Gibson, who spent six months in Graham's office as his first general counsel.

Gibson, who has remained close to Graham through the years, set about planning the process specifically for Graham. This would be the most controversial thing his buddy had ever done, and would likely remain so for years to come. They couldn't afford to screw it up. Gibson went to the prison, outside Starke, walked through the procedure with Warden David Brierton, even visited the death chamber—an antiseptic white room dominated by the dark, wooden chair. In one corner was the executioner's booth, where an anonymous volunteer recruited from the local populace would make $150 to throw the switch on the appointed morning. Facing the chair was a big glass window that opened out on the witness room, where two dozen seats would accommodate those chosen to watch Spenkelink die.

On the wall behind the chair was the telephone that would keep an open line to Graham's office the morning of the deed so Brierton could know instantly whether there was a stay. Gibson knew that the anti-death-penalty movement was in high gear, and that a successful execution here could mark a sudden rush of them around the nation. Would opponents try to sabotage it by somehow getting the number and calling in, pretending to be Graham? Gibson decided to arrange a special code word so Brierton would know it was really the governor. He thought about his and Graham's high school days, when Gibson was senior class president at Edison High and Graham was president at rival Miami High. Miami High's mascot was a stingray. He thought about "stingray" as the password—but then decided that, in the case of an electrocution, perhaps that was in poor taste. Gibson then thought of Graham's youth on his family's dairy farm—and somehow came up with the inventor of the process of safeguarding milk from microbes.

"Louis Pasteur" would be the secret password.[18]

The lawyers on both sides did what lawyers do in these cases. Spenkelink's lawyer, David Kendall,[19] and his team filed their briefs in court after court. Attorney General Smith and his team filed countering briefs, day after day.

In the meantime, Gibson and the rest of Graham's staff tried to keep him above the fray. No matter what the protestors did, no matter how ugly their signs and accusations became—Bloody Bob! Governor Death!—Graham would not respond. He was the governor, merely carrying out his statutory obligation to enforce the duly enacted law of the land. He did so not with pleasure, but because it was his duty.

He would not get into shouting matches, or question-and-answer sessions, or any of that. He had signed the warrant. The warrant spoke for itself. There would be no elaboration.

For the most part, Gibson's plan was followed. Graham, ordinarily a voluble sort when it came to the media, made himself scarce that whole week. "He disappeared," recalled Rick Flagg, a Tallahassee radio reporter and the dean of the Florida capitol press corps. "No one could find him."

Of course, the whole thing nearly fell apart within two days of Graham signing the warrant. It was Sunday, May 20, and an anti-death-penalty group calling itself PAX (People Against Executions) had set up shop outside the Governor's Mansion. Lois Spenkelink, the condemned man's mother, had been driven up from Starke to confront Graham in person—

---

[18]David Von Drehle, *Among the Lowest of the Dead*, Times Books, New York, 1995, p. 14.
[19]Kendall later became President Clinton's lawyer during the impeachment trial.

not realizing that Graham had gone to DeLand for a college commence-
ment address. By the time he returned to Tallahassee, Mrs. Spenkelink had
left the protest.

Eight men, however, remained chained to the Mansion's wrought-iron
fence. Graham watched, and watched, and watched and finally couldn't take
it anymore. He had to go out and talk to them. His aides argued against it,
but Graham was adamant. Before Gibson and Press Secretary Steve Hull
could change his mind, he was out the door.

Calmly, he suggested to the men that they unchain themselves and cross
the street to get to some shade. Unsure how to handle Graham, they com-
plied—and then lit into him. He was being un-Christian, they accused. As
bad as Pontius Pilate.

Graham listened, then quite agreeably disagreed. He told them he did
not think carrying out his duties made him a bad Christian, and that society would be better off if it made clear that brutal crimes would not be tolerated. Then he said: "I respect very deeply the values you share and the
depth of your feelings. . . . I hope God will look out for and care for us all."
Then he offered his hand to one of them.[20]

Somehow, Graham had managed to fulfill the vengeful desires of the
populace while appearing to be nothing if not reasonable. It was the protestors who were shrill and out of touch, not Graham. As if to prove the
point, the man to whom Graham had offered a handshake, Amnesty International's Larry Cox, drew his own hand away. "I can't shake your hand,
Governor. It's got blood all over it."[21]

The television cameras covering PAX's protest captured the whole thing,
and Florida saw it on the evening news.

On Friday morning, May 25, John Spenkelink was down to his final appeal, one last pleading before the U.S. Supreme Court.

In Tallahassee, Graham came to work as usual and went through the
motions of an ordinary day, despite the dozens of protesters who had taken

[20]David Von Drehle, *Among the Lowest of the Dead*, Times Books, New York, 1995, pp. 21–22.
[21]Matt Bokor, Associated Press, May 20, 1979.

over the suite's reception area. Snipers patrolled the rooftops as a precaution. A helicopter sat on the lawn, ready to fly Graham to safety, also a precaution.

Behind the locked doors, meanwhile, as Gibson worried about the banging and chanting outside, Graham went through the morning mail. Suddenly he called for his chief speechwriter, and his aides feared the worst: He's going to back down. He's changed his mind, and he wants a speech announcing it.

The speechwriter came downstairs, and Graham handed him a letter from a woman complaining that her child had to pay a fee to play in the school band. "Could you draft a response to this?"[22]

It was Graham's way of dealing with stress. The worse it got, the more Graham immersed himself in the minutiae. Adele Graham remembers their wedding day, when Graham chattered about Holsteins and Jerseys on the dairy farm when they were growing up. Those around him noticed it again after the September 11, 2001, terrorist attacks. Bob Graham, chairman of the Senate Intelligence Committee, coped with it all by boring down ever more deeply into the gritty details.

Finally, the word came from Washington. There would be no new stays. At a little after 10 A.M., Robin Gibson got warden Brierton on the open line to the death chamber, then passed the phone over to Graham. Graham announced that he was Louis Pasteur, then told Brierton there were "no stays at this time." And then he said, "May God be with us"—words he uttered fifteen more times during his governorship, just prior to every execution he oversaw.[23]

On May 25, 1979, at 10:12 A.M., Graham prevailed. As a hundred protesters crammed into his outer office and another throng in the cow pasture outside Florida State Prison 130 miles away stood by in stunned disbelief, 12 amperes of current at 2,300 volts were zapped through Spenkelink's body. Built from solid oak by inmates in 1923, Florida's three-legged Old Sparky had already dispatched 197 individuals before it fell into disuse in 1964.

---

[22]David Von Drehle, *Among the Lowest of the Dead,* p. 104.
[23]Thomas E. Slaughter, Associated Press, May 26, 1979.

Spenkelink became number 198. Small puffs of smoke rose from the singed flesh around his calf where the electrode was attached, as Spenkelink became the first American since 1967 to be put to death against his will.

Predictably, what people thought about the Spenkelink case depended on what they thought about the death penalty.

"[Graham's] trying to fulfill a commitment to make state murder routine," said Scharlette Holdman, one of Florida's leading anti-death-penalty activists. "The governor is getting very bad political advice. The governor is signing warrants on people who haven't exhausted their legal remedies. The rush to kill these people is violating their due process."[24]

"It was a time when real political courage was necessary, and the governor failed," Kendall said in an interview years later. "His action had all the intelligibility of the Roman emperor's thumbs-up in the Colosseum."[25]

One year after the execution, Graham gave the nominating speech for the reelection of President Jimmy Carter at the Democratic National Convention. Graham has never been particularly good at formal speeches—it is his biggest weakness as a candidate—but in this case it was even worse. For the cameras' and the reporters' attention focused not on him, but on a white-haired lady who had been smuggled into Madison Square Garden: Lois Spenkelink, the mother of the guy Graham had ordered killed.

The protest had little effect on Graham. It didn't matter what liberals in New York or San Francisco thought of Graham in 1980, and the ruckus probably had the opposite effect than was intended on Graham in Florida: It effectively immunized him against that dreaded "L" word, thereby giving him the political maneuvering room to carry out his education and environment agendas.

So, after two terms, what of that agenda? How did he do?

Of the seven Florida governors who have been eligible for reelection, four have succeeded in winning it. Of those four, the one with the largest

[24]Associated Press, June 19, 1979.

[25]David A. Kaplan, "In Florida, a Story of Politics and Death; A Governor Controls the Ultimate Sentence," *The National Law Journal,* July 16, 1984.

reelection margin and the one who seemed to grow ever more popular the longer he was in office was Graham.

He credits his "three E" agenda—education, environment, and economic development.

Reporters who have covered local or state government for any amount of time are understandably wary of "economic development." At its worst, it's blatant corporate welfare. At its best—or least offensive—it's a fuzzy, almost meaningless phrase. Governors always take credit for any upswings in the business cycle during their watches, regardless of whether their policies had anything to do with creating them. Graham was no different.

"When I ran for governor, I had looked at some statistics on how many jobs had been created in Florida. I just sort of arbitrarily doubled the number and said, 'During my first four years in office, we will create 40,000 jobs in Florida.' We actually ended up creating, over the eight years, in excess of one million jobs in Florida. So that was a very successful effort."[26]

Well, maybe. More likely, most of the jobs were created because Florida was growing like crazy, and the construction sector was expanding just to build new tract houses, apartments, and condos while the service sector kept pace to staff all the new Wal-Marts, McDonald's and 7-Elevens.

All governors, Graham included, talk about the high-tech manufacturing jobs they lured to Florida, but the continuing low per-capita wages suggest that the lion's share of those million new jobs were flipping burgers, making beds, and stocking the 40 percent-off aisles.

In any event, while Graham may like to claim—or think it prudent for others to believe—that economic development was a top priority, it wasn't.

Really, there were two top priorities—education and the environment—and in both areas, Graham shone.

Florida, for decades, has been saddled with a dismal public education system. Part of it is the population's transient nature—so many residents are new here that there's little sense of community. In recent years,

---

[26]University of Florida Oral History Project, Tapes N–O, February 21, 1995.

so many of the newcomers speak a language other than English, making the education of their children that much more difficult.

But part of it, probably more of it, is that Florida taxpayers and their elected leaders have been cheap, and in the end, you get what you pay for.

Graham made changing that ethos his top priority. Each year, he recommended spending hundreds of millions more on the schools and universities, even at the cost of raising taxes. His stated goal was to get both school spending and achievement in the top quartile of the fifty states, and he made sure his staff understood his commitment.

Recalls budget director Herndon: "'I don't want a speech without some reference to education in there.' That was the standing order. 'It's got to be in there.'"

Merely speechifying about it, though, wouldn't change anything. It was something even regular citizens recognized. In the January 8, 1979, issue of *Time* magazine's Florida edition, advertising agent Marty Malone placed an ad featuring a photo of his baby boy:

"FLORIDA'S EDUCATIONAL SYSTEM STINKS," the ad read. "THIS IS MY NEWBORN SON. I DEMAND FLORIDA GIVE HIM A DECENT EDUCATION."[27]

No one living in the state at the time could disagree—least of all Bob Graham, who just days before had been sworn in as governor after years of railing against the education system from the legislature. Both he and Adele had attended public schools, as had all four of his daughters. In 1979, Graham finally had the bully pulpit on his favorite issue, and for eight years he made the most of it by targeting specific tax increases, such as the controversial unitary tax, to fund education reform.

Along with the new money came higher standards. A teacher certification test was instituted—over the objection of black teachers who complained that it would discriminate against them. A high-school literacy test required for graduation was made more difficult. The required curriculum for a high-school diploma was upgraded, with three years of math and science needed for graduation. The total number of credit hours for gradua-

---

[27]Associated Press, January 5, 1979.

tion was increased, first to twenty-two, then to twenty-four, and the school day was lengthened from six to seven periods. Class sizes, meanwhile, were reduced, and textbook publishers were pushed to make their books more academically rigorous.

By the mid-1980s, the national rankings had started reflecting these efforts.

Between 1985 and 1986, Florida showed the greatest improvement in SAT scores in the country, with a gain of 11 points. By 1985, per-student spending had climbed to $3,238, putting Florida twenty-ninth in the nation—a move up of more than ten spots during the Graham years. The average student-teacher ratio had improved to 16.6, or twenty-second nationally.

Teacher salaries, likewise, by 1986 had increased to $22,250, ranking Florida thirty-third among the states. Although that figure was still below the $25,313 national average, it was well ahead of where it would have been without Graham, under whose watch teacher salaries increased 60 percent. That works out to an average annual raise of 7 percent, despite state budget cuts that were necessary in 1981 because of a recession.

President Reagan's education secretary, William Bennett, declared: "Florida has also been a leader in the education reform movement by improving teacher quality through testing and through incentive programs and alternative certifications."[28]

Graham's tenure was not just about education, of course. There was that other "E"—the environment.

First there was Save Our Rivers, a $300 million program to buy up environmentally sensitive lands in the watersheds of the state's most treasured rivers, including the Apalachicola and the Suwannee. Then there was Save Our Coasts, a similar, $200 million program to bring stretches of remaining undeveloped beachfront into the state park system.

Years after leaving office, Graham points proudly to the annual ranking of best beaches done by "Dr. Beach," Stephen Leatherman. "Consistently, Florida gets half of the best beaches in the country on that survey. Most of that half are beaches that were purchased under the Save Our Coasts program."[29]

[28]Robert D. Lystad, States News Service, February 10, 1987.
[29]University of Florida Oral History Project, Tapes N–O, February 21, 1995.

Even as he was leaving Tallahassee for Washington, Graham sensed that the one tangible thing he would leave were those tracts of beachfront land, river basins, and Everglades that would remain forever wild because of his intervention.

"I think we certainly will be remembered for environmental programs and specifically land acquisition, because they're going to be the permanent legacies of this generation of Floridians," Graham said.[30]

On other issues, Graham's record is all over the map, but it is generally moderate to liberal.

He pushed hard for legislation in Florida and other states to help Florida banks compete across the Southeast. He tried, without much success, to encourage the growth of solar power and other alternative energy systems.

He tried to persuade the legislature to pass the Equal Rights Amendment, even calling a special session on the matter in 1982. The house passed it, but the senate, led by Dempsey Barron, refused.

He appointed the first woman ever to sit on the Florida Supreme Court, Rosemary Barkett—the daughter of Syrian immigrants who settled in Mexico when they couldn't get into the United States—and the first black woman judge in Florida, Leah Simms, to the Dade County Court.

He pushed for tax breaks to encourage film production companies to set up shop in Florida.

He successfully pushed the legislature to increase prison sentences for drug offenses, from selling paraphernalia to smuggling—to the point that smugglers in Colombia actually plotted to kill him, police learned in 1984.

Republicans, of course, have for years tried instead to focus on what Graham didn't do: build lots of prisons.

Since the early 1970s, Florida had been under a federal consent order to limit the number of inmates it could keep in any given prison. By the early 1980s, the prisons were starting to strain under those limits.

"It was a mess. It was a train wreck," said J. M. "Mac" Stipanovich, a top

---

[30]Terence McElroy, "Great Achiever: Graham Won High Marks, but Alienated Businessmen," *Miami News*, December 19, 1986.

aide to Graham successor Bob Martinez and, more recently, an operative for George W. Bush during the 2000 election recounts. "We basically had to legislate early releases. It was a crisis that had been building for a while, and it certainly was a crisis that continued for a while."[31]

That policy came to bite Martinez hard when Charlie Street murdered two police officers in Miami ten days after his early release in 1988. Street had served just over half of a fifteen-year sentence for attempted murder. He was far from the exception. Inmates were routinely being freed after serving about a third of their sentences. The public outcry was deafening.

Jim Smith—who during Graham's tenure had been the Democratic elected attorney general but who in 1987 became a Republican and joined Martinez's staff after his own run for governor fell short—said the brewing prison problem was well known but largely ignored. "There was a need to build prisons, but we just didn't have the money," Smith said, but then allowed that it was a question of priorities, as well. "It doesn't do you a whole lot of good, politically, to build more prisons."

It's not as if Graham didn't make an effort. In 1981, he proposed in his budget request a $490 million bond issue to build new prisons.

Still, he did not take the forceful action he took on pet issues like education. Staff members said Graham understood that if he raised it as a major concern, the rabidly tough-on-crime legislature would immediately throw every available dollar at the problem, leaving nothing for Graham's top priorities.

Instead, Graham and his top aides left the perennial secretary of corrections, Louis Wainwright,[32] to handle the problem. Wainwright did so with sprawling tent cities for the prisoners as well as something dubbed the "Blue Bird Correctional Institution." The terms of the federal order said that prisoners in transit on the day of a count did not have to be included in the total. So, on days of counts, Wainwright would simply load up prisoners on buses—built by the Blue Bird Corporation, known for its school buses—and drive them around until the count was finished.

Graham remains unapologetic.

"My feeling was that it wasn't our obligation to provide to prisoners a fa-

---

[31]Mark Silva and Tamara Lytle, "The Making of Bob Graham," *Orlando Sentinel*, April 20, 2003.
[32]Yes, that would be the same Wainwright as the one in *Gideon v. Wainwright*, the 1963 Supreme Court case that forced states to provide lawyers to poor people accused of even noncapital felonies.

cility that was better than that which the United States Army provided for our troops. I also felt, as I think history has proven, that this period of escalating prison population was a bubble, not a new, permanent condition, and that we could handle that bubble in less expensive ways than building a lot of new prisons. And that was to use stable, and humane, but nonpermanent facilities. So, for instance, at Raiford, the largest maximum-security prison, we erected tents. And there was never a challenge to that based on a state's obligation to provide appropriate conditions and care for inmates," Graham said in a recent interview. "I thought that was a lot smarter way to proceed than to build a lot of new permanent prisons at very big expense, [with] almost the assurance that if you build a new prison, you will fill it up. It's kind of like the baseball field—build it, and they will come. If you build a prison, whatever happens in the society, you can rest assured that there will be inmates to fill it."

Former aides agree that, to Graham, spending millions to build more prisons was admitting defeat. He truly believed that a focus on education would soon lower the crime rate and solve most of the state's problems. Diverting money to prisons, on the other hand, would make it harder to spend the money on schools.

"Graham was very concerned about the prison system and crime," said Budget Director Herndon. "It was just that the prison system was pitted against education. *Everything* was pitted against education."

Even as he was running for president, where "tough on crime" is the easy mantra, Graham continued to offer proof that his staff read him correctly, that he would rather spend public money building just about anything other than prisons.

He explained about a new concept called "shock incarceration," in which convicts bound for prison for the first time are given terms of four to six months, followed by intensive job training and placement. The idea is that long prison terms teach inmates only those skills that will help them prosper in a community dominated by violent sociopaths. Such sentences, therefore, should be reserved for criminals who are so beyond hope that society's only alternative is to warehouse them.

Said Graham, "If you put a person away for ten years, you have probably signed that person to a lifetime of antisocial behavior."

hroughout his career, Republicans have also charged Graham with raising taxes too much as governor. They recycled that argument in each of his Senate runs, and, upon his entry into the presidential race, both state and national Republicans took up the mantra with enthusiasm: Graham is a tax-and-spend liberal in a moderate's clothing.

Republicans typically do not mention this part, but Graham also *cut* one major tax substantially for most Floridians: the property tax. In 1980, Graham pushed a constitutional amendment to increase the homestead exemption from $5,000 to $25,000 over a period of three years. That change had the effect of cutting property taxes nearly in half for a $50,000 house, which was a typical price at the time. Another amendment Graham pushed that year abolished the inventory tax charged on businesses for their raw materials and unsold goods.

Still, those cuts notwithstanding, there is no denying that Graham raised taxes during his eight years—many different taxes, many different increases.

Graham increased the gasoline tax because he thought the state needed money to expand its highway system. He pushed increases in state university tuition to have students and their families pay at least a quarter of the total cost of the college education. He supported, then stubbornly defended, the enormously unpopular unitary tax as a way to boost teacher salaries. He supported increases in the alcoholic liquor tax, the motor vehicle license fees, and the cigarette tax.

At the time, it should be remembered—and in stark contrast to today— even business groups were on board with some tax hikes. "We're saying: Tax us, and this is how we'd like to be taxed," said Associated Industries of Florida lobbyist Jon Shebel in 1987. "We think it's a corporate responsibility to come forth with a plan."[33]

The retrospective antitax complaints beg the question: Which of the programs Graham instituted or expanded would Republicans not have supported? Increasing teacher salaries? Florida was at the bottom of the

[33]Barbara Marsh, "Business and the Schools Crisis," *Crain's Chicago Business,* March 16, 1987.

barrel. Graham at least put the state in the middling range. How about the environmental programs? This, too, goes nowhere.

Congressman Mark Foley, a Republican who in 2003 briefly ran for Graham's seat, has on his Cannon House Office Building wall a poster commemorating the tenth anniversary of the Save Our Rivers program—a Graham initiative that increased the real-estate transaction tax.

On top of that, the one tax that is most felt by Floridians every day, the state sales tax, has been raised three times in the last four decades: once by Republican governor Claude Kirk in 1968, once by Democrat Graham in 1982, and finally by Republican Bob Martinez in 1987.

House Democrats from that era, meanwhile, still complain that Graham didn't raise taxes *enough* when he had the opportunity. The taxes that did go up were "nickel and dime," former house member Sam Bell says. "They were enough to get us over the hump, but that's all. . . . Graham was always the reluctant partner in each of the tax increases. We in the house were always pushing him."

Graham, though, challenges the fundamental premise that Floridians are antitax cheapskates.

"I think the idea that Floridians are adamantly opposed to new taxes is part of the myth of the state. The fact is, what I think Floridians are opposed to are new taxes for which they do not see an intended purpose," he said seven years after leaving Tallahassee. "People are willing to support taxes—not because they like to pay more taxes, but because they have identified with a problem, they have accepted your prescription to the problem, they accept your price tag for that prescription, and they are willing to pay it." Graham used the metaphor of a supertanker intending to enter a channel from the ocean—the skipper needs to start the turn many miles out at sea if he wants to hit the center of the harbor entrance. "If you want to say, 'By the school year 1985 I would like Florida to be able to reduce the class size of its primary grades,' then you go back to 1981 and begin to lay the steps that will be necessary in order to accomplish that objective."[34]

In any event, Graham does not offer any apologies for those tax increases

[34]University of Florida Oral History Project, Tapes L–M, April 6, 1994.

he either pushed for himself or went along with when they emerged from the legislature. Floridians, he believes, got their money's worth, and did not particularly object while it was happening.

For example, the biggest tax increase under Graham's watch, the penny increase in the sales tax from 4 percent to 5 percent, came in 1982—just months before his landslide reelection. If the populace thought Graham a profligate spender, it surely had its opportunity to say something about it that year and chose not to.

It was his ability to articulate his justifications for a tax increase, Graham said, that won over the electorate.

An analysis of the numbers shows that while the Florida state budget grew from $7.8 billion to $16.6 billion during Graham's stewardship, the state's population increased 23 percent and inflation increased prices 50 percent.

When those two elements are factored in, Graham's constant-dollar, per-capita increase in taxes and spending was just under 16 percent over the entire eight years. So the question Republicans who accuse Graham of taxing and spending too much must ask is whether Florida's residents believed they got 16 percent of additional value in better roads, improved schools, and more conservation of endangered lands for their money.

Republicans posed this question in three subsequent elections since Graham's second term. Three times, they have not liked the answer Florida's electorate has given them.

Fidel

In 1982, film producer Martin Bergman wanted to do a remake of the gangster classic *Scarface*, and set it in Miami amid the Cuban immigration of the 1960s and '70s.

Sounds like something the city of Miami should have eaten up, right? A movie with a heavyweight like Al Pacino shot amid their tax base? All the money the production company would spend over the weeks of the shooting, all that cash seeping into the local economy, turning over several times, cranking up that old multiplier effect—it should make everyone happy, right?

Well, almost.

Everyone was happy—except for one of the Miami city commissioners, who had a slight problem with the story line. It was pretty good, Demetrio Perez, Jr., thought, except for one little part that could stand some rewrite. If Bergman changed the backstory of the villain and made him, instead of simply a Cuban refugee who turned to a life of crime, into an agent provocateur working for Fidel Castro, trying to make the good, hardworking anticommunist refugees look bad—well, now *that* would be more acceptable. And if Bergman didn't make those changes, well, then Perez would ban him from filming on city property.

For anyone unfamiliar with Cuban-American politics Miami-style, the above example pretty much says it all.

It's said that all politics is local. Well, in Miami, for decades now, all politics is Castro. Whether the race is city commission, county commission, state legislature, Congress—it makes no difference. One of the top issues, if not *the* top issue, is which candidate hates Castro more. I am for better schools—and I hate Castro. I support tax cuts—and I also hate Castro.

This is a city where anyone daring to suggest that maybe the United States ought to try to maintain relations with Castro—as we did with places like, say, China, the former Soviet Union, and South Africa—risked getting blown up in his car.[1]

Pediatrician-turned-terrorist Orlando Bosch got ten years behind bars for firing a bazooka at a Polish freighter in the Port of Miami in 1968, but fled the country while he was out on parole in 1974. He later spent eleven years in a Venezuelan jail (although he was never convicted) as the prime suspect in the 1976 bombing of a Cuban airliner, which killed seventy-three people.

Naturally, this made him a local hero in Miami, where city leaders proclaimed Orlando Bosch Day in 1990 and an otherwise sane Jeb Bush (then the chairman of the Dade County Republican Party) successfully lobbied his father to spring Bosch from the federal prison to which he had been returned after he came back to the United States in 1988.

Florida, then, is the only one of the fifty states that for decades essentially has had its own foreign policy, albeit one that focuses almost exclusively on a single country.

Taking a pro-reconciliation stance is tantamount to political suicide in a statewide race. Miami Cubans make up a small minority of voters in the state, about 5 percent, but they often vote as a bloc, meaning candidates can ill afford to risk alienating them.

---

[1] Yes, literally. The 1970s and 1980s saw a spate of bombings in Miami against those who favored dialogue with Castro. Radio host Emilio Milián lost both his legs in a car bomb in 1976 after criticizing exile violence.

To be sure, many statewide politicians aren't really pandering to the exiles when they toe the anti-Castro line—they actually share in a worldview that sees Fidel Castro as a genuine threat to American national security and as a tyrant qualitatively worse than others who have been embraced by the United States. Governor Jeb Bush, former United States senator Connie Mack, and many conservative Republican congressmen from around the state fall into that category—as does Bob Graham.

Typically, there is but limited consequence to these views, regardless of how strident they might be. It doesn't really matter a whole lot what the governor of Florida, or even a member of Congress, thinks about Cuba, unless he or she happens to chair a key foreign relations committee (which Graham does not). The fulminations and venting are basically confined entirely within the sphere of internal Florida politics. The nutty resolutions coming from the Florida legislature declaring this or that, and the outlandish, sometimes bizarre statements the Miami Cuban members of Congress make on the cable news channels[2] are filled with sound and fury but, like Shakespeare's tale told by an idiot, signify nothing.

But a Miami politician as, say, vice president or secretary of Homeland Security?

Usually a candidate running for president who has not previously been vice president is a blank slate when it comes to foreign policy. There is only what the candidate says he will do, but no actual track record to provide any hints.

With Graham, at least, Americans can study his handling of "Florida foreign policy," such as it is, to look for clues as to what he would do with the real thing.

To Graham's credit, he sided with filmmaker Bergman in the *Scarface* flap: "If we, Miami, *Florida*, are going to be taken as an increasingly serious place for movie production, artistic liberties shouldn't be infringed upon by government."[3] (It didn't matter. Bergman, tired of dealing with "amateur

---

[2] Recall Congressman Lincoln Diaz-Balart after the Elián Gonzalez raid, accusing the Immigration and Naturalization Service of drugging the child to make him more docile.
[3] Gregory Jaynes, "Miami Official Objects to Cuban Refugee Film," *The New York Times*, August 24, 1982.

night in Dixie," threw up his hands and shot his $15 million movie in California.)

That stance, though, appears to have been one of the few times Graham has opposed the wishes of the Miami Cubans.

In Tallahassee, five hundred miles and a whole world away from Miami, the exile community's obsession takes on an almost Alice in Wonderland quality. The most pedestrian of issues can somehow become a living, breathing example of Castro's Cuba anytime a Cuban-American legislator from Miami chooses to make it one. A proposed tax cut for, say, agricultural equipment can become A Reason My Family Left Our Homeland. A continued high tax on agricultural equipment, therefore, becomes Something Castro Would Do, while a vote in favor of a tax cut becomes A Vote Against Communism.

Few non-Cubans dare to challenge it. Just as few white lawmakers will dare oppose a new program or building at historically African-American Florida A&M University—"It's a black thing"—so is there a wide berth given to anything that might inflame the Miami Cubans.

In 2002, Democratic candidate for governor Janet Reno visited the state capitol—where she'd served as a staff lawyer three decades earlier—during a swing through Tallahassee. When she was introduced in the house, the entire Cuban caucus walked out in protest of her decision two years earlier to send six-year-old Elián Gonzalez back to his father. Representative Mario Diaz-Balart, now a congressman, declared Reno "the most corrupt attorney general in the history of the United States"—a time period that presumably includes the Watergate-era tenure of John Mitchell.

Lost in the mists of Florida-tinted revisionism are the actual facts of Cuba's long and tortured history since the Spanish-American War.

Forgotten is the 1934 coup in which Fulgencio Batista first came to power. Most decidedly forgotten is the 1952 coup that reinstalled Batista, with tacit American support, as Cuba's dictator. Forgotten are the corruption and the repression Batista inflicted on his country over the next seven years, or the co-counsel role played by American organized crime in running the casinos and the prostitution rings.

To the contrary, the exile community and their elected legislators paint a pre-Castro Cuba brimming with democracy and freedom—a veritable Switzerland of the Caribbean. Amazingly, no one challenges them.

Lost also are the class and racial undertones of those who left Cuba in the years following Castro's ascension and those who stayed. Cuba's population is 62 percent black or mulatto, yet the exiles who came to Florida in the 1960s and '70s are overwhelmingly white—the moneyed class, the propertied, and the professionals.

And lost are the nuances of Castro's break with the United States. In 1959 and 1960, Castro twice visited the United States on a mission to secure foreign aid. The Eisenhower administration mistrusted him—a natural reaction, perhaps, after having backed Batista—and ultimately an aid package was not agreed to. Historians continue to argue whose fault that was.

In 1960, Castro instead signed a deal with the Soviet Union to get oil. The American-owned refineries there refused to process any Soviet oil. Castro nationalized the refineries. Historians continue to argue whose fault *those* things were.

But in 1961 came the Bay of Pigs plot to overthrow Castro, a plan hatched by Eisenhower's CIA in 1960 and left to newly elected John F. Kennedy to approve. Kennedy gave the go-ahead, and on April 14, 1961, a fleet of B-26s (chosen in a somewhat lame attempt to disguise American involvement—the planes were of a type common at the time in Latin American air forces) bombed Cuba's airfields, wiping out most of Castro's air force. Two days later, 1,400 Cuban exiles—many of whom had received paramilitary training in the Everglades or Louisiana—arrived aboard five ships at the Bay of Pigs. Two of the ships were sunk, including one loaded with most of the supplies. And when Kennedy refused to provide American air support, the "invasion" was doomed. Within three days, all the exile troops had been killed, wounded, or captured.

In 1959 and 1960 Castro had to invent excuses for breaking off relations with the United States, but after the Bay of Pigs, he did not need to invent them any longer. Here was living proof of what the Imperialist Yankee was capable of. Round up the usual suspects!

For most of the country and, indeed, the world, times have started to change. The Red Menace is gone. The East-West prism through which every populist or land-reform movement in the Third World was seen has largely been discarded. In most places on the planet, a reasonable person can reasonably make the argument that perhaps it was wrong for the United States to commit an unprovoked act of war against a neighbor.

This is not yet the case in Florida.

The latest Castro proxy, the Elián Gonzalez melodrama, provided a fresh litmus test for politicians, and the party that took Castro's side in the dispute—that would be the Democrats—have in the 2000 and 2002 elections suffered their worst beating among Cuban-American voters since Walter Mondale's 1984 showing.

All of which is to say that Graham's position on Castro is pretty much that of most American politicians over the last forty years: Fidel Castro is an evil man who must be isolated and confronted until he is forced from power or dead.

And, like the fulminations of most American politicians who feel they must pander to Miami's Cuban exile community, Graham's anti-Castro diatribes might ordinarily be taken with several grains of salt. Sort of the way politicians visiting Iowa are invariably in favor of gasohol and those passing through Milwaukee are great lovers of bratwurst, so candidates visiting Miami's Little Havana are expected to demand to see Castro strung up by his thumbs.

Except that with Graham, the rhetoric seems more than just expedient political talk to win support. His words and deeds seem almost personal— which, in fact, they might be.

Even before he was born, Cuba had played a role in his family history once, and almost played an even larger role a second time. In the 1890s, recall, it was Cuban unrest that caused sugar companies to build beet sugar mills in the Midwest, including one in Croswell, Michigan, his father's hometown. It was the experience working at that mill that led Ernest Graham to become an engineer, a career path that ultimately led to Miami. And in the 1930s, in the midst of the Great Depression, Cap Graham received an offer to run a mine in Cuba. "He seriously thought about taking that position and then decided to stick it out with the dairy. I have often thought about what a difference in our family life would have been if he had done that."[4]

As it was, Bob Graham's dealings with Castro were not quite as personal as they might have been had he been born and raised in Cuba, the son of an American mine engineer.

Rather, Graham was in high school in 1953 when Castro launched his quixotic attack on the Moncada barracks. He was in his senior year at the University of Florida in the first days of 1959 when Batista fled to Miami and Castro rolled into Havana. He was in his fourth semester in law school at Harvard in 1961when Kennedy refused to provide air support at the Bay of Pigs.

And he was working at his family's newly launched Miami Lakes project in 1962, looking for industrial park tenants, when the missile crisis brought nuclear-tipped rockets to South Florida. Those tense days nearly sank the Miami Lakes project before it had a chance to float. Who, after all, wants to buy a new house right next door to a military airfield flooded with troops and armed to the gills in anticipation of a possible thermonuclear conflict?

In time, the fears subsided and residents began flocking to Miami Lakes to buy single-family homes and town houses, thereby ensuring the financial well-being of Bob Graham and his family and his progeny for generations to come. Yes, Castro (with Khrushchev's help) had nearly brought financial ruin upon the Graham clan. But that wasn't his unforgivable transgression.

That came later—exactly seventeen years and six months later.

Governor Graham got his first sign of trouble at an April 1980 dinner in Washington when the State Department official there kept getting interrupted with urgent, whispered messages in his ear. Graham asked what was the matter, and was told about a crisis brewing in Havana.

Some malcontents had stormed into the Peruvian embassy looking for asylum, and Fidel Castro had declared, perhaps offhandedly, that anyone who wanted to leave Cuba could go right away to the Peruvian embassy.

---

[4]University of Florida Oral History Project, Tapes A–E, February 13, 1989.

The compound was now crowded with more than 10,000 would-be immigrants—thoroughly embarrassing Castro, who never dreamed so many residents of his Socialist Paradise would want to live anywhere else.

Graham did not think much more of it until a few days later, when he was in Miami. By now, Castro had expanded upon the invitation to leave, had designated Mariel Harbor as the embarkation point for all Cubans who wanted out, and had invited exiles in the United States to sail on down if they wanted to take their relatives away with them. Graham had just finished cutting a public service announcement when a cameraman offered to show him some video he had just shot.

The tape was an aerial view of hundreds of boats leaving Key West bound for Mariel, and finally the scale of what was about to happen began to sink in.

On April 23, trying to ward off the influx, Carter administration officials warned that skippers bringing Cubans back to Florida could face felony charges and fines of as much as $1,000 per refugee. Boat captains, some of whom were charging as much as $1,000 per refugee for that ride across the Florida Straits, largely ignored the threats. Graham, not wanting to see refugees drown because they were dropped off near the surf line so as to let skippers make a quick getaway (as had happened with Haitian refugees earlier), told President Jimmy Carter that prosecution threats were a bad idea.

On May 5, Carter, facing criticism from Republican opponent Ronald Reagan, reversed himself and declared that the United States was a "country of refugees," and that the nation would continue "to provide an open heart and open arms" to those fleeing Cuba.

The floodgates were officially open.

All summer long, the boats streamed back from Mariel. Shelters quickly filled up in Key West, then Miami. Refugees started being airlifted to Eglin Air Force Base near Fort Walton Beach in the Panhandle. Others were flown to Fort Chaffee, Arkansas. Some drowned on the way back across the narrow but treacherous Florida Straits, where an easterly wind can create enormous, breaking waves on the Gulf Stream.

Thousands of refugees arrived every week, and thousands more would have come had they had the chance, those who made it said. "If the people of Cuba have the opportunity, Castro will be the only one left there," said seventy-seven-year-old refugee José Antonio Arse.[5]

Graham started complaining ever louder for Carter to do something— to stop the flow, to spread more of the refugees across other states, to help Florida's straining social services budget.

For months they kept coming, an average of 5,000 a week. Boats hired by exiles hoping to bring family home were told by Castro's forces that they had to take so many strangers back with them, too.

Finally, in September, President Carter got Castro to shut Mariel down. Since April, 125,000 Cubans had jumped across the ninety miles of ocean to Florida. Another 35,000 or so Haitians had come across, too, taking advantage of the chaos. Florida was going broke, and Graham was openly telling Carter that unless he helped Florida fast, he needn't bother trying to campaign in the state come autumn.

In October 1980, Carter, the impending election looming ever closer, finally approved $100 million of federal aid to reimburse states for the costs of caring for the refugees. Of that, $80 million came immediately to Florida.[6] Another $160 million came Florida's way under President Reagan over the next three years.

Those were just the costs of providing to the refugees the basic assistance that anyone down and out in this country in that period had a right to expect—food stamps, a cot in a shelter, and basic medical care. Graham contended that Florida bore an additional $150 million by educating all the children of the refugees and paying other local expenses.

Much greater costs were yet to come.

Starting in the summer of 1980, police in Miami started noticing an increase in crime. Not just petty crime, like theft, but dangerous, sociopathic crime. It got so bad that Graham was forced to send a hundred state troopers to Miami. The troopers did basic patrol work, allowing the local police to investigate the worst of the worst.

[5]Dan Sewell, "Refugee Flood Grows as Tent City Readied," Associated Press, May 2, 1980.
[6]For Carter, it was not nearly enough. He had won Florida in 1976, but lost it in 1980 by a wide margin to Reagan.

In the months and years to follow, this pattern began to repeat itself around the country, wherever there happened to be large clusters of *marielitos,* as the refugees came to be called.

Soon, officials started realizing the extent to which the rumblings they had been hearing during the actual boatlift were true: Castro had taken the opportunity of this massive exodus to export most of his violent criminals and mental patients.

U.S. News & World Report put together one of the most comprehensive analyses on the subject in 1984, interviewing police detectives from around the country and presenting a horrific catalogue of crime.

New York City, for instance, reported 7,000 arrests of *marielitos* since 1980. Las Vegas detectives said that the 3,000-member *marielito* community there had taken over a quarter of the narcotics trade and accounted for 22 of the previous 100 murders. And in Miami, police charged 3,232 *marielitos* with a total of 14,035 felonies, misdemeanors, and criminal traffic violations in less than three years.[7]

"Absolutely the meanest, most vicious criminals we have ever encountered," one Los Angeles detective told the magazine.

"So vicious are the bandidos, police say, that even hardened American criminals are terrified of them," the magazine wrote. "Authorities in the Southwest report that *marielitos* are beginning to run their prisons, dominating black and Mexican-American gangs."[8]

One *marielito* burglar in Los Angeles, surprised by a returning housewife, shot her in the head. The baby in her arms fell to the ground, unharmed, and then the killer started tearing the clothes off the dead woman's nine-year-old daughter, hoping to rape her. A neighbor happened in on this and ran home to call police, sending the killer fleeing. The man shot another victim who refused to give him his motorcycle before he was gunned down by police.[9]

So among the honest, hardworking refugees like José Arse that came over, how many killers and lunatics were there?

---

[7] John S. Lang, Joseph L. Galloway, Linda K. Lanier and Gordon M. Bock, "Castro's 'Crime Bomb' Inside U.S.," *U.S. News & World Report,* January 16, 1984.
[8] *Ibid.*
[9] *Ibid.*

Estimates varied. The Reagan Justice Department ultimately generated a number of 24,000 *marielitos* who had spent time in Castro's jails—but took pains to point out that a number of those were political prisoners or gays, people who would never have been imprisoned in the United States.

Police were more expansive, putting the number at more like 40,000 who were either criminals or dangerously insane—or nearly one of out every three refugees who came over during those six months. Another 3,000, according to a former Cuban agent *U.S. News* interviewed, were operatives sent specifically to traffic in drugs and otherwise undermine American society.

Castro was evidently quite pleased with himself. Top Cuban official Eugenio Rodríguez Balari had bragged that Havana used to have thirty-five robberies each day prior to the boatlift, but that the number had fallen to two or three daily in the years since.

"So we can say that Mariel was very beneficial for Cuba," he said. "If we could make an arrangement with Reagan, maybe we could have another Mariel to get rid of the rest of these bad elements."[10]

Graham and other U.S. officials were quite naturally perturbed by all this. "Castro emptied out his prisons and dumped them on Bob Graham," summarized Charlie Reed, Graham's longtime aide.

Graham actually proposed rounding up all the criminals—more than a thousand of them were being held in a federal prison—and flying them to the U.S. Naval Base at Guantánamo Bay on the eastern tip of Cuba, opening up the gates, and shoving them through.

And what if there was a confrontation?

"I can't think of a better place to have a confrontation than our own military base," Graham said.[11]

Reagan administration officials had problems with that approach—for example, it would break the terms of the 1903 treaty that Castro wanted to terminate anyway—but empathized with Graham's woes.

---

[10]*Ibid.*

[11]James Gerstenzang, "Florida Governor Suggests Cuban Refugee Criminals Forced Back to Homeland," Associated Press, February 24, 1981.

"Why should the United States have inflicted on it, not legitimate refugees fleeing Castro tyranny, but people who are pushed out of the jails and put on boats to come to this country?" wondered then vice president George H. W. Bush. "It's totally unreasonable."[12]

Reed recalls the time Graham thought he saw an opportunity to get even—following the American invasion of Grenada in 1983. The Cuban construction workers building a new airport on the island were to be loaded aboard military transports and airlifted back to Havana. Graham got wind of this and had an idea: Military transports are big planes, and there were only a few hundred construction workers. Why not fill up the remaining spots on the planes with, say, mental patients and criminals from, say, the Mariel boatlift? When they landed in Havana, the whole lot of them would be shooed out and the planes would take off for home before Castro or his goons were any the wiser.

Graham actually took this plan to the Reagan State Department but was rebuffed.

"He was so mad," Reed recalled of Graham's feelings toward Castro. "He hated him."

Of course, no story of Castro and Florida is complete without the made-for-television tragicomedy that was the Elián Gonzalez affair of 2000. Here again, the absurdity of South Florida politics was whipped into a foamy froth for all the world to admire. And Graham found himself on the opposite side of what the overwhelming majority of Americans saw as decency and common sense.

A six-year-old boy, found floating in an inner tube in the Gulf Stream, was one of the few survivors of an overloaded boat trying to escape Cuba. His mother had drowned, and upon his rescue he was given to relatives he had never met in Miami. His father, still in Cuba and panicked over his disappearance, was relieved to hear he was alive.

Most Americans intuitively empathized here with, first, the boy, and

[12]David Broder, "Bush Says Reagan Administration Favors Idea of Returning 'Undesirable' Cubans," *Washington Post*, March 16, 1981.

second, his father. The child had lost his mother in a traumatic ordeal. The father almost lost his boy. Boy loves his father. Father loves his boy and, by all appearances, is a good father. Forget for a moment that what his mother did would, in our society, be illegal under most custody arrangements. Particularly when there is joint custody, one parent can't up and leave the state with the child, let alone the country, without the agreement of the other parent. Forget for this discussion what Juan Gonzalez's reaction must have been when he discovered that his ex-wife had taken his little boy off on a dangerous trip across the Florida Straits. Given the terrible results of that journey, what should have happened next is a no-brainer.

Brains, unfortunately, are rarely employed when the discussion turns to Cuba in South Florida. There, thousands of exiles, fanned on by their right-wing enablers in Washington, took to the streets to insist that, no, the boy should stay in Miami in the care of his none-too-stable relatives. The relatives, thus encouraged, defied the Immigration and Naturalization Service's command that they return the boy to his father.

To some observers, what was going on was starting to look an awful lot like kidnapping—people refusing to return a minor child to his lawful parent. But in Florida, nary a politician would say boo. Both Graham and his Republican colleague in the Senate, Connie Mack, pushed a bill that would have given Elián permanent residency status—thereby allowing the relatives to sue for his custody in state courts.

With both presidential candidates in full pandering mode—agreeing that the issue should be settled in family court—Attorney General Janet Reno tried to have calmer heads in Miami turn the boy over. But each time it seemed as if a deal was close, the relatives would come up with a new demand. Finally, on April 22, a full five months after Elián had been plucked from the sea, Reno's troops went in and returned him to his father.

In most of the state—indeed, the nation—the vast majority said: "It's about time." Not so in Miami, where the exile community went ballistic and, amazingly, dragged a number of ordinarily sane politicians like Bob Graham with them.

While protests hit Miami city government for its "complicity" with the raid—in other words, having its police force help carry out Reno's order—Graham joined some of his Republican colleagues on Capitol Hill, calling for an investigation. He complained about the Clinton administration's du-plicity. In a meeting with the President, Graham said that Clinton himself had assured him they would not do the one thing that Graham believed would wreak total havoc—and that was to come in under cover of night and snatch the boy.

Three weeks later, that was precisely what happened. "I was just stunned because that was exactly what they warned against. My relationship with the Clinton administration never really recovered from that experience," Graham said. "This is just inexplicable to me, what their motivation was to act in such an aggressive and precipitous way."[13]

Graham's main beef was that Clinton had told him "we can do that" when Graham asked for a commitment against a midnight raid. White House spokesman Joe Lockhart, in response to Graham's complaints, said that "we can do that" should not have been inferred as a firm commitment.[14]

In either case, polls at the time showed that most people—including most Floridians—ultimately supported Reno's decision to forcibly remove Elián from the "Miami Relatives" and hand him back to his daddy. Throughout the five-month saga, the Relatives and their handlers had bar-gained in bad faith, substituting one demand with another. They wanted sole custody of Elián. They made and released what amounted to a hostage video. They wanted joint custody with Elián's father. They wanted several weeks where they would all—they, Juan, Juan's new wife and baby, and Elián—live together in a house in Miami.[15] Reno finally decided that enough was enough—that no amount of talking was going to make the ex-ile community give the boy back.

And once that decision was made, most people understood the safety reasons for doing so in the middle of the night. The crowd outside the house would be at its smallest, and the people inside would be at their least combative.

---

[13]University of Florida Oral History Project, Tapes W–X, January 26, 2001.

[14]Graham, given everything that had transpired to that point with Clinton, probably should have asked what the meaning of "can" was.

[15]The new Mrs. Gonzalez, Nercy Carmenate, thought this last one was truly nutty. "Who would want to live with them?" she scoffed, according to *Newsweek*'s May 1, 2000, issue.

A year later, Graham's analysis of the political fallout over Elián was as follows: "If you had set out and said how can we most irritate the Cuban-American community, they did exactly that thing which would have accomplished that objective."[16]

That's probably correct—as is the analysis that the Elián raid cost Gore the election that November. In 1996, Clinton had received 40 percent of the Cuban-American vote. In 2000, Gore barely got 25 percent. The difference, according to Florida International political scientist Dario Moreno, translates to about 65,000 votes. Even a small fraction of those breaking for Gore would have put him in the White House.

"Elián Gonzalez has created a huge problem for the Democratic Party in Florida," Moreno said, and not just with Cuban voters, but with all Hispanics, who saw the issue not as a custody fight but a referendum on immigration. The Hispanic point of view on immigration is simple, Moreno said: "You don't send people back."

That said—for a man who eschews focus groups and government-by-polls as much as Graham does, is he suggesting that Reno, with Clinton's backing, ought not to have done what she thought was correct? Never mind that Graham, having already publicly sided with the Relatives on the custody issue, really could no longer be considered an honest broker on the matter.

Normally, political pandering to Miami's exile community has very little obvious consequence. If a continued embargo means the people of Cuba remain impoverished and hungry, well, that's not so troublesome. They are a faceless mass, and a communist one at that. But with Elián, the exile community's obsession took on a human face—that of a precious six-year-old who might never see his father again.

If before Elián the exile community was viewed by the rest of the country as pursuing the noble goal of freedom for their homeland, the whole sorry episode changed that image. Mention Miami Cubans now, and many

---

[16]University of Florida Oral History Project, Tapes W–X, January 26, 2001.

people north of the Broward County line think: "Oh, right, those are the wing nuts who would tear a little boy from his daddy to make a political point."

In the eyes of most Americans, this was not a muddy issue. Right and wrong were crystal clear, and George W. Bush and Al Gore and, yes, Bob Graham were wrong, and Janet Reno was right.

For years, American foreign policy toward much of the Third World has been codified in the slogan, probably apocryphal, as it has been attributed to so many leaders over the years, "He may be a son of a bitch, but he's *our* son of a bitch." Our sons of bitches have included such gems as Anastasio Somoza in Nicaragua, the Shah, Mohammad Reza Pahlevi, in Iran, Augusto Pinochet in Chile, and, off and on for twenty-five years leading up to 1959, Fulgencio Batista in Cuba. Ruthless, murderous dictators all, but, because they were anticommunist, viewed as valuable allies.

These and other unsavory friends—many we have merely cozied up to after they seized power; others we have actually installed—may well be the reason the rest of the world views American sanctimony about individual freedom and democracy with a somewhat jaundiced eye. It's a hard sell, that the United States is truly interested in advancing the cause of liberty, when United States–supported dictators have had so many people tortured or "disappeared" over the years.

In the case of Graham, the hypocrisy, at times, was all the more stark.

In December 1984, China's consul general for the southern United States came to Florida to help Graham plan a trade mission to China. He got a warm welcome in Tallahassee, meeting with Graham and other top state officials. In Miami, he got the cold shoulder.

"The People's Republic of China, the last time I checked, is a communist country," said Marie Petit, a top aide to Puerto Rican–born mayor Maurice Ferré. "The mayor's decision and his policy is that he does not meet with representatives of communist countries or of South Africa. These governments are affronts to our constituents."[17]

---

[17]"Chinese Diplomat Gets Cold Shoulder from Miami Mayor," Associated Press, December 21, 1984.

Ferré had a point. Was China in those years less repressive than Cuba?

Earlier, in September 1981, Graham had visited Haiti in an attempt to persuade Jean-Claude "Baby Doc" Duvalier to modernize his economy and thereby cut back on the stream of impoverished refugees to Florida's shores. Graham met with Duvalier, who was then only twenty-three years old, at a special guest house for heads of state Duvalier kept in the mountains overlooking the Caribbean. Graham later sent a team of agronomists, led by Lieutenant Governor Wayne Mixson, to help Haiti improve its economy, sort of a foreign-aid package from Tallahassee.

"We're mad as hell," Graham said, explaining his foray into diplomacy. "Clearly a state has no legal basis to conduct foreign relations, but we've had to try to influence treaties and get involved in foreign affairs because the federal government has abdicated its responsibilities. We can't just sit back and let Florida just be devastated."[18]

Now, an argument can be made that Graham's visit probably had the potential of much benefit (a stronger Haitian economy) with a limited downside (somewhat increased legitimacy for Duvalier). Similar arguments have been made by this country regarding American trade and cultural exchange with China, the Soviet Union, South Africa, and Saudi Arabia, among other repressive regimes.

But in the measuring of dictators, was Baby Doc so much less bad than Castro that it was okay to break bread with one but not the other? After Duvalier was deposed in 1986, Graham acknowledged that he was a "repressive" autocrat. Nevertheless, he continues to defend his attempts to work with Baby Doc while flat-out dismissing Castro. What's the distinction?

Baby Doc Duvalier "didn't have much of a driving set of philosophical tenets," Graham explained during a recent interview just outside the Senate chamber in the Capitol. "He was mainly interested in protecting the economic status that his father had achieved."

And Castro?

"I think Castro, in my judgment, was a more evil person, in that he not only repressed his people, whereas Duvalier was at least trying to build an

---

[18]Art Harris, "Boatlift Bloat Sends Angry Florida Officials into Tropical Politics," *Washington Post*, December 22, 1981.

economy that would have given the people of Haiti some better prospect, and probably would also have undermined his regime as it has in so many other authoritarian governments—Castro has shown no real interest, in fact has resisted the kind of reforms that most other communist countries made, those in Central Europe, even the Soviet Union itself, and particularly China," Graham said. "So I think that Castro was a more evil figure. He also had international aspirations, such as the large contingent that he had fighting in Angola and the support that he gave to radical elements in other parts of Latin America and the Caribbean. Duvalier didn't have any focus of attention beyond Haiti itself."

And so, from Graham in the first decade of the twenty-first century, comes the same distinction between authoritarian (read: anticommunist) dictators and totalitarian (read: communist or socialist) dictators made popular by Reagan's United Nations ambassador, Jeane Kirkpatrick, in the 1980s.

According to the theory, an authoritarian regime could, over time, be transformed, softened, molded into a democratic nation. Therefore, the United States had a legitimate interest in "constructive engagement" with such countries. Totalitarian regimes, on the other hand, were lost causes. Therefore, the United States should isolate, if not actively undermine, those governments.

Critics pointed out that the distinction also just happened to distinguish between dictators with whom American corporations *were* doing business and those dictators with whom American corporations were *not* doing business.

Chile's Augusto Pinochet, he of the infamous soccer stadium killings, for example, was an authoritarian dictator and therefore "okay" to deal with.[19] Nicaragua's Daniel Ortega, who couldn't possibly have killed anywhere near as many people, was a totalitarian dictator and therefore had to go.

Even Dario Moreno, the Cuban-American political scientist at Florida International University who is generally sympathetic to the exile cause,

---

[19]Or perhaps he was okay to deal with because, as declassified documents now prove, the CIA orchestrated the violent coup that killed democratically elected Salvador Allende and put Pinochet in power.

agreed that authoritarian repression is probably indistinguishable from totalitarian repression, if you happened to be the one being repressed.

"Whether you're killed by a right-wing dictator or a left-wing dictator makes very little difference to the victim," said Moreno.

In fairness to Graham, his stance on Cuban-American issues goes beyond the anti-Castro rhetoric.

Graham for years has been a fixture at Little Havana's Activities and Nutrition Center. His Senate Web site is and has been available in Spanish. Graham himself made a concerted effort to learn Spanish early in his Senate career, including a two-week immersion course in Costa Rica.

"I remember many times hearing him say, 'We don't work for the Democratic Party, we work for anybody paying taxes. We treat them all the same,'" Lula Rodriguez, Graham's former Miami district director, told the *St. Petersburg Times* in 2000.[20]

That faithfulness to the exile community's issues, Castro and otherwise, has paid off politically for Graham over the years. During his first run for the United States Senate in 1986, Graham won only 26 percent of the Cuban-American vote. Six years later, he increased that to 74 percent. He managed to win 70 percent of it in 1998—a year that saw Cuban darling Jeb Bush on the Republican ticket for governor.[21]

"Cubans are part of his constituency," Moreno says, adding that the feelings have been mutual. "He's always been well supported by the Cuban-American community."

Graham's position on Castro and Cuba has also been consistent through the years. In 1994, he told his oral history biographer at the University of Florida: "The most effective way to deal with authoritarian regimes—whether they were in South Africa or in Czechoslovakia or in Havana—was through a policy of isolation, politically and economically, while you tried to pour in as much information and person-to-person contact as you

[20]Bill Adair, "Graham Steps out of Middle at Odd Time," *St. Petersburg Times,* April 30, 2000.
[21]*Ibid.*

could. And I think that policy worked in Central Europe. I hope it is going to be the catalyst for a transition to a truly democratic union of South Africa, and I think it will eventually work in Havana."[22]

Which is not to suggest that Graham has not been keenly aware of the various political implications of Cuban refugees, both good and bad. Controlled immigration from Cuba has been okay—Graham even believes, the Elián Gonzalez affair notwithstanding, that the Democratic Party can once again make inroads into the Cuban-American community.

Once Castro eventually steps down or dies or is forced out, that, too, will reconfigure Florida politics, Graham believes. The one factor that kept Miami Cubans in the grasp of Republicans will have vanished, and then Cuban-Americans will start seeing politics without the Castro lens.

"They will no longer have that foreign policy basis as their dominant political philosophy. They will be more like the second or third generation of other domestic groups . . . more concerned with domestic issues, jobs, their children's future, and so on."[23]

A mass migration like Mariel is another story. Tens of thousands of refugees would cost Florida hundreds of millions of dollars in social services and incalculable loss of goodwill among those already here and struggling. Graham attributes the 1980 riots in a black ghetto of Miami at least in part to the money, time, and jobs flowing to the new refugees while longtime citizens got nothing. He attributes then-Governor Bill Clinton's 1980 reelection loss in part to Mariel, as well—some of the refugees were being housed at Fort Chaffee in Arkansas, where they rioted.

Graham is also cognizant of the historical precedents of the Miami exile community's single-minded obsession with Castro. He points to the city of Milwaukee, and the German immigrant community that refused to vote Democratic for decades because they were so upset by Woodrow Wilson's siding with the British and French against Germany in World War I.

"So the influence of the Cuban-American community on U.S. Cuban policy fitted a long tradition of certain components in our population, with a strong interest in a particular foreign policy, exercising their influence."[24]

[22]University of Florida Oral History Project, Tapes L–M, April 6, 1994.
[23]University of Florida Oral History Project, Tape P, November 11, 1995.
[24]University of Florida Oral History Project, Tapes Q–R, January 11, 1996.

The comparison points to the hyperbole implicit in any discussion of Castro in South Florida. Routinely, Cuban-American state lawmakers have compared Castro to Stalin and Hitler during floor debate. Here, Graham compares Castro's revolution, driven primarily by the repression of Batista, with German expansionism in 1914.

In South Florida, it is not just Castro who is evil personified. Pretty much any left-of-center government is lumped into the same category. And for the most part, Graham has gone along with this line of thinking.

In Nicaragua, for example, the Sandinistas led a popular uprising against longtime U.S.-backed dictator Anastasio Somoza in 1979. Yet Graham, again reflecting Miami sensibilities (Somoza and much of his hated Guardia Nacional fled to—where else?—Miami), called the Sandinistas "an illegitimate regime that has taken power by force and without credible support by the Nicaraguan people."[25]

It was this rationale that put Graham squarely behind President Reagan's efforts to arm the *contra* rebels, and squarely against the efforts of many Democrats in Congress to stop the proxy war.

Graham supported Reagan's invasion of Grenada, such as it was, and the first President Bush's invasion of Panama. In 1990, he supported the first Bush's original Gulf War, again going against many of his Democratic colleagues in the Senate.

So what, then, would a Graham-tinted foreign policy mean? Should he become vice president or, say, Homeland Security secretary?

Until September 11, 2001, it would not have been completely clear. As a governor and a senator, he has known that his positions in this area did not have much effect on U.S. policy, so even his harshest statements are tough to judge. In the Senate, he has concentrated on Florida issues, particularly Medicare, the Everglades, and the state's share of federal funding, largely to the exclusion of foreign policy questions.

[25] *Ibid.*

That changed in the aftermath of the terrorist attacks. As chairman of the Senate Intelligence Committee, Graham saw and learned in some detail those things that are typically the province of the president and his national security staff. And, as his now-famous "Blood on Your Hands" speech prior to the Iraq war resolution in 2002 shows, what he learned changed him forever.

With pointing fingers, waving arms, and much un-Graham-like shouting that stunned aides and family members alike, Graham implored his colleagues not to go along with President Bush's focus on Saddam Hussein's Iraq and to instead focus on al Qaeda and other terrorist groups that could actually harm Americans.

"If there was one major mistake we made in the 1990s, it was allowing al Qaeda's training camp to be a sanctuary where every year thousands—*thousands!*—of young people were converted into hardened assassins," Graham railed. "If that's the criticism that we're going to have, because in the 1990s we allowed that to go on month after month, year after year, what is going to be our excuse *today*—when similar training camps are in operation in Iran, Syria, Syrian-controlled areas of Lebanon!"[26]

West Virginia senator Jay Rockefeller has known Graham for nearly thirty years, stretching back to the late 1970s when they were governors together, and is Graham's closest friend in the Senate. Both Graham's words and his tone startled even him.

"It was one of the best speeches I've ever heard him give," Rockefeller said later. "I've never seen him so angry. And he wasn't running for anything at the time."

Graham's message was simple: The everyday politics of Washington was going to get Americans killed. That central lesson, that inaction or misguided action against the wrong targets could leave the United States with smoking ruins where skyscrapers once stood, will no doubt continue to color his worldview for years to come.

That said, it is important to remember that Graham is a walking encyclopedia of American and world history. He has probably forgotten more facts on those subjects than most elected leaders in Washington have ever known.

---

[26]For the full transcript, see Appendix C.

So how would Graham use this knowledge on a grander stage? On the one hand, he clearly believes that America has an obligation to help poorer nations win a leg up. His Florida scholarship program for Caribbean students was a good example. Helping these students bring expertise in business and the sciences back to their home nations was not only the right thing to do, Graham thought, but it also fostered goodwill toward the United States in the coming generation of leaders as well as increasing trade and mutual prosperity.

Graham could bring a more evenhanded approach to elements of the antiterror war. For instance, he has been willing to hammer[27] Saudi Arabia for its ties to the September 11 terrorists. Saudi Arabia, a repressive monarchy, has been immune from Washington criticism for decades because of American reliance on its oil reserves.

Graham appreciates the need to work with allies and act with the support of a consensus. He also speaks about credibility, and the importance of speaking and acting based on solid information. He has criticized President Bush for failing on both counts.

On the other hand, Bob Graham has never been a peace-love-and-understanding dove. Far from it. A Graham-influenced Cuba policy could well be less tolerant of Castro than that of any administration since Kennedy's. This could become a real factor, with Miami's exile community in 2003 lobbying President Bush for the sort of "regime change" in Florida's neighbor to the south that Bush was willing to spend billions on, in a country halfway around the world.

And, again, in the matter of terrorism, watch his speech on the floor of the Senate on October 9, 2002, and it is clear that he opposed the war against Iraq not because he thought it too much, but because he thought it too *little*.

"I am concerned by those who see only one evil," Graham said. "I urge my colleagues to open their eyes to the much larger array of lethal, more violent range of foes that are prepared to assault us here at home."

---

[27]Hammer by implication, that is. As of the summer of 2003, the pages relating to Saudi Arabia in the congressional report on the September 11 attacks were censored by the Bush administration. Graham said he would be thrown into federal prison if he revealed the name of the nation involved, but officials familiar with the report told reporters it was, indeed, Saudi Arabia.

Since then—and particularly since the July 2003 revelations that the Bush administration had hyped the intelligence data regarding Iraq's weapons of mass destruction—Graham has refined that statement to say that he opposed the war because, while Saddam Hussein was an evil man and potentially a threat to the United States, he was nowhere near the threat that al Qaeda and Hezbollah and Islamic Jihad were.

In April 2003, he suggested lobbing "a few cruise missiles" at Hezbollah training camps in Syria if Assad's government does not shut them down.

On the face of it, such action seems a bit extreme. Is Graham suggesting that the United States should go after Hezbollah and Islamic Jihad for its attacks against Israel? Should America also go after the terrorists fighting Indian occupation of Kashmir? How about the terrorists fighting British occupation of Northern Ireland?

But Graham, as a former Intelligence Committee chairman, could well know details about those terror groups' operatives and plans that would frighten and galvanize Americans into doing exactly as Graham suggested.

One thing is clear: Graham's chairmanship after September 11 has clearly had a toll on him. Both Adele and brother Bill have noticed it. Is the unease a result of his knowledge of a large, free country's inherent vulnerabilities? Or are there specific threats and plans he has come to learn of through his position that would terrify the rest of us if we only knew?

Perhaps his experience on the committee will push a politician who was already a "hawk" even farther into that camp. Or maybe exactly the opposite: The knowledge he has gained will make him more of an internationalist, and lead him to decide that fewer instances of unilateral American force overseas, not more, will make the nation safer.

Graham refuses to talk about what he has learned on the Intelligence Committee,[28] so it's impossible, for now, to know the answer.

---

[28]He is, in fact, prohibited from doing so by law.

River of Grass

No matter what else happens in his life, there is one thing that Bob Graham can point to as his legacy to Florida, and that is the slow, dark, six-inch-deep, hundred-mile-long river that runs down the central part of the state south of Lake Okeechobee.

A marsh, a swamp, the largest continuous wetland in the continental United States, the Everglades is unique, and if it survives in a form that in any way resembles what it was when Bob Graham was a child, or even when he was the newly elected governor, that will be a tremendous accomplishment, perhaps the biggest of his career.

Because what Graham managed to create in his years in the Governor's Mansion, and then helped maintain from Washington, was the idea of the Everglades as a pressing government priority, as something so important that all thinking people would agree to its fulfillment—with the critical corollary that if you *didn't* see it as a pressing priority, then you clearly were not a thinking person.

Because that is now the state of affairs in Florida when it comes to the Everglades. If you are running for any statewide office, you must at the bare minimum mouth the words from the Everglades hymnal.

There are other, more pressing needs doesn't cut it anymore. Likewise with *there needs to be more study*. Even the most pro-development of candidates, who deep in their hearts would like nothing more than to pave the damned place over and put up another string of Wal-Marts, now must nod and appear interested when courting the environmental vote. And court it they must, because the environmental vote in Florida is too significant to ignore, and cuts widely across party lines.

And right there is the fundamental sea change Graham was able to bring about in Florida—astonishing, really, particularly considering his background.

The three things most damaging to the Glades are suburban encroachment, cattle ranching, and sugar farming, which dump, respectively, stormwater runoff, cow manure, and phosphate fertilizer into a fragile ecosystem ill equipped to handle them. Graham's family wealth is based squarely on all three.[1]

The Pennsylvania Sugar Company brought Graham's father, Ernest, to the company town named Pennsuco in an area ditched and drained out of the Everglades. After the company abandoned its cane fields and essentially gave the land to him if he agreed to pay the taxes, Cap Graham turned to his old family business from Michigan, milk cows. The Graham Dairy over the years became one of the best-known businesses in Dade County. And when property values in South Florida shot sky-high, the Graham sons turned much of the land into the planned community of Miami Lakes, which over the years multiplied their millions.

Despite this, or perhaps because of it, Graham became the first governor to champion the massive task of restoring the Everglades, a task that, a quarter century later, even conservative Republican governor Jeb Bush must at least claim to support.

"One of the things I am pleased about is that these [Everglades] initiatives were not cult-of-personality initiatives—lots of Floridians bought into them. The very phrase 'Save Our Everglades' has become a very common description of our efforts," Graham said.[2]

---

[1] A fourth threat to the Everglades, lime-rock mining, is not something the Grahams have taken part in themselves, but they have profited from it indirectly by selling their lands to rock-mining companies.
[2] University of Florida Oral History Project, Tapes N–O, February 21, 1995.

I t is amazing, especially for people who recall the wholesale carnage being inflicted on the state's wilderness in the 1960s and '70s, but true. Politicians hoping to run for statewide office in Florida today—or even local office, for that matter, in South Florida—must make the obligatory canoe trip amid the sawgrass and the tree hammocks to show their commitment to restoring what's left of the Glades to their original condition.

Bob Graham doesn't have to make that sort of effort. All he has to do is think back to his childhood and tell audiences about when he and his brother Bill could swim in the Miami River canal that ran by their house, the water was so clean.

Then, as a young boy, he would awaken on summer nights and look out his window across the great swamp. The house his father had built for them was made of coral rock, a material ideally suited for pre-air-conditioned South Florida because its porosity captured moisture at night and allowed it to evaporate off in the daytime, serving as a sort of natural air-conditioning.[3] Still, on the steamy nights of July and August, sometimes there was no getting around it, coral rock or no. It was hot.

"There is a certain tendency to romanticize the past, but it was clearly different and in some ways much harsher—mosquitoes eight or nine months of the year," Graham recalled in a 1994 newspaper interview. "I remember a lot of nights sitting in my bedroom sweating and looking out the window, and you could see the Everglades burning, which is a recurrent thing there. And fire makes it a very stark kind of environment."[4]

That was the scene when there were droughts. It was something else entirely after the periodic hurricane, when the house, as solid as could be built, served as a shelter for those who lived nearby in wooden structures.

"In 1947, we had two hurricanes in close proximity. The first had left a lot of water behind, and the second *really* left a lot of water. Waking up, there was a walkway around the south and east sides at the second level of the house. The walkway was the roof over an enclosed patio. I remember

---

[3]There are some who are not quite sold on this explanation—among them Bill Graham, who actually grew up in said house. "It's a great theory," he says of the natural air-conditioning.
[4]Anne Groer, "Teflon Bob," *Orlando Sentinel,* January 8, 1995.

opening the door and walking out onto this walk area [of] about ten or fifteen [feet] width and looking as far as you could look to the south and to
the east and it was just a sheet of water. We were an island," he recalled
years later. "One of the adults, a woman, said, 'Today is Columbus Day. If
Christopher Columbus had come in 1947 instead of 1492, and if he had
come here instead of to the Bahamas, he would have turned his damn boats
around and gone back to Spain.'"[5]

In Graham's mind there is little doubt what effect those years had on
him. "I think my emotional feelings for the Everglades were a direct result
of having grown up in Pennsuco."[6] Those feelings are best understood with
a "before and after" study.

Bob Graham's childhood home, a two-story structure with stone arches
over the porch and a circular window at the top, essentially marked the
western frontier of Dade County. Living at the settlement were maybe a
hundred or so dairy workers in a bunkhouse for single men and small
shacks for families. Graham Dairy Road ran eastward toward civilization.
In all directions, there was only soggy cow pasture and, beyond that, the
natural Everglades vegetation. During the wet summer months, the soggy
pasture turned into black, gooey muck—the original state of the Glades
prior to Governor Napoleon Bonaparte Broward's drainage canal scheme.

In 2003, Cap Graham's coral rock home is dark with mildew, its win-
dows broken and boarded. Ominous cracks have appeared in the arches, the
result of decades of vibrations from nearby blasting. Concrete companies
prize the particular, hard limestone underlying the muck that makes for
good road material. Huge, rectangular quarries dot the landscape, bringing
with them the ancillary streams of heavy dump trucks and rail cars to
carry off the pulverized rock.

Part of the old Graham Dairy Road is now a small segment of Interstate
75. The Miami River canal Bill and Bob used to swim in as children is now
a litter-strewn ditch on the other side of U.S. Highway 27, which has

---

[5]University of Florida Oral History Project, Tapes A–E, February 13, 1989.
[6]Anne Groer, "Teflon Bob," *Orlando Sentinel*, January 8, 1995.

grown from its original two lanes to six. Its service road comes to within a few yards of the front door. Where before the Graham house stood virtually alone in the wilderness, now it is dwarfed by nearby cell phone towers. Across the highway is an industrial park, acres and acres of warehouse space. To the east is continuous development right to Biscayne Bay, and each mined-out quarry to the west becomes a potential "lakefront" housing development around the inundated hole.

Brother Bill Graham, who moved into the house when he was six months old in 1924, finds the sight so depressing that he refuses to go out there anymore. Bob Graham described his own feelings about his first home like this: "It is almost like Tom Sawyer: What the Mississippi River was to Tom Sawyer, the Everglades were to my childhood."[7]

Translating those feelings to action was another matter. Developers, real estate agents, indeed the whole "concrete coalition"[8] had held and continue to hold tremendous power in Tallahassee. Getting them to buy into a proposal to protect hundreds of thousands of acres from development, to return the "channelized" Kissimmee River to its original, meandering course, to *increase* the real estate transaction tax to help pay for it all—in short, to do just the opposite of where their natural proclivities would lead them—was an impressive feat by any definition.

Graham did this by appealing to their baser instincts: their bottom lines. He pointed out that South Florida without a stable supply of water was a South Florida where people would no longer come to live and work and buy affordable single-family homes with all the modern amenities. The same fresh water the Everglades needed to survive was water the concrete coalition would need to thrive in the decades to come, and without a long-term plan to fix the whole system, the home builders and road pavers and all their associated allies may as well just pack up and find someplace else to make their money.

The strategy worked. Graham in 1983 passed the Save Our Everglades

---

[7]University of Florida Oral History Project, Tapes W–X, January 26, 2001.

[8]The term has, in Florida politics, referred to the pro-growth leaders of the Florida Keys, but it could just as easily apply to anywhere and everywhere in Florida, a state where growth itself is a growth industry.

act through the Florida legislature. His stated goal then was simple but ambitious: "By the year 2000, the Everglades will look and function more like they did at the turn of the century than they do today."[9]

To understand the scope of this, it is necessary to appreciate what the Everglades looked like in 1900.

Then, there was no Miami. Or Fort Lauderdale. Or any of their vast, sprawling suburbs that stretch twenty miles in from the ocean. Instead, along the Atlantic was a narrow strip of dry land, in places only a couple of miles wide, sandwiched between salty ocean on one side and flooded, sawgrass swamp on the other.

This marsh stretched most of the way across the Florida peninsula, until it merged into cypress swamps south and east of a ridge of relatively high ground on the west coast. This was the Everglades, Marjory Stoneman Douglas's "River of Grass."[10] It was essentially a sixty-mile-wide, 130-mile-long river, running from Lake Okeechobee south to Florida Bay.

In the rainy season, which typically lasted nine months, water would lap over the southern lip of the lake, feeding the so-called "sheet flow" that varied from a few inches to a few feet in depth. The change in elevation over those 130 miles was only twenty feet—working out to a mere two-inch drop per mile—producing a lazy flow to the sea. As it flowed, it also seeped down through as much as a dozen feet of peaty muck, topping off the underground aquifer that stretched to the east and west.

During the brief dry season in spring, the standing water would almost disappear in areas, creating pools teeming with small fish. Wading birds would time their nesting season around these dry spells, because it was easier for baby birds to feed in these pools.

Then Governor Broward implemented his plan to drain the Everglades to create more room for cities and farms. When the new cities and farms

---

[9]Philip Shabecoff, "Program Aims to Rescue Everglades from 100 Years of the Hand of Man," *The New York Times,* January 20, 1986.
[10]The 1947 book that first popularized the idea that the Everglades was something beautiful and majestic and worth saving, rather than a mosquito-infested swamp.

flooded, the Army Corps built a giant dike around the south side of Lake Okeechobee. When the cities and farms still flooded, a long levee was added, running north and south the length of South Florida, to hold back the summer waters from the newly inhabited areas. The newly dry half million acres just south of the lake was turned over to sugar growers, with controlled releases from the lake providing irrigation at the correct times.

The system of canals and levees and pumps made South Florida safe for humans. It also began killing the Everglades.

The natural cycle? Nine months wet, three months dry? Gone. Now, during rainy season, Flood Control District managers would dump excess water out the canals to the Atlantic and the Gulf and, when necessary, down through the Glades to ensure that the homes along the southeast coast were not flooded. And during dry season, district managers would make sure the farmers and the cities got the water they needed, typically leaving little or none for the Everglades.

By the 1970s, fully half of the original Everglades was gone—replaced by suburbs in the east and sugarcane fields in the north. What was left was sick. With too much water in the summer and fall, the "tree islands"— those small, teardrop-shaped mounds of dirt dotting the shallow river— were swept away, along with the animals that lived there. The wading birds, their natural cycle disrupted, were largely gone as well.

And the rich peat soil? Without the constant submersion in water, it dried out, subsided, even burned. The soil levels were down some fifteen feet in the agricultural areas, about three feet elsewhere. The marsh that remained too often had cattails and other invasive plants crowd out the native sawgrass—the result of too many nutrients in the water from farm and ranch runoff.

And that's pretty much the Everglades as Bob Graham inherited them when he put together his coalition to save them in 1983.

To be sure, doing so was not as hard as it would have been in the 1940s or 1950s—when growth and development were almost universally regarded as a panacea: a way to increase revenues without increasing taxes.

"Up until the mid-1960s, Florida had largely been thought of as a commodity, and the state cabinet . . . every time we met would sell off another bay or another piece of Florida, of state-owned property, to encourage development," Graham said.[11]

Ironically, perhaps, the credit for starting the environmental movement in Florida, according to Graham, should go to Republicans. So many of the ruling Democrats through the middle decades of the twentieth century were beholden to the interests that made money by despoiling the environment that it was left to Republicans like Nathaniel Reed, of Hobe Sound, to start pushing to protect what was left. Graham credits GOP governor Claude Kirk for, among other things, appointing Reed to what was then called the Water Pollution Control Board and which eventually became the Department of Environmental Protection.

"Reed had a great deal of influence on Kirk and got Kirk to be the spokesman for a number of environmental issues in the state."[12]

That trend slowly began gathering momentum, then picked up a great number of converts in 1970 and 1971, when a drought burned some 500,000 acres of the Everglades. Suddenly, there came the realization that the unchecked development in South Florida seemed to have fundamentally altered the area's water supply, possibly with dire consequences.

Governor Reubin Askew held the first conference to study the Everglades issue—a full quarter-century after Marjory Stoneman Douglas published her cautionary *River of Grass*.

For the record, Graham's environmentalism does not come from his father. Cap Graham came to Florida and saw in the Everglades a soggy mess that was making it difficult for his employer to make a profit. In other words, he saw it the same way that the state's political and business leaders had seen it since the idea of settling South Florida became desirable.

One of Cap Graham's projects, in fact, was to figure out a way to boost

---

[11]University of Florida Oral History Project, Tapes F–I, May 24, 1989.
[12]*Ibid.*

the nitrogen content of Pennsuco's soil to increase its cash crop productivity—exactly the opposite of what conservationists hope to do to restore the marsh to the way it was.[13]

"My dad had the idea that the muck in the Everglades would have a significant commercial value if you could increase the nitrogen content. I think muck, naturally, is about two or three percent nitrogen, and his theory was that if you could get it up to seven or eight percent it would be useful for fertilizer and other things." Bob Graham, years later, well understood the irony: "It was probably a good thing [that he failed] because it would be hard for me as such an interested person saving the Everglades, to also be associated with somebody that was out there trying to dig up big pits of the muck."[14]

"My father is what I would call an accidental environmentalist," Bob Graham said, explaining his father's insistence that the Tamiami Trail project—the first roadway to cross the Everglades—be built with culverts to let water cross the dike, and his later opposition to the Cross Florida Barge Canal.

In the first instance, Cap Graham saw what all the retained water would do to his land in hurricanes, and in the second case, he realized how bad it would be for South Florida military installations if the federal government built a canal across Florida just south of Jacksonville.

"So on two important environmental projects, water management through the Tamiami Trail and the Cross-Florida Barge Canal, Dad was on the side of the angels," Bob Graham recalled, "but not necessarily" for the right reasons.[15] "He came to the right conclusion, but some might question whether his motives were as green as they should have been. They were green, but they were green for dollars."[16]

Graham is quick to defend the motivations and goals of his father's generation as products of that time. Even Hamilton Disston, who started the work to drain the Glades, should not be vilified.

---

[13]Sugarcane and other crops weren't growing well in the soil, it was later learned, because of a deficiency of copper and other trace minerals. When this was solved, the Everglades peat became tremendously productive.

[14]University of Florida Oral History Project, Tapes A–E, February 13, 1989.

[15]*Ibid.*

[16]University of Florida Oral History Project, Tapes S–T, December 11, 1996.

"I imagine that Hamilton Disston, who was a Philadelphia industrialist, when he came and first saw the Everglades, that he might well have thought, 'This does not look like central Pennsylvania,' and that the purpose of man is to convert this formidable swamp called the Everglades into useful land like central Pennsylvania so that it can serve man's purposes," Graham said. "The reality was that the people in previous generations who had been making decisions on the Everglades were not evil people who had as their goal destruction. They had a different value system."[17]

That Bob Graham would wind up "on the side of the angels" is in itself high irony.

A quick review of Graham's financial picture shows just how rich he and his family have become by, well, despoiling the Everglades. In his 2003 filing with the Federal Elections Commission at the start of his campaign for president, Graham showed stock holdings (belonging to Adele) in a well-diversified portfolio worth, in aggregate, at least $1.3 million.

That, though, is not where the big money is. The big money is Graham's piece of the Graham Companies, the privately held entity that owns a pecan farm, timberland, and a Black Angus cattle breeding ranch in Albany, Georgia; some 1,800 acres primarily in dairy cows in Moore Haven, Florida; and, most significant, much of the town it started developing from scratch in 1962, Miami Lakes.

Graham's shares of the Graham Companies (originally known as Sengra, for "Senator Graham"—Cap Graham) stock are worth about $5 million, with Adele owning another $600,000 worth.[18]

All of which means that Bob Graham is uniquely qualified to speak about the factors destroying the Everglades, insofar as his family has taken an active financial interest in three of the most destructive ones. By stepping out of that background to become a champion of conservation, Graham essentially rejected his past.

---

[17]University of Florida Oral History Project, Tapes U–V, October 24, 2000.
[18]Kris Hundley, "Graham Profits from a Modest Image," *St. Petersburg Times*, July 13, 2003.

"He turned his back on his roots a little bit," agreed Tom Lewis, who ran Graham's Department of Community Affairs, the state agency in charge of managing growth, during Graham's second term as governor.

Starting in 1921, Cap Graham began the effort that would not come to fruition for several decades, which was to turn much of the vast acreage of the Everglades into a domestic source of sugarcane. Graham's lack of success presaged the end of Pennsylvania Sugar Company's efforts along those lines, but others continued. Particularly after the massive flood-control efforts following the 1947 hurricane, growers were invited into the Glades to cultivate sugarcane in the newly drained muck.

This time, the efforts took hold, and the "Everglades Agricultural Area" now has 460,000 acres—720 square miles—growing sugar, propped up by federal price supports that keep domestic growers in business despite a world market price that is much lower.[19] About 700 of these acres in Glades County, somewhat over one square mile, are owned by the Graham Companies, which since 2000 has leased the land to U.S. Sugar for a cut of the profits.[20]

Of the Everglades' killers, sugar is probably the least lethal. What's choking the Everglades and, by extension, Florida Bay to the south, is fertilizer that has run off from farms and lawns and golf courses into water that should naturally be very low in phosphorous. The higher phosphate levels cause the growth of algae and invasive plants like cattails, which in turn dry up marsh and destroy habitat for the fish and birds that require it.

Acre for acre, the phosphate fertilizer required to grow sugarcane is less than what's needed for crops like tomatoes and other vegetables that are also grown in South Florida and which contribute to the runoff problem.

And sugar is positively benign beside the next thing Cap Graham got into: cattle.

Cows each day produce manure, which, when it runs off into the Everglades, dramatically increases the nutrient load in the water, thereby once

---

[19]A recent General Accounting Office study put the cost to American consumers of the price supports and their associated programs at $1.9 billion annually.

[20]The value of the Florida sugar crop averages about $1,800 per acre, meaning the Graham Company acreage grosses about $1.26 million a year. The net profit to the Grahams, subtracting production costs and the share paid to U.S. Sugar, could not be determined.

again encouraging the growth of algae blooms and weeds that are literally choking the marsh to death.[21] Cap Graham's cows numbered a few thousand head at any given time, but he was not the only dairyman or cattle rancher. Far from it. Along the shores of Lake Okeechobee, and thence northward along the Kissimmee River basin, were hundreds of thousands of acres devoted to cattle. Hundreds of thousands of cows, dumping millions of pounds of manure, all of it in the watershed that eventually empties out via the Everglades.

Yet, in the end, the problems of the cane and the cows can likely be solved—maybe not completely, but the ill effects can be dramatically reduced by catching and treating the nutrient-laden runoff in so-called feeder marshes before its release into the Everglades. Indeed, Bob Graham himself has played a major role in bringing those concepts to fruition.

What cannot be solved with any such innovative fix is the biggest threat to the Everglades: urban sprawl. And that is the thing that made Bob Graham rich. For the Graham Companies' remaining dairy herd in Moore Haven and the ranch in Georgia contribute but a tiny fraction to the business's overall, $80 million annual revenues. The vast majority of that stream flows from apartment rentals and commercial leases from a five-square-mile city about fifteen miles northwest of downtown Miami—Miami Lakes.

When Cap Graham originally got his land from the Pennsylvania Sugar Company, there was the "Muck Farm" and there was the "Sand Farm," separated by a dirt road five miles long. The Muck Farm was at the original Pennsuco settlement along the Miami River canal. As the name suggests, the land was dark, Everglades soil, sort of a soggy peat. It had an average elevation of three feet above sea level, and therefore during the rainy season was frequently flooded. Cows don't like to eat grass that is underwater, so each year during the summer months, Cap Graham would drive his herd to the southeast, to the Sand Farm closer to Hialeah. There, at a lofty five feet above sea level, the cows could graze until the dry season.

[21]Hard-core environmentalists would also argue that the methane in cow flatulence is a leading destroyer of the Earth's protective ozone layer, and that the increasing demand for beef cattle is each day wiping out some 10,000 acres of rain forest in South America—but that's another story.

In the mid-1950s, as Dade County property values started going through the roof, middle son Bill, who by then was running Graham Dairy, started considering doing what so many of the other agricultural land owners around them were doing: selling their land to developers who were offering astronomical amounts of money so as to build and sell tract homes and shopping centers.

Bill Graham, though, had some reservations. He was seeing a lot of the construction taking place in Dade County, and he wasn't impressed. He had also read a book about the "new town" concept that had taken hold in Britain and Scandinavia—where a community would be built incorporating both housing and businesses, a more organic approach—and decided to explore that further. Then, with the concurrence of his sister and brothers (Cap Graham suffered a debilitating stroke in 1959), he pushed ahead with the idea. Rather then sell the land to developers and pocket the cash, the Grahams would instead develop the entire 3,000-acre Sand Farm themselves, with the profits from one phase paying for the development of the next, over a period of many years.

As developments go, Miami Lakes is a pretty good one, particularly by the Florida standards of the 1960s.

The streets all have sidewalks. Because four-way intersections cause accidents, they were avoided whenever possible. At many corners are pocket-sized parks—some with only a few benches, most with a piece of playground equipment or two. On some roads, the strip of land between the sidewalk and the curb is extra wide and irregularly shaped to follow the shoreline of one of the many irregularly shaped lakes. Most impressive are the shade trees. Every residential block has them—Bill Graham insisted on them, even though they cost money to plant (which is why most developers at the time were *not* planting them). "I can't imagine this place without trees," he says, waving a hand at them on a tour.

Bill Graham's experience on the zoning board in Miami Springs, where he lived after college, taught him that churches often made bad neighbors because they rarely had enough parking. Parishioners would simply park on nearby lawns, irritating the residents. So brother Bob, when he was positioning churches, located them near the schools, so there would be ample parking on Sundays when the schools were closed and wouldn't need their lots. Of course, Bob also worked to bring in schools for the children of new residents to attend. This sounds logical, and maybe in the rest of the country it is a given. But in Florida, many developers to this day do not voluntarily work to bring in schools, and they cry bloody murder if the county attempts to impose an "impact fee" to make them pay for new schools. Miami Lakes was decades ahead of that curve.

And then there are the lakes, named for Ernest Graham's daughters-in-law (there is a Lake Patricia, a Lake Katharine, a Lake Adele) and Bill Graham's daughters (a Lake Sandra, a Lake Cynthia, a Lake Carol, a Lake Elizabeth). Every single one is artificial, but again, the difference between the lakes in Miami Lakes and the lakes in surrounding developments is obvious from the air: Miami Lakes' ponds are irregularly shaped, with curves and fingers jutting every which way. Bill Graham said the town's architect, Lester Collins, believed that the entire extent of a lake should not be visible from any one point along the shore. Being unable to do so would add a sense of mystery for the viewer—make the lake appear larger than it was.[22] The lakes at neighboring developments are rectangular—the obvious remnants of quarries that have been mined for the limestone rock that is used to build roads all over Florida.

Only one of the Grahams' lakes was ever a rock quarry (that particular parcel was owned by one of the early financial partners). All the rest were gouged out for the dual purpose of building up the remaining area of the town to the required seven feet above sea level as well as creating a landscape feature for which home buyers were clearly interested in paying a premium. That, Bill Graham said, was one lesson of Palm Lakes, a small-scale dry run the family built in the late 1950s (it was, in fact, the site of Bob and Adele's first home after his graduation from law school in 1962). "What we learned was that people like to live on lakes," Bill Graham said. "People didn't want to buy the dry lots, but would stand in line to buy the lake ones."

A large percentage of Miami Lakes' houses, town houses, and condos are waterfront—and those that aren't generally have easy access thanks to the

---

[22]An irregular shoreline also provided a financial benefit: a longer lakefront perimeter for a given surface area. A longer lakefront meant more waterfront houses.

paved easements that Collins designed into the original plan. Many have small sandy beaches for swimming, and the town's rules allow nonmotorized craft like small sailboats and paddleboats. According to the 2000 Census, the city had nearly 23,000 residents and a median household income of $61,000, which is about 70 percent higher than the typical family income in Miami–Dade County. People generally like living there. Particularly for parents with young children, the town offers some refuge from the urban jungle that surrounds it.

All of which is to say that if you're going to pave over the Everglades and build something, a community like Miami Lakes is probably as good as it is going to get.

Tom Lewis, who after Graham left office for Washington went on to manage Disney's planned community "Celebration," said Miami Lakes was the first real planned community in modern Florida. "They did it right."

Hard-core environmentalists would argue that it doesn't matter what is being built and whether it has decent sidewalks and well-positioned schools and churches. The fact that it has been built at all on land that used to be beneath six inches of water is why the Everglades as an ecosystem is in such trouble—and they would be right. It is, of course, about eighty years too late to be making that kind of argument.

For Graham, the Everglades go beyond politics. They are personal, and he takes personally—and with rare anger—suggestions that his commitment to the project is not as it should be.

In late 1995, the widow of millionaire conservationist George Barley and billionaire environmentalist Paul Tudor Jones were making a full-court press to end government price supports for domestic sugar. Their interest was not merely a philosophical opposition to subsidies—it was an attack on the mother's milk of their political enemies. Without the price supports, it is doubtful that Florida growers would see a profit. The way Mary Barley and Jones saw it, that would ultimately lead to more acreage coming out of production and into the hands of the state and federal government for Everglades restoration.

With this in mind, they hired lobbyist Curt Kiser—an ardent environmentalist in his own right from his days in the Florida legislature (where, in the early 1980s, he served as house Republican leader—or Graham's assigned tormentor in Tallahassee). They accompanied Kiser to Washington to lobby the Florida delegation, ending their long day in the suite of Senator Bob Graham.

They knew from the start that Graham would be a hard sell. He had always supported price supports, and Kiser had no reason to believe he would change his mind now. But before Kiser and his clients could start their pitch, Graham had a complaint to register regarding the harsh newspaper and broadcast ads the Everglades people had taken out in Florida. They named Graham among a host of other lawmakers as beholden to Big Sugar.

Graham was not amused.

"He lit into us," Kiser recalled. "He said: 'Curt, who was the first governor who actually made the Everglades an issue?' I told him he was. Then he said, 'Curt, when I ran for governor for the first time, you know how much sugar gave me?' I said, How much? He said, 'Zero.' And then, 'Curt, when I ran for reelection for governor, you know how much sugar gave me? Zero.' And then he said, 'Curt, when I ran for the Senate the first time, you know how much sugar gave me?' And I said, Well, I'm going to presume zero. He said, 'That's right. Zero. When I ran for reelection in 1992, they finally gave me money. And the only reason they gave it to me was they figured they were stuck with me.'"

Kiser got the message. Graham was not going to budge on the price supports, and he was tired of getting accused of being on the take because of it. So what did Kiser think of the tirade?

"Well, he was right. Everything he said was true."

Graham acknowledges that he finds environmentalists' attacks on him over the Everglades a bit much to take. "Sometimes a person in my position, who is trying to reach agreement, gets irritated with those groups, because they seem to be too strident. But I also have an appreciation for the role that they play and the overall contribution that they make."[23]

---

[23]University of Florida Oral History Project, Tapes W–X, January 26, 2001.

The Everglades activists, nonetheless, insist that Graham could have done more to guarantee the restoration project had he supported either one of the two efforts to make the sugar industry pay for a larger share of the cleanup.

The 1995 federal legislation, which had the Clinton administration's support, would have levied a two-cents-per-pound tax on sugar grown in the Everglades—an amount that would have totaled about one-third of the subsidy created by the federal price supports, according to its proponents. Instead, Graham and Florida's junior senator, Republican Connie Mack, offered a three-tenths-penny-per-pound tax on *all* sugar grown in the United States.

"Instead of making Big Sugar pay its fair share to clean up the Everglades, senators Mack and Graham want Florida taxpayers to pay the bill. In the next five years, 133 Florida sugar growers will make over $1 billion in profits because Washington props up the price of sugar," Mary Barley said at the time.[24]

Graham objected, explaining: "I felt that if you were going to have a tax, the primary purpose of that tax would be to clean up the water that the sugar industry discharged. Since it was a state responsibility to clean up the water, that ought to be a state issue, not a federal issue."[25]

Fair enough, critics charged, but then how to explain what happened the following year, when Graham opposed a separate *state* ballot initiative that would have imposed a *state* penny-per-pound tax on sugar grown in the Everglades?

Graham, nearly a decade later, maintains that with the 1994 passage of the Everglades Forever Act—the broad outline that finally put to paper a consensus on how to fix the Everglades—it was critical to hold together the coalition that supported that law's basic framework.

"We spent about ten years fighting and litigating over the Everglades

---

[24]Everglades Trust press release: "Mack/Graham Everglades Proposal Called Unacceptable and a Sham," November 3, 1995.
[25]University of Florida Oral History Project, Tapes S–T, December 11, 1996.

and nothing positive happened," he said. "The lesson that I learned from that is that you've got to have an inclusive policy that includes all the stakeholders in the Everglades, one of which is the agricultural interests that are currently using the Everglades Agricultural Area. So I get a bit concerned when we're not doing that by shutting out or discounting the views of some of the key players in the future of the Everglades."

His friends say that Graham makes no apologies about supporting sugar, just as he makes no apologies about supporting farmers period. "That's where he came from. He saw himself as a farmer," Charlie Reed said. "He saw agriculture as Florida's economic foundation."

Buddy Shorstein said Graham also believed it was unfair for the sugar industry to bear the heaviest burden in the cleanup because it was not the worst polluter. "They're part of the problem, but they're not near the problem that development is," Shorstein said.

The Everglades, while perhaps the crown jewel of Graham's environmental record, is not his sole accomplishment.

Two important precursors were Save Our Rivers and Save Our Coasts, begun in 1981 and 1982, respectively. They were, as their names imply, created to preserve the state's sensitive river basins and at least some of the natural shoreline from rampant development.

Save Our Coasts, particularly, has kept in a pristine condition miles of dunes and beach that otherwise would be sporting high-rise hotels and condominiums. As the years pass, and unspoiled oceanfront land vanishes, the decision to purchase such tracts as North Beach, in heavily built Broward County, will seem ever more foresighted.

Save Our Rivers, in some respects, was an even more important accomplishment. It's relatively easy to sell even those who do not consider themselves environmentalists on the idea of preserving natural shoreline. After all, there is something majestic in the roar of an ocean against a virgin dune line.

It's a lot harder to convince people about the importance of protecting river basins, particularly in Florida where most rivers resemble, well, swamps. It's a lot harder, but actually a lot more important. Florida's rivers and their interrelated underground aquifers are vital not only to the state's ecological balance but also to its economic vitality. If the "recharge" areas for the aquifers are degraded, clean water soon becomes a scarce commodity. It was that simple fact that Graham sold to a skeptical business community and legislature. More important, he sold with it the tax on real estate transactions that has served as the basis for every major environmental program since them. Save Our Coasts relied on an expansion of the "documentary stamp tax." So did Save Our Everglades and, under the guidance of Graham's Republican successor, Bob Martinez, do did Preservation 2000, a further continuation of the land-buying efforts.

Those are the programs that are easy to explain. One somewhat more complicated, but in the long run probably even more critical, was Graham's success in 1985 at pushing through what was, at the time, the toughest growth-management law in the country.

The act required every county to implement a master plan, tried to keep growth contained within existing developed areas, and, most important, gave the state veto power if local governments tried to grant permits beyond their comprehensive plan. Given the raw political power that Florida developers possessed in the mid-1980s (and, indeed, still possess today), it is hard to overstate Graham's achievement in getting this through the legislature.

"The physical quality of this state, both on the development side and the environment side, is much better than it would have been," said Tom Lewis, who, as Graham's last secretary of community affairs, saw the long-discussed plan finally become law.

In the intervening two decades, critics on both sides of the issue have called the law a failure. Developers argue that it created a Byzantine bureaucracy, and environmentalists say it has not stopped urban sprawl and growth that hopscotches into undeveloped areas critical for aquifer recharge.

Lewis agreed that it has not worked out as well as it was hoped. That blame must fall on local and state agencies that look for ways to get around the law's restrictions. A diet, after all, is only as effective as the dieter's self-discipline.

"Everybody stayed on the diet a little better, but if you wanted to sneak a Baby Ruth every now and again, you could do that," Lewis said.

As he ran for president in 2003, Graham also returned to a theme that showed up earlier in his tenure as Florida governor: that the nation is inevitably, and in the not-so-far-distant future, going to run out of oil, and should therefore start planning for that day before it is too late.

"We are beginning to see the darkness at the end of the tunnel, and that darkness is that America has been using up many of its natural resources," he told New Hampshire business leaders. "The most dramatic example of that is petroleum. We have two or three hundred years of estimated reserves of natural gas. We have only approximately fifty years of remaining reserves, at the current rate of consumption, of our domestic petroleum."

Graham made similar assertions during the 1979 energy crisis, but found little support and, frankly, little portfolio as governor of Florida to make serious changes to national behavior. His opposition to oil drilling in environmentally sensitive areas, particularly the Florida Gulf Coast offshore waters, strikes a sharp contrast with President Bush and his oil industry allies. Graham, as a top presidential adviser, would have the ability, using the federal tax code, to encourage further the wind and solar energy research that he described for a receptive New Hampshire audience.

"We need to begin to aggressively develop alternatives to fossil fuels," Graham said. "I think a key point of any national energy policy has got to be to stretch that fifty-year period as long as possible. . . . The place to start is out there in the parking lot with all those automobiles."

Closest to Graham's heart, though, has been his Everglades project. In Washington, Graham has pushed to expand the federal role in the Everglades restoration, with good results. Graham and the rest of the Florida congressional delegation, against the odds, have been able to win a commitment to a joint state-federal restoration plan, with United States taxpayers matching the state's $200-million-a-year share over two decades. He has had less luck putting in place a permanent source of money to accomplish this, such as the royalties received from offshore oil drilling. Without this, he fears, the federal commitment could dry up if money gets tight or if the Everglades fall out of vogue.

"Right now, the Everglades are very popular, they are nonpartisan, they are increasingly being seen as a national treasure with full national support. But twenty years is a long time, and we might run into a sustained period of economic downturn or [see] a president get elected who is not sympathetic," Graham said. "To me, while we are in this period of good feeling about the Everglades, we ought to try to lock it in."[26]

Which is not to say that, even in an era of good feeling about the Everglades, keeping the massive project moving forward is easy.

A full twenty years after he started it, holding the disparate Everglades coalition together is no simple task. By the summer of 2003, Graham's original estimates for the project's costs had fallen by the wayside as hopelessly optimistic. The projected cost of restoration, which he had pegged at $100 million in 1983, was now $8.4 billion over two decades. Even the Kissimmee River proposal, which Graham had hoped would cost no more than $82 million in 1983, by 2003 had a $518 million price tag. It had also been delayed by the Army Corps of Engineers' unwillingness to undertake environmental projects—a mind-set Graham needed to undo with legislation after he moved to the U.S. Senate.

Environmentalists, urban and suburban property taxpayers, and sugar growers continue to squabble over who in Florida should pay the lion's share of the cleanup costs.

And, even at this late date, there is still the occasional feeling from environmentalists that the whole thing is a con job, designed not for the Everglades but for the builders and business community of South Florida.

In June 2002, the *Washington Post* took a four-part, critical look at the project and concluded this way:

"It's not remotely clear whether the Everglades restoration plan will actually restore the Everglades. Most of the plan's ecological benefits for the Everglades are riddled with uncertainties and delayed for decades, though

[26]University of Florida Oral History Project, Tape Y, June 18, 2001.

it delivers swift and sure economic benefits to Florida homeowners, agri-businesses and developers."[27]

Unlike the Kissimmee River project (to restore the "channelized" stream to its natural, meandering course), which is well under way and accomplishing its stated purpose of bringing back wildlife and helping clean up the water flowing into Lake Okeechobee, the Everglades project in late 2003 was still beset by worries that, in the end, it would not accomplish even a little bit of actual restoration before Congress, tired of spending money with no results in sight, winds up pulling the plug.

That's just one danger. Another is that one member or another of the fragile coalition that shepherded the whole package through legislative bodies in Tallahassee and Washington will bail out and seek to advance its own interests.

In the spring of 2003, sugar industry lobbyists rammed a bill through a pliant Florida legislature[28] that even a federal judge agrees is full of "weasel words" that would effectively postpone the clean-water requirements. Graham, from afar, was unable to dissuade the legislature from passing the bill or Governor Jeb Bush from signing it.

Mouthing the right words on the Everglades, obviously, goes only so far.

"The current leadership in Tallahassee talks the talk but is reluctant to take the steps necessary to save the Everglades, and has in fact put the partnership of the state of Florida and the federal government at risk," Graham said.

As obstreperous as Big Sugar may remain toward meeting its obligations for the cleanup, the more fundamental problem will continue to be the insatiable urge to build more and more stuff.

There is too much money to be made by paving over land and erecting strip malls and health clubs and single-family tract houses on streets with wilderness-sounding names for the Everglades ever to be safe.

---

[27]Michael Grunwald, "A Rescue Plan, Bold and Uncertain," *Washington Post*, June 23, 2002.

[28]This is not particularly difficult. The Florida legislature has always been cheerfully pliant for interest groups that provide hundreds of thousands of dollars in campaign contributions.

In recent years, a new controversy has arisen involving some of the biggest money players in the pro-growth coalition, the "lime rock" mining industry. To non-Floridians, the very existence of this industry might seem odd. It is, however, literally the bedrock of development in the state. The particular type of hard limestone underlying the Everglades in South Florida is much prized for its qualities in concrete—the sine qua non of Florida growth.

The mining companies dig deep, rectangular pits straight into the bedrock, using explosives to loosen the stone and giant excavation equipment to lift out the rubble. Every day, one after the next, the pulverized bits are shipped out in rail cars and dump trucks, providing the state's construction companies with the material they need.

And it is this rock that has become a new front in the Everglades war. The mining companies have persuaded regulators that they should be allowed to dig in what is now undeveloped wetland for the next three decades. When they are done, the pits would be used as giant reservoirs to store the water that will be needed to quench Miami's thirst and to ship into the Everglades in times of drought.

Environmentalists are livid, incredulous that the politically connected rock companies have been able to win the right to destroy 15,000 acres of Everglades swamp. They are also suspicious of the reservoirs—in the past, these holes in the ground have become "lakes" on the shores of which developers have quickly thrown up more new houses. In the summer of 2003, a lawsuit was pending to stop the mining plan.

Graham's response to the fuss? The rock mining is going to happen one way or another—as it has been happening for decades. Proponents of Everglades restoration may as well try to salvage something useful to the project like the reservoirs.

"The politics are very tricky. We walk a fine line," John Ogden, the water district's chief Everglades scientist, told the *Washington Post*. "I'm not saying we've got a perfect plan. I'm saying that some very idealistic ecologists have worked on this for ten years, and this is where we are."[29]

---

[29]Michael Grunwald, "An Environmental Reversal of Fortune," *Washington Post*, June 26, 2002.

Even if the restoration plan proceeds as currently outlined, the Everglades still won't *really* look like the Everglades of 1900. That is physically impossible.

For one thing, you'd have to expel the better part of six million South Florida residents to do so. Entire communities in Dade, Broward and Palm Beach Counties—including Wellington, Weston, Sweetwater and, yes, the Graham family's own Miami Lakes—would have to be emptied, the levee that keeps the flood waters out demolished, and the whole region inundated.

If somehow this could be managed, there is still the major problem of the lowered elevation throughout the Everglades, and particularly in the area where sugarcane has been grown. With so much of the peat soil burned off, washed away, or simply oxidized into thin air, the topography of the area, if simply allowed to flood, would not revert to the historic sheet flow.

Rather, there would form a wide, shallow lake in what is now the Everglades Agricultural Area south of Lake Okeechobee and extending southward. Which means that the only way to approximate a natural look and function to the half of the original Everglades that is left is to unnaturally and very closely control the amounts and timing of freshwater that flows through the system.

Still, as Graham points out, half an Everglades, looking and working like it once did, is better than none, which was where the state was headed before he and other environmentally minded leaders stepped in.

He makes a valid point.

Environmentalists who reasonably enough point out the problems with the restoration plan and chide Graham for not being an aggressive enough advocate for its actual restoration components would probably do well to consider what might have happened if Graham *hadn't* been governor in the 1980s. Would either of the likely winners of that 1978 election worked as hard—or at all—to preserve what most people still considered a nasty, mosquito-infested swamp?

How much of the Everglades actually winds up surviving into the twenty-second century, and in what condition, is an open question, one that probably still accurately reflects what *River of Grass* author Marjory Stoneman Douglas posited: "The Everglades is a test," she wrote. "If we pass it, we may get to keep the planet."

If we do pass, and the final history of the River of Grass is written, there is little doubt that among the names of the first pioneers—Marjory Douglas, Art Marshall, Nathaniel Reed—will be the politician who actually made it happen, Bob Graham.

Senior Senator

For the better part of two decades, Bob Graham has held membership in the most exclusive club in the world, the United States Senate, one of a hundred persons able to pass laws and budgets that affect a quarter of a billion citizens; consent to or deny presidents their appointments, approve or reject men and women who would sit as the highest judges in the land, ratify or refuse treaties with foreign potentates.

And for the better part of two decades, Bob Graham has fought the rap that he has not done much with the job.

Sure, he's won reelection twice by huge margins. Sure, he's liked and respected in Washington. But why, given all his potential, hasn't he done *more* with it?

Right there is the heart of it. Bob Graham showed in his two terms as governor that he could learn, and adapt, and grow, and by the end wind up high on the list of Florida's best chief executives. He did that in eight years. January 6, 2004, will mark seventeen full years in the Senate.

Randy Schultz, chief editorial writer at the *Palm Beach Post*, distilled the criticism to its most cogent nut in 1998, after Graham made his obligatory public criticisms of President Clinton in the Monica Lewinsky scandal:

"The sequence of events left Senator Graham just where he likes to be—in the safe position. Having never lost an election, he would say that no lawmaker can get anything done if he's not in office. Another view is that, given all the skill Senator Graham has displayed getting elected, you'd like to see him actually do something in keeping with his talent," Schultz wrote.

"Yet Senator Graham keeps most of that political capital in his mattress. He has offered sensible compromise legislation on many key issues but stands out on none of them. His last big risk was that run for governor, and he had $750,000 of his own money (lots, back then) to help him. . . . Lawmakers tell voters that the unpleasant parts of the job—fund-raising, occasional pandering—are necessary to keep themselves in office so they can do great things. With the ever-safe Bob Graham, we're waiting to see them."[1]

It's not particularly fair, to be damned by high expectations. But yet, there it is.

Never does anyone see that kind of criticism of Florida's junior senator, Democrat Bill Nelson, because he has never been viewed with the kind of regard reserved for Graham.[2] He will likely win plaudits if he merely keeps his seat in 2006.

Graham, long before he officially declared his U.S. Senate candidacy in early 1986, was already being sized up for bigger and better things. The era of governors running for president had begun with Carter and continued with Reagan. Who better as a Democratic candidate than a former Florida governor who could, like Carter, break the Republican stranglehold on the South?

Such were the musings. As for 1986, that was the year Democrats picked up a total of eight seats in the Senate to retake control of that chamber after six years on the outs. Graham's contribution to that takeover was counted as virtually in the bag as early as 1985.

Adele, for one, pretty much figured their next home would be Washing-

[1]Randy Schultz, "In Scandal, Graham Fills Usual Role," *Palm Beach Post,* September 13, 1998.
[2]Nelson, a former congressman from the Space Coast, ran for governor in 1990. *Florida Trend* magazine did a cover story on him. The illustration was an empty suit.

ton, D.C., years before he got around to even raising the subject. "He has not told me, but I assume he will run," she predicted in 1984.[3]

Graham says he never seriously considered the U.S. Senate until the summer of 1985, when he attended a dinner sponsored by Al Neuharth, chairman of Gannett newspapers, in Miami Beach. There, he chatted with board member Howard Baker, who told him he had left the Senate when his term ended that January because it was becoming unpleasantly partisan. But Baker said that rising stars like Richard Lugar from Indiana and Bill Bradley from New Jersey would likely make it an enjoyable place to be again.

"His observations, what he thought the new Senate would be, were a significant factor in my decision to run."[4]

Once the decision was made, Graham set about the task with typical organization and efficiency. First off: He had to learn a bunch of stuff.

As governor of Florida, he knew all about state budgeting and education funding formulas and the sales tax and buying environmentally sensitive land. But of the things that Congress concerned itself with, the federal budget and the income tax and Medicare, Graham knew very little. His only real experience with the military, for example, was the Florida National Guard, which he had called upon numerous times during hurricanes and riots and so forth, but never, obviously, in any foreign-affairs role.

So Graham fell back on one of his greatest strengths: He studied. During that autumn, he laid out a series of breakfast meetings to learn about foreign policy and various weapons systems and the myriad federal domestic programs. He drew from experts in the Carter administration, who would come brief him on these subjects until Graham felt comfortable taking positions on the issues.

"By the time I became a candidate, I was able to respond to most questions that would likely be asked by a general audience or editorial board with some degree of confidence and knowledge of what I was talking about."[5]

Of course, getting in the race was one thing. Next there was the technical matter of getting past the incumbent senator, Paula Hawkins.

---

[3]Mike Ollove, "The Turning Point," *Miami Herald*, December 9, 1984.
[4]University of Florida Oral History Project, Tape P, November 11, 1995.
[5]*Ibid.*

When Ronald Reagan swept into the White House in 1980, his coat-tails dragged with him a healthy gaggle of Republican candidates into the United States Senate. Six years later, all of them had to face their first reelection on their own, without the benefit of Reagan's name at the top of the ticket.

Among them was Paula Hawkins, the self-styled "Housewife from Maitland" who had managed to leverage her years on the state's Public Service Commission into a successful campaign for one of the nation's highest political offices. She and Graham already had some history. Prior to 1978, the state's PSC, which regulates phone, electricity, and water utilities, had been an elected office. Paula Hawkins had won it twice on the strength of her pro-consumer reputation. She knew what it was like to pay bills and manage a household budget, and she had stuck up for housewives and families all over the state against the big, bad utilities.

In the summer of 1978, she was chosen by Republican candidate for governor Jack Eckerd as his running mate—a smart move, it was thought. After all, she was the only woman in Florida history to have won statewide election.

Maybe she helped, maybe she didn't. On the one occasion when both governor candidates and both lieutenant governor candidates participated in a joint forum, Hawkins did manage to irritate Graham with some ridiculous milk-price accusations—which he finally put a stop to with some equally ridiculous notebook price accusations against drugstore magnate Eckerd.[6]

So a few months later, after Graham had taken office and was looking at candidates to nominate to the now *appointed* PSC, Graham understandably passed over Hawkins and chose commission staff attorney—and Democrat—John Marks (who twenty-three years later became the first black mayor of Tallahassee).

Within a year of losing her job, Hawkins was being recruited for a new

---

[6]See the chapter "The Notebooks" for more details.

one. The Republican Party needed a candidate for Senate against incumbent Richard Stone. Would she be willing to run? She was still the only woman to have won statewide office, and her name recognition was fairly high from the governor's race. She accepted—and then watched along with the rest of her party as Democratic Insurance Commissioner Bill Gunter ran hard against Dick Stone in a primary. The result was a vicious campaign that Gunter won—but won so ugly that he was vulnerable in November. Hawkins, with the help of Reagan's performance in Florida, won, 51 percent–49 percent, in the general election.

That was 1980. By 1986, Hawkins was vulnerable. Befitting her style, she had gone up to Washington to "shake things up," and apparently decided that spitting at Senate protocol would be a good way to start things off. Senate tradition was for a newly elected member to be "sponsored" by the state's senior senator on swearing-in day. But Hawkins didn't want Democrat Lawton Chiles. She insisted on Republican Bob Dole.

"That was considered to be *very* impolite and bad protocol," Graham recalled. "It probably contributed to chilling the relationship between Lawton and Paula."[7]

Things got even worse, quickly. This was the start of the Reagan years, when much was made of the welfare queen driving around in her Cadillac, collecting food stamps. Hawkins took the parable literally, and decided to push legislation mandating prison terms for food-stamp cheats. She announced this at a luncheon featuring catered steak.

"The press had a field day drawing the comparison. Paula Hawkins was after food stamp defrauders, while she had this taxpayer-financed lunch with steak. That was a gaffe that haunted her throughout her six years in the Senate."[8]

Hawkins ultimately came to see the media as a hostile force, best avoided. Not many politicians have been able to get away with this strategy, which be-

[7]University of Florida Oral History Project, Tapes Q–R, January 11, 1996.
[8]*Ibid.*

comes even more perilous when facing an iffy reelection. Hawkins was never able to pull it off—particularly against a governor who genuinely liked and was liked by the press.[9]

Hawkins also had had the misfortune of a painful neck injury in 1982. It was at a television studio in Orlando, and Hawkins was doing an interview when a prop fell from the wall and hit her in the back.

The chronic pain wound up plaguing her throughout the campaign. In spring, while Graham was tied up in Tallahassee with the annual legislative session and Hawkins should have been out campaigning, she was instead recuperating from surgery she had undergone at Duke University Medical Center. That ordinarily would have won her some sympathy points.

But with Hawkins, nothing was ordinary. She had snuck off to Duke, her press aides in Washington passing out some cover story, and checked in under an assumed name. This was broken all too easily. When a *Washington Post* reporter called Duke and asked if Hawkins was there, a nurse told him: "She's here, but under an assumed name."[10]

And so she turned something that might have helped her into something that made her seem silly anew.

A similar thing happened later, again with the neck injury. For reasons that still remain elusive, Hawkins sued the television station for pain and suffering—and then tried to have the courts seal the case to keep it out of the press.

Bad idea. That merely got the media lawyers' backs up and shone a bright spotlight on a case that otherwise might have been relegated to the inside pages. When finally the documents were unsealed (there were never any justifiable grounds to keep them secret), it came out that Hawkins and her husband were suing the station for, among other things, "loss of consortium and companionship."[11]

---

[9]In the final days of the 1986 Senate campaign, when his internal polling showed he had built an insurmountable lead, Graham was so ebullient that one morning he asked the press contingent traveling with him: "So, where does everyone want to campaign today?" Someone shouted out, "How about Key West?"—so Key West it was. Graham spent the day glad-handing tourists. The reporters had a blast.

[10]Bill Peterson and Edward Walsh, "Hawkins May Need Spinal Surgery," *Washington Post*, February 12, 1986.

[11]"Hawkins Goes to Trial After Election," United Press International, October 14, 1986.

Governor Bob Graham sings his campaign song while campaigning for the U.S. Senate, 1986. (Photo by Lenny Cohen/*Palm Beach Post.*)

Suffice it to say: Yes, Graham had to beat an incumbent to get to the Senate—but on the other hand, that incumbent was Paula Hawkins.

Graham's polling[12] showed him, at one point, with a lead of only five points. But apart from that dip, he had a healthy lead from the time he announced to the time the votes were counted, giving him a ten-point victory.

There's simply no getting around one basic fact: that the United States Senate, indeed, the Capitol itself, is an awesome place.

Inside the rotunda, the scrollwork rises to dizzying heights, with Bru-

---

[12]The Graham-Hawkins race in 1986 also showcased two political consultants who a decade later put together the powerful Clinton-Gore reelection campaign. Bob Squier once again was doing the media for Graham. Dick Morris was Hawkins's pollster. At one point a few months prior to the election, Morris released numbers to the media showing that Hawkins was barely half a point behind Graham. Squier, seeing numbers from pollster William Hamilton showing Graham with a strong lead, accused Morris of cooking the numbers like Julia Child.

midi's *The Apotheosis of George Washington* painted on the "eye" of the dome overhead. Wall-sized paintings depict the Spanish conquest of the New World, while larger-than-life statues of the Founding Fathers overwhelm visitors with a sense of majesty. Everywhere there is marble—marble staircases, marble columns, even marble banisters—and the floors are tiled with ceramic mosaics.

Within the Senate chamber, the polished mahogany desks, the oak doors with the brass trim, the skylight with the design of the United States seal—all of it suggests two hundred years of tradition and history, of significance and heft.

And yet—the United States Senate is burdened with precisely the same flaws that weigh down the Florida senate, and probably every other legislative chamber in the nation. Much, if not most, of the legislation is written by a ubiquitous corps of professional lobbyists serving the various moneyed interests. The laws that come out at the other end of the pipeline too often have nothing to do with the public interest. And at an astonishing number of congressional office desks sit the young, attractive females who, for whatever reason, appear to be eminently more qualified for legislative staff work than are, say, fat, balding men.

It is a club, imbued with a sense of self-importance that far outweighs any public good that could possibly derive from it, and a rigid hierarchy for its new members. Seniority is everything, from better office space and parking spots to committee assignments to committee chairmanships. The longer you've been there, the more you can get done, and even those members with the seniority and the clout to effect change must still fight both the lumbering bureaucracy and the well-oiled influence machine lined up to protect the status quo.

It is a club, and Bob Graham's not much of a joiner. He should have known going in that there would be some problems.

Things started out promisingly enough. Graham headed to Washington with much optimism and cheer, evidently not at all worried about returning to a legislative body after an eight-year reprieve. Even a bout of what turned out to be a case of giardia the night before his swearing-in (contracted on a ski vacation with his family in Colorado the previous month) could not dampen his enthusiasm.

Florida's rules of public office had forced Graham to resign the governor's office three days early so his Senate service would not overlap with the governor's term—thereby allowing eight-year sidekick Lieutenant Governor Wayne Mixson to serve a weekend as governor before handing over the reins to Republican Bob Martinez.[13] Graham got sworn in by vice president George H. W. Bush, using the heavy, 1890 Bible that came down from his mother's side of the family, and declared himself ready to work.

Still, there were already hints that Graham's personality might not be particularly well suited for the backslapping camaraderie that brings success on Capitol Hill, just as it wasn't well suited for the horse-trading that spells success in the Florida senate.

In November 1986, barely two weeks after winning the office, Graham said during his first post-election visit to Washington that he had a few thoughts on how to streamline the Senate's cumbersome rules. "I have some ideas about procedures," Graham said at a news conference. "But I only got here at 8:30 this morning, and I'm not about to tell an institution that is 200 years old that it ought to start changing its rules."[14]

As in most legislative chambers, new members are expected to learn the customs and rules and not necessarily contribute to the dialogue. One of the ways to make them do this in the Senate (while still making use of them as warm bodies) is to force them to preside over the chamber. Someone has to do it. Why not make the freshmen?

Graham, with characteristic nerdiness, decided to make lemonade out of this lemon: "A lot of my colleagues, particularly those who had been in the House for a number of years, really despised presiding. They thought it was tedious and a waste of time. I rather enjoyed it, because it was a way to learn how the institution operated and a way to listen to some of the people who had a reputation of being the more effective and persuasive members, and see how they went about doing their business," Graham explained in an

---

[13]Mixson took this about as far as he could. He presided over a Cabinet meeting and made more than a hundred appointments. He even had cards and stationery printed up: "Governor Wayne Mixson."
[14]Larry Lipman, "Graham's First Capitol Visit as Senator-Elect Low-Key," *Evening Times*, November 20, 1986.

interview a decade later. "I presided a lot. They give you a golden gavel when you preside for a hundred hours during one calendar year of the Senate. I was one of the first members in 1987 to get a golden gavel."[15]

Graham had a lot of time to spend presiding because, frankly, he was unable to get onto the high-profile committees that demand lots of time and attention. Not having been a member of the Congress prior to his election, he was near the bottom in terms of seniority, both among his freshman class as well as overall. In a chamber of 100, he was Number 98.

His strategy was to get on the Finance Committee—fellow Floridian Lawton Chiles was chairman of the Budget Committee, so Graham figured Florida was covered there[16]—and Graham thought he would be able to represent his constituents on such matters as taxes and Medicare. Graham wrote letters to the powers that be explaining why he'd make a good member of Finance. Fellow Senate freshman Tom Daschle made personal visits and schmoozed. Guess which one got named to the Finance Committee?

Graham downplayed the disappointment and homed in on the committees he did get: Environment, Veterans Affairs, and Banking. The first two, actually, were committees he wanted to serve on. The environment was his great love, and veterans' concerns were critical to the many military retirees in Florida.

So it was viewed as a stumble when his first controversy in the Senate was over a vote on the Environment Committee—a vote counter to the wishes of the environmental groups that had loudly praised his arrival in Washington. It was over billboards, and whether the federal government ought to mandate their removal from interstate highways. Graham, fresh from twenty years in state government, took a states-rights perspective on the matter, arguing that the decision should be left up to the state and local governments, not the federal bureaucracy. He seemed genuinely surprised when the environmentalists publicly attacked him.

---

[15]University of Florida Oral History Project, Tapes Q–R, January 11, 1996.

[16]A bad assumption, as it soon turned out. Chiles, burned out and suffering from depression after three terms, announced he would retire in 1989. Graham, after only two years in Washington, became Florida's senior senator.

Whatever hurt feelings that engendered, it couldn't begin to compare to the humiliation that came as a result of his membership on the Banking Committee.

It was there that Graham got his first real taste of the smallness of Washington politics. First came the shock of any Florida elected official who then goes to Congress and learns that Florida's tradition of "Government in the Sunshine" is virtually unheard of in the nation's Capitol. Whenever it was time to amend bills, the committee chairman simply adjourned the public meeting and then convened everyone in a back room.

"In our government, with the Sunshine [Law], all of us would have been put in jail. . . . And here I was—the youngest in seniority on the committee getting exposed to this culture," Graham said.

Then there was what he actually *saw* in those back rooms: On one occasion, a senior member of the committee got down on the floor and banged his arms and legs over something Graham did not consider vitally important. "I wondered, 'What in the hell have I just done? I have just spent all this time and a lot of my friends' money to get elected to an institution that behaves like a kindergarten.' So I was very happy to get off the Banking Committee."[17]

He got off the committee, but not before suffering his one real taste of scandal in nearly four decades of politics.

The issue was the savings-and-loan industry and its looming problems, problems that had been building for years but were only coming to a head as Graham joined the oversight panel in 1987. Over the years, the federal government had allowed its deposit-insurance limit to increase from $40,000 to $100,000 but had not required a corresponding increase in the premiums. That was the financial cause of the resulting ruin when it turned out that the S&Ls had been playing with depositors' cash like it was Monopoly money.

Graham was also able to witness firsthand the disaster's political cause: "The committee was a very undisciplined legislative body. The leadership of the committee spent a lot of its time trying to blame somebody else for

---

[17]University of Florida Oral History Project, Tapes S–T, December 11, 1996.

what was happening to the nation's savings-and-loan industry while those things were happening under their watch."[18]

At the same time, a Florida savings-and-loan chief named David Paul was, unbeknownst to Graham, getting help from Graham's office in dealing with regulators. A March 1987 meeting, it came out later, was arranged by Steve Josias, who happened to be Graham's special counsel at the time.[19] Graham had used "special counsels" since his first term as governor, encouraging private-sector lawyers to take six-month stints in government service. He thought it was a good way for lawyers to get a taste of public service while at the same time giving his office a perspective from the "real world."

As it happened, Josias also had previously done extensive legal work for Paul's CenTrust, and arranged the meeting with regulators who were (as it turned out, with good reason) looking into CenTrust's finances. The message of the meeting, and of a subsequent letter Graham signed to regulators, was that it was not fair for the government to take a harder line with CenTrust than it did with other thrifts.

Graham said he knew nothing about the meeting until three years had passed—when it was disclosed by NBC News—and thought the letter was a matter of fairness. The implications were obvious: Here was a United States senator, helping to bail out a well-connected rich guy who essentially had stolen his customers' money and used it as a personal slush fund.

It was "the single most personally unpleasant experience in my years in the Senate, and it was maybe the most unpleasant experience of my entire political career," Graham said later. He conceded that signing the letter on Paul's behalf was done "maybe with a significant lack of judgment which I will say was based largely on our newness to these issues and to Washington."

"I personally do not think that allegation was correct, but it was very embarrassing and personally distressful," he said.[20]

It got even worse. After one committee hearing in December 1987, Graham's flight back to Miami had been canceled. Legendary Florida lawyer

---

[18] *Ibid.*

[19] Charles Elmore, "Graham Denies Doing Favors for ex-CenTrust Chairman," *Palm Beach Post*, August 8, 1990.

[20] University of Florida Oral History Project, Tapes S–T, December 11, 1996.

Chesterfield Smith offered Graham a ride back on his plane, which Graham accepted. Except it wasn't Chesterfield Smith's plane. It was CenTrust's.

The fact was that David Paul, during the 1986 race, had given money not to Graham but to Republican Paula Hawkins. And any personal connection to Graham was incidental—chance meetings at social occasions. It didn't matter. Graham was hounded by the issue through Paul's conviction and into the first run for reelection.

"I kept saying, 'My God, here is a guy who I hardly know and who supported my opponent, and yet . . .' "[21]

Graham got through that mini-scandal, and the later sale of his Miami Lakes home (with the kids grown and moved out, he and Adele didn't need so much room anymore) to a "businessman" who later turned out to be a Chilean arms dealer accused of selling cluster bombs to Iraq. Graham said he had no idea who Carlos Cardoen was until he read the allegations in the newspapers, and that the house had sold for market value. Although his campaign opponent in 1992 tried to make it an issue, there was never any indication that Graham was telling anything other than the truth.

It helped that in neither 1992 nor 1998 did he have much of an opponent—a function of his perennially high poll numbers. During his first reelection, the best the Republicans could come up with was Bill Grant, a former congressman from North Florida who was drummed out of office after switching parties.[22] Graham beat him 66 percent–34 percent, sweeping all sixty-seven of Florida's counties. Grant's campaign complained in the aftermath that the national party reneged on $1.1 million to help buy television ads. The National Republican Senatorial Committee no doubt came to the conclusion that the money would be wasted against Graham.

And in 1998, the GOP came up with a state senator from St. Petersburg as their sacrificial lamb. Charlie Crist had a penchant for pumping out

---

[21] *Ibid.*

[22] Grant, who was telling voters in 1992 that Graham was a lousy senator, had four years earlier, as a still-Democratic congressman, told everyone how wonderful Graham was and how Michael Dukakis should make Graham his running mate.

news releases on pretty much every topic, but the one that caught journalists' fancy was his proposal to bring back chain gangs to Florida prisons, arguing that hardened, violent criminals might be shamed into giving up their ways—or at the very least deter others from committing crimes—after seeing how humiliating it was to pick up trash and cut weeds along the side of the highways. Department of Corrections officials eventually wondered aloud whether putting such criminals out on the highways wasn't perhaps a dumb idea. Crist's grand chain-gang proposal ultimately disappeared, but the nickname "Chain Gang Charlie" stuck.[23]

Not that it mattered. Graham beat him 63 percent–37 percent, despite all the new residents who had come to Florida since his last election who were putting Republicans into power in most other offices. In that election, Jeb Bush became governor, the cabinet became Republican for the first time since Reconstruction, and Republicans solidified their grasp on the state house and senate.

Graham said that despite the caliber of the opposition, he ran each reelection as if he were the underdog. "You get ready for Abraham Lincoln or Franklin Roosevelt," he said, "and if by chance they should not appear, then you face whoever does."[24]

In 1998, Graham raised and spent about $4 million, three-quarters of which went for television ads explaining to 1.8 million new residents in Florida since the 1992 election who Bob Graham was and why they should vote for him. He called the effort a "moderate campaign."

"There are a lot of people in the political graveyard who thought they had the campaign won before the votes were cast."[25]

After each reelection, Graham was free to continue the sort of low-key work in Washington that he says he purposefully set out to accomplish. This was partly a result of his early lack of seniority—he probably couldn't have passed high-profile legislation if he'd tried: to wit, his at-

[23] Crist in 2000 ran for and won the state commissioner of education cabinet post, and in 2002 ran for and won attorney general, that despite having needed three tries to pass the bar exam. Well, this *is* Florida.
[24] Howard Troxler, "Senators Try on Their New Roles," *St. Petersburg Times,* January 24, 1997.
[25] University of Florida Oral History Project, Tapes U–V, October 24, 2000.

tempt in 1987 to add a prescription drug benefit to Medicare—and partly his decision to concentrate on Florida issues.

"I have tried to pick issues that are primarily federal and where there is a noticeable difference in either the quantity or quality of the application of that issue to Florida."[26]

This is Graham-speak for: Florida was getting screwed, and I tried to fix it.

One such area was transportation. There is a federal gasoline tax, and there is an allocation of money for federal programs like the interstate highway system. The value of one from a particular state did not necessarily have anything to do with the value of the other.

"Every year, Florida sends about $2 billion to Washington and gets back about $1.5 billion," Graham said in 1996.[27]

In the early 1990s, the federal road money distribution formula was drafted based not on 1990 Census data but on 1980 data. The intent was obvious: New York's population had gone up from 17.6 million to 18 million in the decade of the 1980s. West Virginia had actually lost population, from 2 million to 1.9 million. Florida, on the other hand, had gone from 9.8 million to 12.7 million. So for an additional five years, Florida and other high-growth states would continue to funnel money to those places people either were not moving to anymore or were flat out leaving.

Graham fought for and won a minimum-allocation guarantee that a state would get back at least 90 percent of the money it sent to Washington—a floor that worked out to 83 percent after a couple of built-in loopholes were factored in.

"The good news is 83 percent is better than the 75 percent we had gotten before, but it is not as good as 90 or not as good as 100."[28]

Graham found a similar setup with the allocations for Veterans Administration money. Those states where veterans *used* to live were getting more money than states veterans were actually moving to. Here Graham found a powerful ally—Arizona senator John McCain, who was happy to sponsor an identical bill in 1996. Arizona was similarly getting the shaft on veterans'

---

[26] *Ibid.*
[27] University of Florida Oral History Project, Tapes S-T, December 11, 1996.
[28] *Ibid.*

issues—the difference was that McCain was a Republican war hero in a Republican-controlled chamber.

"One thing that I have found in the Senate is that if you want to get something accomplished, you need to be prepared to defer the credit to somebody else," Graham said, citing the veterans bill as a perfect example. "It is exactly the same bill, but the realities are that the Republicans have more votes than we do, and we need their votes if we are going to pass anything, so you better find a Republican friend."[29]

Of course, complaining that states like West Virginia and New York are robbing the nation blind tends to irritate senators from places like West Virginia and New York. And that, in turn, tends to diminish the complainer's popularity in a collegial, hail-fellow-well-met place like the United States Senate, where public sucking up to one's elders is the expected behavior.

Graham made an enemy of New York Democrat Daniel Patrick Moynihan over the roads bill, and West Virginia Democrat Robert Byrd over Byrd's general propensity to transfer as much of the federal infrastructure as possible to his home state. Graham actually accused Byrd of sticking "piglets" into the budget that would one day grow up to be full-blown "pork." Byrd wasn't amused.

"One of the things in the Senate that is hard to balance is the degree to which you want to have good relations with your colleagues, particularly colleagues that are in influential positions, such as Senator Moynihan and Senator Byrd, and at the same time be a forceful spokesman for the interest of your state even if those interests are at variance with a New York or a West Virginia."[30]

He did not, of course, make enemies of everyone. Senator Jay Rockefeller, of West Virginia, is among Graham's closest friends in the Senate. Richard Shelby, who was a Democratic congressman from Alabama when he was elected to the Senate with Graham in 1986, has remained an ally, even after switching parties in 1994.

---

[29] *Ibid.*
[30] *Ibid.*

And certainly fellow iconoclast McCain is a big fan of Graham. "I found him from the outset to have had a broad view, a bipartisan approach, because of his experience as governor," McCain said of his fellow Class of '86 freshman. "I found him immediately a pleasure to work with and appreciated his efforts on many issues, not just veterans, but immigration and a number of other international issues."

He agrees that Graham hasn't gotten the credit he deserves because it's not Graham's style. "His nature is not to try to seek the limelight," he said, harkening back to a distinction made by former House speaker Carl Albert. "There are two kinds of senators, a showhorse and a workhorse, and he's a workhorse."

For the record, Graham's "by the numbers" vote history in the Senate is mixed. Graham supported President Reagan's efforts to arm the Nicaraguan *contra* rebels and lauded the invasion of Grenada. In the administration of the first George Bush, Graham bucked party leadership—he was one of only ten Democrats to do so—and supported the resolution authorizing the Gulf War to expel Saddam Hussein from Kuwait.

He has generally supported presidential nominees to judgeships and cabinet positions. However, on two big litmus tests—votes on Supreme Court nominees Robert Bork and Clarence Thomas—Graham voted with Democrats against confirmation, although in these, as in most controversial issues, Graham was slow to announce his decision after studying the question from every conceivable angle.

Environmental groups have always ranked Graham high on their lists, as have education groups. Traditionally conservative groups have put him in the middle or lower—which, by the standards set by the typical Florida delegation, make him seem quite liberal among the state's lawmakers.

In 1992, the National Taxpayers Union ranked Graham sixteenth among big spenders in the Senate, saying he sponsored a net $51 billion in spending (defined as proposed new spending less proposed cuts) during the eighteen-month period of their study. The average senator sponsored $49.8 billion in spending and $6.8 billion in cuts—for an average net of $43 billion of spending—during that period. Mack, Florida's other senator, a conservative Republican, ranked sixty-second, with proposed net spending of $10.5 billion.[31]

This ranking notwithstanding—at the time, Graham was pushing several expensive Everglades restoration projects—Graham has been known as a "deficit hawk," perennially warning against the perils of long-term debt on the economy that will be handed down to future generations.

After seventeen years in the Senate, however, and countless floor votes, one piece of Graham's record becomes clear—the part that isn't there.

With nearly three complete terms under his belt, Graham has yet to bring to a president a bill so big and so important that it becomes known by his name.

Everyone has heard of the Gramm-Rudman-Hollings deficit-reduction act. And for years the names McCain and Feingold have been synonymous with campaign finance reform. Middle-class savers are certainly aware of the Roth IRA. Where is the "Graham" anything?

It gets back to what some observers have felt all along—that Graham has never really been happy in Washington.

Sam Bell, who served in the Florida house in the years Graham occupied the Governor's Mansion, said Graham's personality was better suited for the executive branch than the legislative. "He didn't really do well in a collegial body. Where he shone was as governor."

West Palm Beach congressman Mark Foley, who in the summer of 2003 was running for Graham's seat, said that is also the consensus view of the Florida congressional delegation. "That's been one of probably all our collective thoughts, that he never really liked the Senate. He liked being governor," Foley said.

A governor can make things happen with a stroke of a pen. A lawmaker must cajole and convince a number of others to even start the process of making anything happen. "That was never in his skill set," Fo-

---

[31]Andrew Mollison, "Floridians on Hill Called Big Spenders," *Palm Beach Post*, September 7, 1992.

ley said. "He hasn't been aggressive enough to get something done in his name."

Foley said he remembers the first time he met Graham the governor, and then the first time he met Graham as a United States senator. The former was shortly after Graham took office in 1979. It was in Tallahassee, maybe a couple of blocks from the state capitol, and Graham had in tow the entourage that surrounds any governor—a security officer or two, a gaggle of aides. Graham pinned a miniature graham cracker, his symbol during the campaign, onto Foley's lapel. Eight years later, Foley ran into Graham on the streets outside the U.S. Capitol. Graham was by himself.

"It was a different Bob Graham," Foley said. "It wasn't this kind of *figure*. He was now just this lonely man in a big city."

Adele concedes that it was somewhat of a letdown to go from being the biggest fish in the fourth-largest state to Number 98 fish in the Senate. "You go from having everyone recognize you and hold chairs for you to attending events where no one even knows you're there," she said.

Graham himself did point out in a 1995 interview that the decision to run for the Senate came only a year before election day—a sharp contrast to his governor's run, which had been planned, seemingly, his entire life.

"Up until a year before the 1986 election, I was quite uncommitted to running for the Senate. I loved being governor. Every day I woke up excited about what I was going to do."[32]

Yes, he was having fun. Particularly after he got past the rough patch in the first couple of years, he was having a blast. Which explains why, in many ways, getting to the Senate must have been disappointing. After eight years of running a large state, of proposing and championing and bringing to fruition ideas as vast as the Everglades, Graham was, again, in a legislative body, with all the deal-making and ego-soothing that entails— in short, all the things Graham hates doing.

"For someone like my father, who has been chief executive, that's frustrating," said Gwen Logan, who along with her husband, Mark, shared a town house with Graham his first year in Washington.

---

[32]University of Florida Oral History Project, Tape P, November 11, 1995.

Graham himself explained his frustrations with the chamber in a 1996 interview with his University of Florida biographer: "The Senate has a hundred members. About 80 percent of the ability needed to get things done is concentrated in maybe the twenty to twenty-five members who are the most senior. Those twenty to twenty-five people are the ones who are the most distant from the lives of most Americans by their age, by the length of time they have been in Washington, and by the sort of personal changes that come after twenty-five years of having people deferring to you because of your title."[33]

Graham, who never thought much of hometown projects for legislators when he was governor, said he has been appalled at how openly senators flaunt the power that lets them divert tax money back to their states. "We had some of that in the Florida legislature, but when people did it, they felt a little bit embarrassed about it, in the sense that they did not want to talk about it very much. Whereas in the Congress, rather than a source of shame, it is a source of pride if you have been able to get some kind of a turkey or pork project in your state or district."[34]

Buddy Shorstein, a college friend who served under Graham in both Tallahassee and Washington, said Graham truly enjoys the policy side of the issues—learning the details of a problem and then writing legislation to fix it—but could never get used to a town in which so much was determined by polling and focus groups and making friends with the right people. "He is extremely interested in legislation. He likes the crafting of legislation. He likes the idea of legislation," Shorstein said. "In many respects, he is almost too cerebral for the Senate."

It is a view Graham both agrees with and disputes.

No, he hasn't pushed big, controversial national legislation because he has, by design, concentrated on those things that most benefited Florida. And second, he hasn't gotten much attention for his work because he hasn't

---

[33]University of Florida Oral History Project, Tapes S–T, December 11, 1996.
[34]*Ibid.*

made it a priority to get the credit. The veterans issue, for instance, was pushed through at a time when Republicans controlled the Senate. Therefore, he sought out Republican McCain to get the bill through, even if it meant not being able to use it on his résumé. It probably did not matter in any case, in terms of his popularity. A new road formula, after all, was hardly the stuff of compelling campaign commercials.

"These are fairly complicated, complex issues. They do not lend themselves to thirty-second spots," Graham said.[35]

As to which he enjoyed better, that probably became evident during a 1992 plane ride Graham shared with Lawton Chiles, who stepped down from the Senate in 1989 and the following year ran for and became governor. Asked who had the better job, both Chiles, the current governor and former senator, and Graham, the current senator and former governor, pointed a finger at Chiles.

Ironically, the most attention Graham has received, either nationally or in Florida, has been on those occasions over his Senate career when it appeared he might leave—specifically, the three times over a dozen years when he has not been chosen as the Democratic vice-presidential candidate.

His first brush with greatness came a year and a half after he had been in the Senate—the summer of 1988, when old Harvard Law School mate Michael Dukakis considered him along with Lloyd Bentsen, Jesse Jackson, Al Gore, Lee Hamilton, Richard Gephardt, and John Glenn.

Jackson, of course, had to be considered, given how well he had done in the primaries and how much noise he was making about *deserving* to be considered. No one really took it seriously. As much of a loose cannon as Jackson was, the prospect of him as the *vice president*, first in the line of succession to the presidency, pretty much ruled him out from the start.

Graham was another matter. Early on, when Dukakis was ahead in the national polls, Florida polls actually showed that Dukakis might be competitive there. He had, after all, won Florida in the primary over Al Gore

[35] *Ibid.*

and Richard Gephardt. The thought was that Graham might bring Florida and its twenty-one electoral votes into the Democratic column, thereby screwing up the electoral math George H. W. Bush was counting on.

In the summer of 1988 (well before the Bernard Shaw rape question, before Boston Harbor, before Willie Horton, before the silly tank ad with the Snoopy helmet), it seemed a real possibility. Sure, Reagan had won Florida in 1980 and 1984, but Carter had won the state in 1976. And Graham had just two years earlier taken on a well-funded Republican incumbent and beaten her. Public opinion polls showed he was still riding high in his home state.

Despite all of it, Dukakis picked Bentsen—seen at the time as somewhat of a bizarre move. After all, Bush was *from* Texas—or at least, most recently from Texas, as far as public office went. Why would Texans vote for Bentsen in order to have a Texan *vice* president? They'd already *had* a Texan vice president for eight years, and now they had the chance to get a Texan president.

Graham explained the reasoning years later. It turned out that the Dukakis camp—obviously a rather humorless sort—had gotten nervous about Graham's brief appearance in singer Jimmy Buffett's 1985 music video for the song "Who's the Blonde Stranger?"[36] Graham conceded that perhaps it hadn't shown the best judgment, but that he happened to be in Key West, and his friend Buffett was shooting this video, and he asked Graham to be in it. Graham, a big ham at heart, said sure, why not, and that was that and it wasn't any big deal.[37]

But that wasn't the problem the Dukakis campaign had. They were more concerned about Graham's financial disclosure statement for that year. He had not listed his earnings from the video.

---

[36]Somehow, this appearance has over the years morphed into a quasi–shaggy dog tale. According to the majority of recent press accounts of the role, Graham plays an adulterous husband captivated by a blond island girl in Key West. Hooey. Graham appears for exactly 1.15 seconds wearing a flowered shirt and silly tourist hat, one arm around a woman, the other raising a pineapple cup in toast to singer Buffett. Now, there *is* an adulterous husband in the video, rolling in the sand with a gorgeous blonde, but it's not Graham. It's Will Jennings, one of the coauthors of the song. Jennings *does* wear a Texas A&M football jersey with the name "GRAHAM" on the back. Maybe that's where people got confused.
[37]Like most Buffett videos, it never actually appeared on television.

"I said: This is Jimmy Buffett we're talking about," Graham recalled a decade later. "You think he *paid* me?"

Four years later, Graham was once again on the short list of potential running mates for the Democratic ticket, this time for Arkansas governor Bill Clinton.

Once again, the whole running-mate selection process cranked up—this time, Clinton started with a list of forty names that included (not wanting to leave anyone out) blacks, Hispanics, women, as well as a few white-guy governors, mayors, and senators—and once again Graham was given a ride through several weeks of "could it be" publicity. Clinton and Graham both became governors in 1978. Clinton had lost a 1980 reelection but had come back two years later and, without term limits, had continually won reelection since.

Clinton aides let it out that Graham was under close consideration, along with Al Gore, Lee Hamilton, Jay Rockefeller, Bob Kerrey, and Harris Wofford. Days before Clinton made his choice, rumors had it that Graham would be the pick. The *Boston Globe* even had a story saying Lieutenant Governor Buddy MacKay would jump in to run for Graham's Senate seat.

Eventually, Clinton called Graham late one night and told him he'd chosen somebody else. Graham told him that was great (he didn't find out until the next morning that it was Gore) and then went back to sleep.

With Clinton's win, and then easy reelection in 1996, it was a solid eight years before the Gore campaign came knocking. Graham went through the gyrations yet again, this time with the chance of playing second fiddle to Gore.

The Florida media, certainly, were led to believe that Graham was a serious contender, and speculation again flew that he was among the finalists, along with Evan Bayh, Joe Lieberman, John Edwards, and John Kerry. In the end, it was Lieberman. Some speculated that it was Graham's infamous notebook habit[38] that nixed his chances, but Graham aides said later they

---

[38]See the chapter titled "The Notebooks."

learned that Gore was never seriously considering Graham but merely wanted Florida voters to know how important the state was to him.

In retrospect, the consequence of Gore's decision is crystal clear, even to Republicans.

Said Congressman Foley: "There's no doubt in my mind, if Graham was on the ticket, it would be Gore-Graham. In a state where he's very popular, there's no question he would have been able to pull 537 votes out of his hat. It would have been more like 100,000."

Perhaps because of the consensus that Graham was never quite thrilled with the Washington experience, there were two additional times that he was thought to be considering leaving his Senate seat.

Oddly, both involved the possibility that Graham would return to Florida to run for the governorship again. Each time, his opponent would have been Jeb Bush. The first was in 1996, when party activists in Florida worried that Lieutenant Governor Buddy MacKay, as competent and as nice a guy as he was, would be no match for Bush in 1998. Bush, the thinking went, had almost beaten Lawton Chiles in 1994, and Buddy was no Lawton.

Graham, in characteristic Graham fashion, appeared to seriously consider the possibility for a time—every moment of which, the party faithful's confidence in MacKay continued to slide. When finally Graham announced that he would run for reelection to the Senate, the Buddy-can't-win whispers had become Buddy-can't-win shouts—and helped weaken an already hurting campaign.

Four years later, as Bush looked nearly invincible heading into a reelection, some party honchos again turned to Graham. This time, the consideration seemed less serious, and Graham quickly announced that he was not interested. Instead, a Tampa lawyer named Bill McBride challenged Clinton attorney general Janet Reno, beating her in another controversial, marred primary, but then got clobbered by Bush in the general election.

In both instances, Gwen Logan says, her father never really gave the idea of trying to win back the Governor's Mansion much thought.

"I don't think that it was even a serious possibility, because he never looks back. He always looks forward," she said.

Perhaps. But at least in 1996, it was a serious enough possibility that Graham did not dismiss it out of hand, and instead played the announcement of his decision out over some time—which, maybe more than anything, gives credence to the idea of Graham's ambivalence about being in the Senate.

So why, then, has he stayed? Part of the answer must be that Graham's happiness or unhappiness in the Senate cannot be considered in a vacuum. Chances are pretty good that had he gone there directly from the Florida senate, he would have been utterly thrilled with the change. True, they are both legislative bodies, with the inherent drawbacks therein—but come on: a Florida senator in Tallahassee versus a United States senator in Washington? It's not a tough call.

But Graham did not go to Washington directly from the Florida legislature. He went there after two successful terms as Florida governor. He said so while he was governor, and he said so afterward: He pretty much loved every minute. Each day was a new opportunity as head of the fastest-growing state in the country.

During his Senate campaign, the Hawkins camp said that Governor Graham, had there not been term limits, would have happily run for a third term. There is probably more than a little truth to that.

And yet this does not seem a fair criticism of Graham's tenure in Washington. Okay, he was happier as governor, but does that mean he should not have sought and kept a different job when it was done? After all, he had to do *something*. Where would he have been happier: in the United States Senate, warts and all? Or leasing commercial real estate in Miami Lakes?

Former Republican senator Connie Mack, who served twelve years with Graham as Florida's junior senator, agreed that the common perception that Graham was unhappy in the Senate was not quite accurate.

"I think that's overstated." He said that Graham, like many former governors, loved being governor and thought that was the best job he'd ever had. But that did not mean Graham actively *disliked* life at the Capitol. "He's too talented a guy to have hung around seventeen years just for the hell of it."

The litmus test here should be: Whether he was ecstatic about the job or not, has he served those who sent him to Washington well? On that, the general consensus in Florida has been a resounding yes.

On a crisp Tuesday morning in September 2001, Graham was at a top-secret joint meeting of the House and Senate Intelligence Committees. Graham had become chairman of the Senate committee earlier that summer, when Vermont Republican Jim Jeffords had switched to become an independent, giving Democrats control of the Senate.

On that particular morning, on the fourth floor of the Capitol in the secret meeting room, Graham and his fellow committee members were grilling a Pakistani general about a variety of subjects—poppy cultivation in Afghanistan, the nuclear arms race with India.

Graham wrote in one his notorious notebooks:

"8:05—Issues re Afghanistan"

They talked a little about the Taliban:

"focused on hereafter, whether their current life will assure eternal glory"

But then:

"9:04—Tim gives note on 2 planes crash into World Trade Center, NYC."[39]

Suddenly Bob Graham the unknown, boring senator who cared only about Florida issues and who nobody outside the Capitol even recognized became one of the most important people in the nation.

Overnight, Florida's senior senator became America's senior senator. As chairman of the Senate Intelligence Committee, Graham would be privy to top-secret briefings conducted on the Capitol's fourth floor and in the steel-vaulted committee room in the Hart Office Building. He, and very few others in the country, would see much of what the president was seeing. He would get briefings from CIA Director George Tenet on secure telephones installed in his town houses on Capitol Hill and in Miami Lakes.

Simultaneously, overnight he was given the national audience that for a decade and a half in Washington had eluded him. Few in the national

---

[39]Michael Grunwald, "Running Scared," *Washington Post*, May 4, 2003.

press much cared what Bob Graham thought about any issue prior to September 11. Afterward, they couldn't get enough of him. The afternoon of the attacks, he held a press conference outside Florida House, the state's "embassy" in Washington. Two days later, he was on NBC's *Today* show, supporting a relaxation of the country's ban against assassinations.

By mid-August of 2002, Graham had appeared on more than eighty nationally televised news programs to discuss terrorism and national security. CNN's Larry King had him on his program ten times in fifteen weeks.[40] Graham similarly found that his stature had risen among his colleagues. He successfully pushed a series of amendments onto the major antiterrorism (and, according to critics, anti–civil liberties) Patriot Act that made it easier for the FBI, CIA, and other agencies to share intelligence about potential attackers.

The attacks also gave urgency to a piece of Graham legislation that had not quite managed to find its way into law earlier. In December 2001, the Senate finally passed a seaport security bill designed to better monitor the 7.5 million cargo containers that enter American ports annually, although, by the time it got to the President's desk, it did not have a source of money to pay for it. The bill grew out of a blue-ribbon commission that Graham had pushed President Clinton to create in 1999—which in turn grew out of a "workday" that Graham performed at Tampa Bay's Port Manatee in 1997.

Like most things that accrue to the more senior members, Bob Graham's office in the Hart Office Building is an impressive thing.

By dint of the size of his state, and the gradual improvement of his seniority over the years from Number 98 to Number 31, Graham rates a two-story suite that faces east, overlooking historic St. Joseph's Church. The dominant decor is a tribute to Florida's natural environment—a giant painting of a mangrove island covers the north wall of his inner office, while a landscape of the Fakahatchee Strand covers the west wall. Then

[40]Larry Lipman, "Year Later, Graham Stays on Top of Terror Fight," *Palm Beach Post*, September 8, 2002.

there are the grandchildren. Everywhere are the bright, shining faces of the offspring of Gwen, Cissy, Suzanne, and Kendall, many with Bob or Adele, or both, among them.

On his government-issue oak desk is the small block of granite carved by a German prisoner of war as a token of gratitude to his father, inscribed: "War in France, 1918, Capt. E. R. Graham," below a black Iron Cross.

It was not an easy thing to get from Number 98 to Number 31. With another reelection, with the retirements and assorted defeats of incumbents, Graham likely would have risen into the twenties, providing even more choice committee assignments and—in the event the Democrats retook the chamber—perhaps even a significant chairmanship.

Had there not been a September 11, it is unclear whether Graham would have considered abandoning the near certainty of a fourth Senate term for the chance to take on an incumbent Republican president. True, the incumbent may have been substantially more vulnerable to a challenge had there been no terrorist attacks. On the other hand, a more vulnerable president may well have drawn even more credible opponents—and Graham, without the visibility provided by his leadership of a key committee, likely would not have been among them.

Eighteen years is a long time to be any place, particularly someplace you've always thought of as a stepping stone to get someplace else. Would Graham have decided to call it quits regardless, had there never been that short but draining presidential run? It's doubtful even he knows for certain.

Graham did not dwell on any of this that afternoon he announced he would not seek reelection. He acknowledged that the "premature conclusion" of his presidential campaign was disappointing, and that the decision to retire had been difficult.

He reminded everyone that he still had another fourteen months in his term, and promised to make good use of them. "I will return to Washington with renewed knowledge and commitment to helping America rebuild America," Graham said. "We are about to commence the process of rebuilding the schools, the roads, the bridges of Iraq. If we can do that, we can also invest in rebuilding the schools, the roads, the bridges in America, for Americans, by Americans."

And then Graham touched on the hours he had spent that morning as part of his 391st "workday," when he had helped construction workers build the framework for Lincoln High School's new roof.

"From the roof you get a new horizon, a horizon of the opportunities that are available in this great country," he said. "This day has shown me the possibilities of the new role of service for myself—that new role of service at the end of the beginning. Thank you."

From someone who even his political opponents concede is a classy guy, it was a classy finish.

The Notebooks

There is in the Marathi language of west central India the adjective *nadishte*.[1] It is used to describe someone who takes an ordinarily good habit a bit beyond the bounds of common sense. The noun form is *nadishte-panha*.[2] An elderly grandmother who insists that a key be hung from its special hook *at absolutely all times* it is not actually in use is being a little *nadishte*. A three-year-old who isn't happy until his shoes are all in a row, arranged by increasing size, is exhibiting some potentially major-league *nadishtepanha*.

With his little, color-coded, spiral-bound notebooks filled with the specifics of his life, Bob Graham is clearly *nadishte*. Every single waking hour, of every single day, of every single year of Bob Graham's existence for the past quarter-century has been logged in minute—at times minute by minute—detail.

Want to know what brand of cereal Graham had for breakfast on that second week of July in 1989? Graham can tell you.

---

[1]Pronounced "NAH-dthish-tuh."
[2]The ending *panha*, pronounced "PUH-nha," translates roughly as "-ness."

How about which hotel room Graham stayed in during a vacation to Hong Kong in October 1983? Graham can you tell you that, too.

And if for some inexplicable reason you cared to know how long it took for the jetliner that Graham rode back to Miami after a Senate session in May 1998 to get airborne, Graham can almost certainly tell you that, as well. He can tell you the exact time his wife Adele phoned to tell him that eldest daughter Gwen had been accepted into law school. Or the score of the Dolphins game the night that second daughter Cissy had a baby boy.

Twenty-six years of notebooks. Two and a half days per notebook. Close to 4,000 notebooks—that's 450 *pounds* of notebooks—and counting.

Yes, sir. *Nadishte.* No doubt about it.

In the beginning there were the "workdays," the campaign gimmick that would propel Graham to fame and a long-shot governor's race victory. Part of the workdays campaign was to write a book about them, which would then be published and sold as the election drew closer.

To make sure he had the details right for the book, Graham began keeping an accurate log of his new jobs—the names of his coworkers, descriptions of what he had seen, and details about the actual work.

And Graham saw that keeping such a record was good. So good, in fact, that even after the campaign was finished and Graham had won, Graham kept on going with the notebooks.

Maybe it was for the sense of history—it's a pretty big deal, after all, being governor. People might actually care, someday, what his daily life was like. Maybe he kept on with it because by then he had a nice streak going. Somewhat like Cal Ripken's consecutive-game streak—after so many days in a row of keeping a log, it would be a damned shame to quit now. Maybe, and this ought not be discounted, he just plain *likes* keeping track of everything he does. Some people like following the value of their stocks.[3] Some people like to monitor which soap opera character is being unfaithful to

---

[3]Although, in the last few years, this hobby seems to have fallen out of favor somewhat.

whom. Bob Graham likes to know what he ate and where he slept and at what times he changed into what outfits.[4]

Whatever the reason, Graham does love taking his notes. He writes down names of buildings he has visited, books and magazines he has read, and the names and characteristics of the people he meets.[5] He will ask for addresses and phone numbers so that he can follow up. Graham logs how long he has spent doing the various tasks in his day. This includes even the time he has spent logging his notebook entries. He knows the odometer reading on his 1999 Mercury station wagon at each fill-up. When he has a free moment, he will whip out his notebook *du jour* to update times and details of the previous few hours, before he forgets.

He seems to have a particularly keen interest in airplanes. He could probably produce, with some research, a "minutes airborne" total for the thousands of flights he has taken over his years as governor and senator.

On the 1998 campaign "fly-around" with the other statewide Democratic candidates (he was pretty much the only one guaranteed an easy win; even during his first reelection in 1992, the Republicans had all but given up on trying to beat him), he was recounting a story about Jimmy Buffett when the turboprop stopped at the head of the runway and began racing its engines as it started down the strip. Graham stopped in midsentence and punched a button on his digital watch. At wheels up, he punched the button again, whipped out his little notebook, and jotted down the time. Then he picked up his train of thought exactly where he had broken off.

His wife, Adele, tells about the time during his governorship when they were flying from Brasilia to Rio de Janeiro on a South American trade mission. Suddenly the pilot was on the intercom. Adele, fearing a crash, reached to grab her husband's hand—but he was busy, writing down the pilot's exact instructions.

---

[4]This actually makes complete sense, given his personality. He doesn't like throwing anything away, ever—campaign trinkets, T-shirts he has been given, you name it. (During his governor years, Adele had to secretly box things up and ship them off to the state archives, so as to manage the Mansion clutter.) He reads his newspapers in the same exact sequence each Sunday. He keeps the stack of books by his bedside in a very particular order. This is what *nadishte* people do.
[5]This is particularly unnerving for a reporter interviewing him for the first time. Rarely do you have to take notes in an interview in which the subject is simultaneously taking notes about you.

A reporter later asked to see the notations. They read: "2:39 P.M.—Pilot announces hydraulic failure. Must make emergency landing," followed by "3:20 P.M.—Take bus to hotel."[6]

For the record, here are the basic notebook facts:

Each notebook has eighty pages. Each white page is ruled with sixteen faint blue lines, which are spaced half a hair less than one-quarter inch apart.

The pages and both front and back covers are exactly three inches wide and five inches long. Pages and cardboard covers are rounded off at each bottom corner with a half-inch radius, and each page and cover has at the top twelve small, oval holes, through which a wire spiral binds the notebook together. Each oval hole is one-eighth inch wide and five-thirty-seconds of an inch long. The wire spiral, it should be noted, adds one-quarter inch to the notebook, producing an overall length of five and a quarter inches.[7]

When new, the notepaper heart of each notebook is one-quarter inch thick, meaning each sheet of notepaper is approximately 0.003125 inches thick. The back cover is a heavy manila cardboard one-thirty-second of an inch thick, while the front cover is either green, red, yellow, or blue on the outside, white on the inside, and one-sixty-fourth of an inch thick.

This gives each notebook overall dimensions of three inches wide, five-and-one-quarter inches long, and nineteen-sixty-fourths of an inch thick, with a weight of 1.8 ounces.[8]

---

[6]Maureen Dowd, "From Florida, a Senator of Note," *New York Times*, January 7, 1987.

[7]The thickness of the wire that makes up the spiral binding is one-thirty-second of an inch. However, the length of the wire could not be measured through nondestructive means, and the author was unwilling to employ destructive testing. A crude mathematical formula, however, produced an estimate of 20.07 inches in length, including the quarter-inch bits at each end that are tucked back inward to prevent injury and damage to clothing.

[8]The weight was measured using the electronic scale at the United States Post Office at the northeast corner of College Avenue and Bronough Street in Tallahassee, Florida, on Sunday, July 27, 2003. The National Weather Service at the Tallahassee Regional Airport at the hour of the weighing showed a relative humidity of 93 percent. However, the Post Office interior was air-conditioned, resulting in a significantly lower humidity. The Post Office does not have installed a hygrometer in the publicly accessible area on weekends, so it could not be determined what the interior humidity was. Nor could it be determined what effect this lowered humidity had on the measured weight—presumably, the notebook weight would have been slightly higher outside, as notepaper is slightly hydrophilic.

When Graham cracks open a new notebook, he writes his name, his mailing address at the Hart Senate Office Building, and his various telephone numbers on the inside cover in the upper right quadrant.

Graham uses a blue, push-button ballpoint pen to write with, and has a small, neat script.[9] Both pen and notebook are kept in the breast pocket of his shirt.[10] The main part of each day's entry is a log of events. Separate "to do" lists are created for himself and his staff, as is a list of things to discuss with Adele. Each "to do" item is prefaced with a circle, so that he can check it off when it has been accomplished. Graham also has developed a sort of shorthand for himself: "MLTH" is his Miami Lakes town house. "LVM" is left voice mail.

Just as there is a method to the notebook writing, so there is a method now for notebook storage. The ones from his earlier years are kept in Tallahassee, where Graham maintains a district office. The more recent ones are stored in closets of his Hart Senate Office Building suite.

There are four colors of notebooks, denoting each of the seasons: blue for winter, green for spring, red for summer, and yellow for autumn. No, that doesn't mean Graham uses only green notebooks in spring or red ones in summer. It means he uses a green one after he's filled up a blue one, a red one after he's filled up the green one, and so on. This is so that if he has two notebooks on his person at any given time (which he frequently does), he knows instantly which one is the more current, and which one he is carrying around in order to pass along some piece of information or instruction.

After two or three notebooks are filled up, they are consigned to a six-inch-by-nine-inch manila envelope, which also contains copies of the corresponding official schedules, business cards of people he has met on those particular days, and other pertinent papers. The six-by-nine envelopes, in turn, go into white storage boxes, each the size of a toaster oven, with the boxes arranged chronologically.

---

[9]Well, it would *have* to be small, wouldn't it. With the lines slightly less than a quarter-inch apart.
[10]No, the pen is not inserted through the wire spiral.

While the notebooks were originally purchased from Eckerd's drug-stores in Florida (back then, brown was the autumn color in the sequence, not yellow),[11] in the early 1990s Graham learned that the manufacturer would no longer make the particular style that he likes. Graham's aides got in touch with North Carolina Paper Company in Clayton and bought up the remaining stock.

People looking through the notebooks for some deeper meaning are bound to be disappointed. There are no great insights into the American political psyche, nor any diatribes against those who have wronged him, nor even pithy observations of his colleagues.[12]

They are not so much a journal, filled with emotions and thoughts and impressions, as they are a ship's log, filled with times, measurements, and other factual details.

Some have theorized that it was oldest brother Philip's manic depression and 1963 suicide that brought out in young Bob a need to be as ordered and controlled as possible—exactly the opposite of Phil. But Graham himself discounts that idea.

"I can't say I ever incorporated that experience into my personality and went through a period of reflection and self-examination," Graham said in a 1984 interview.[13]

The notebooks are, depending on your point of view, either utterly utilitarian or utterly useless.

An obvious case can be made that they are useless. They contain so much trivia—room numbers of hotels Graham has stayed at, the flavor of muffin he had for breakfast, and the precise amounts of times it takes to do certain things, like walking from town house to office or back.

---

[11]Graham's staff tried to order some from the Senate commissary for him, but Graham rejected them. The blue cover was not the correct shade.
[12]A rare exception may have been during the Clinton impeachment debate in 1999, when Graham wrote of Senate Minority Leader Tom Daschle: "emergence as an effective leader—a unifying force."
[13]Mike Ollove, "The Turning Point," *Miami Herald*, December 9, 1984.

Graham and his friends concede that, okay, it is true Graham records some details that may not necessarily be relevant to much of anything a few months or even a few minutes after they are jotted down. But amid that jumble are bits of information that are critical to the efficient functioning of his office and his political livelihood. The notebooks, the counterargument goes, are the pre-electronic-era equivalent of the Palm Pilot. Graham was hyperorganized before being hyperorganized was cool.

In the pages of the notebooks are checklists of instructions for his chief of staff, his press secretary, his policy directors. And new staff members who think maybe Graham might forget something he asked about a couple of days ago will soon learn that that is not likely to happen. The notebooks make sure of it.

In fact, Graham's jottings are his way of entering data into the computer program his office uses to track projects. Everything the office is doing or checking into is kept up to date on the computer—a system that actually was instituted by Dick Burroughs, the man who whipped some organization into then–Governor Jello's staff.

The notebooks have also played a big role in Graham's impressive reelection margins. In view of Florida's rapid growth, the six-year Senate terms mean that each time an election rolls around, a significant percentage of the electorate are people who weren't even living in Florida during the previous election. The seat Graham holds, for example, had a new senator each of the three previous elections prior to his winning it. Ed Gurney held it from 1969 to 1975,[14] Richard Stone held it from 1975 to 1981, and Paula Hawkins held it from 1981 to 1987. Graham has had it since then, winning landslide reelections both times.

Some of that margin must be attributed to the notebooks, which became the repository of the name and mailing address of nearly every person Graham would meet. That notation, in turn, would within a day or two lead to a personalized note from Graham. As anyone who knows politics can attest, this personal contact matters. For every person who gets such a

---

[14]Although Gurney's demise probably had more to do with his involvement in the FBI's Abscam sting operation.

note, ten friends and neighbors might actually see the letter and a hundred acquaintances may eventually hear of it.

In 1987, not long after he'd been in the Senate, Graham sent letters to all fifty-one people he met on a one-day trip from Tampa to Vero Beach. "I enjoyed seeing you at the Orlando Airport March 21," Graham wrote in one missive. "Thank you for the material which you gave me on Jehovah's Witnesses and mankind's future. I appreciate having this very enlightening information."[15]

Over the years, Graham has sent out thousands of such letters.

The notebooks' usefulness was called into question during one instance when they might have served to settle a campaign argument.

It was in the heat of Graham's 1986 run against incumbent Paula Hawkins, whose camp was charging Graham of having supported a 1984 National Governors Association resolution at its annual meeting in Nashville calling for a freeze in Social Security payments to help reduce the federal deficit. The resolution had no real effect—the NGA made and continues to make meaningless resolutions all the time. However, Social Security has long been the "third rail" of Florida politics—touch it at your own peril. Graham turned to his trusty notebooks for proof that he had not supported the resolution.

The research was in vain. The notebooks mentioned nothing about Social Security. Duly recorded, though, was what Graham had to eat that day.

Eight years earlier, however, notebooks and Graham's intimate familiarity with them let him score political points in an impromptu debate.

The adversary then, too, was Paula Hawkins, Republican gubernatorial candidate Jack Eckerd's running mate. Eckerd, Hawkins, Graham, and his running mate, Wayne Mixson, were all together at a West Palm Beach forum. Each, by turn, was to give a brief presentation to the audience. Graham, Eckerd, and Mixson all gave relatively innocuous remarks, Graham recalled.

"When Paula got up, she began to attack Wayne Mixson and myself,

[15]David Dahl, "Graham: Mr. Inside on the Outside," *St. Petersburg Times*, October 13, 1991.

both of whom had come from an agricultural background, for having been personally responsible for the high cost of milk and all of the bad things that were happening to Florida's children because of that high cost of milk," Graham said. "And she went on and on. Then her time was up, the meeting was over and I was walking out, and she kept right behind me, berating me about this high cost of milk and the inflation that was occurring in the food that children had.

"So we got out on the sidewalk, she was continuing on, and I said: 'Look, Paula, let me show you two things here. First, here is a notebook which I purchased, as I generally do, from Eckerd's. It's got 80 pages and it cost 49 cents. Here is a book that I just have gotten from Rite Aid, which has 100 pages and costs 39 cents. By my quick calculation, that's almost 50 percent less expensive than the one from Eckerd's. And you're accusing *me* of contributing to inflation?' Well, it was not a very rational argument, but it was good enough to end the discussion about inflation and milk prices."[16]

The issue never came up again.

A s with many trends in snarky political journalism, poking fun at Graham's notebooks appears to have begun on a national scale with the *New York Times*'s Maureen Dowd, who, after trailing Graham on his first day in the United States Senate, wrote a 976-word feature about the fresh Florida face in the upper chamber.

She detailed for readers Graham's hours, as recorded in a yellow notebook:

> 7:30, awake at Willard Hotel, room 928, maid looks for misplaced laundry.
> 8:30–8:40, Willard Hotel lobby, TV with Channel 6, Tallahassee. Staged dressing for first day.[17]

---

[16]For the truly *nadishte* out there: The Eckerd notebooks were 57.1 percent more expensive than the Rite-Aid notebooks. The Rite-Aid notebooks were 36.3 percent cheaper than the Eckerd notebooks.

[17]Graham evidently was not willing to let Channel 6 *really* watch him dress, so they got to shoot a video of him putting on his Florida tie.

> 8:40–8:50, Cab to Hart Office Building with driver, Tom Bowman of States News Service doing story for Miami Herald, Channel 6 cameraman.
> 8:50–9:05, Hart Senate Office Building, room 313, talk with [chief of staff] Buddy Shorstein.
> 9:15–10:45, Democratic caucus, continental breakfast (coffee, orange juice and doughnuts) Bob Byrd presides.
> 10:45–10:55, Walk subway to Hart Senate Office Building.
> 10:55–11:10, Hart 313. Talk with staff.

By the standards of her columns in recent years, Dowd was downright gentle: "Senator Graham usually begins his daily entry with his weight (about 182 pounds). But he says he is not recording it this week because he has two scales at home in Florida that he trusts and does not want to risk using a scale in Washington that would be off by a pound or two. . . . The senator agrees it is confusing at first to understand the point of some of the things that he regularly writes down. But he says you never know when you might want to know the exact hotel room you stayed in several years ago."[18]

For years, Graham made the notebooks available to reporters who asked to see them. The reporters who saw them (almost always Florida reporters) typically poked mild fun at them, but almost always in the context of a much longer article. Here is our governor, or here is our senator, Bob Graham, and this is how he got elected, and here is his record, and this is what people say about him, and oh, by the way, here is this one really goofy thing that he does.

Graham is beloved in Florida, and generally liked and respected by the press corps. This is easy to understand. In a state where a criminal indictment of an elected official is, unfortunately, a fairly routine event, and where weak ethics laws allow egregious conflicts of interest to go completely unpunished, journalists come to an understandably cynical view of politicians. Add to that the secretive, even combative tone so many elected

---

[18]Maureen Dowd, "From Florida, a Senator of Note," *The New York Times,* January 7, 1987.

officials take with the press, and Graham's open, bantering style is a re-freshing change. Reporters who know Graham have a tough time justify-ing an article making fun of the notebooks without also pointing out that the notebooks keep him organized and help him stay focused.

A good example is a feature on Graham's notebooks by *St. Petersburg Times* reporter Bill Adair on February 23, 2003—easily *the* definitive "notebook" story. It went into the minute details of Graham's peculiar note-taking but pointed out that the peculiar note-taking, when it occurred on October 14, 1997, during a "workday" at Tampa Bay's Port Manatee, ac-tually had a tangible result. During Graham's stint as a Customs inspector, the port workers told him that because the various federal agencies did not share information well, there remained a high risk of drug smuggling or terrorism. Graham wrote in his notebook: "No sharing of info—why? . . . Budget depends on # of arrests . . . conflicting agencies: Customs, ATF, DEA, locals."[19]

When Graham got back to the Capitol, he started asking questions. In 1999, a blue-ribbon commission was appointed to make recommendations. Those recommendations became law in 2002 when Congress passed the Port Security Act.

This dynamic, the balancing of the notebooks' silly with the serious, the useless with the useful, did not apply when Graham's name entered the national arena in 2000.

Although Graham was a possible vice-presidential nominee in both 1988 and 1992, he was seen as a much more serious contender in 2000, when Al Gore's campaign made it clear that it had no intention of ceding Florida to the Republicans just because the governor there was George W. Bush's little brother.

The national media took a renewed interest in Graham. On July 17, 2000, *Time* magazine took a renewed interest in his notebooks.[20]

The article explained the obligatory journalistic facts—who Graham

---

[19]Bill Adair, "Dress in Gray Suit, Discuss CIA, Mingle," *St. Petersburg Times*, February 23, 2003.
[20]Ann Blackman, "Take Note of Bob Graham," *Time,* July 17, 2000.

was, what offices he had held, and so on—but then spent nearly one-third of its 701 words quoting verbatim from Graham's notebook entry from Sunday, September 4, 1994.

It was, as it happens, the day the second of his four daughters was having a baby. Graham's notations detail the time he had his breakfast, the sort of muffin he ate, the fact that he returned a rented video, *Ace Ventura*, and even how long it took to rewind *Ace Ventura* before he returned it.[21]

Other national reporters followed suit with their own notebook stories. This was only natural. Anytime a candidate from south of Washington, west of Philadelphia, or north of Boston appears on the national scene, the national press feels compelled to ridicule him. It's a form of District of Columbia–centric hazing: You've been covered by backwoods bumpkins all these years, Candidate-Boy, now welcome to the big time.[22] An outsider, any outsider, is given this treatment—at least at first.[23]

Whether these articles really mattered is debatable. Many among the Washington and New York–based punditry declared that Bob Graham's notebook fetish did him in—he was just too weird for prime time. Other political insiders concede the notebooks coverage may have been a factor but that Gore never really intended to pick Graham in the first place. He just wanted Floridians to believe their state was so important to him that he would consider their favorite son as his running mate.

Florida voters, of course, don't care about the notebooks. They've known about that and all of the other Graham quirks from his days as governor, and have continued to vote for him by huge margins. In 2003, he remained Florida's most popular elected official, according to opinion polls.

Nor does his family care about the note-taking. Ask brother Bill about notebooks, and he'll whip one out of his own pocket and explain that he and Bob got the habit from their dad, who would carry a small notebook

[21]Actually, *Time* reported that it took fifteen minutes, from 1:30 to 1:45 P.M. to rewind the movie—which begs the question: Did Graham rewind the video by hand? If not, what in the world kind of VCR takes fifteen minutes to rewind a single video? What was this, *Ace Ventura: The Director's Cut?*

[22]The crows-on-a-telephone-wire theory about reporters also comes to mind. When one lands, they all land. When one flies, they all fly.

[23]Witness former Vermont governor Howard Dean, who got fairly harsh treatment from the political press (particularly after his roughing-up on NBC's *Meet the Press*)—until he raised more than $7 million in the second quarter of 2003, which thereby bought his entrée into the "first tier" of serious candidates.

around with him to jot down which cows needed attention or what fences needed mending.

Fair enough. These are reasonable things for a cattleman to write down. But is Bob Graham really trying to tell us that his father wrote down what he ate for breakfast or the time, to the hundredth of a second, it took him to walk from his house to the barn?[24]

Bill concedes that muffin flavors go somewhat beyond a farm "to do" list. "Bob goes a little further than we all do. But the notebook thing is a family trait."[25]

Even Adele will rib her husband about the level of detail in his logs. Once, when Bob was explaining about watching *Ace Ventura*, she reminded him: "And you rewound it, too."[26]

In any event, after Gore picked Connecticut Senator Joe Lieberman, the notebook issue receded once again into dormancy, where it remained until Graham decided in late 2002 to run for president.

There was a time when Graham did not care one iota what other people thought of his note-taking.

In 1984, when a *Miami Herald* reporter was researching a lengthy profile for the paper's Sunday magazine, Graham actually seemed to get a charge out of explaining the organizational scheme behind the notebooks.

"This one is really going to blow your mind," he told the *Herald* writer. "These books come in four different colors. Blue, green, red, and brown. Winter, spring, summer, and fall. I never use them out of that sequence. Winter, spring, summer, and fall." At the time, Graham did not at all attempt to attach significance to it: "It's just habit, a curiosity," he said. "I've been doing it a long time."[27]

---

[24]There is, by the way, a protocol in the physical sciences regarding the use of "significant" digits when recording data, which says that neither a data point nor a calculation using it ought to exceed the precision of the least precise data source. With all due respect, it would seem that the stopwatch function on the senator's wristwatch is not sufficient to produce accurate measurements down to one-hundredth of a second. Prudence dictates, therefore, that such times be recorded only to the nearest tenth of a second.

[25]Mark Silva and Tamara Lytle, "He Has Been Long Shot Before," *Orlando Sentinel*, April 20, 2003.

[26]Todd S. Purdum, "An Elder Statesman Offers Steadiness, Not a Jolt," *New York Times*, March 4, 2003.

[27]Mike Ollove, "The Turning Point," *Miami Herald*, December 9, 1984.

The *Time* article in 2000 probably should have been seen as a harbinger of things to come, notebook-wise. If Graham realized this, he did not appear to be terribly concerned. When the *Washington Post* arranged to take a photo for their Sunday magazine cover story on him in May 2003, Graham agreed to pose—holding a notebook. It wasn't really that odd. His official portrait hanging in the Florida capitol also has him holding a notebook. Some of his campaign ads have featured him busily writing in them.

But with the *Time* article still near the top of the "notebooks and Bob Graham" Nexis query when Graham started considering the race, the national political press corps was bound to get into their typical tail-chasing frenzy. They did not disappoint.

Again, television news outdid itself the following morning, when Katie Couric asked Graham about his notebook entries from the previous day, the ones recording: "12:17 . . . Ascend stage, stumble, regain balance. 12:18, applause. Where the Streets Have No Name plays, U2. 12:19, Clap. Wave. 12:20, Adjust tie, red white stripes. 12:21, double thumbs up. 12:22, sing along with national anthem. Right hand on heart."

"What—what do you do this for?" a perplexed Couric asked.

Of course, Graham *hadn't* made those entries. Couric was actually reading from a *Washington Post* article parodying what Graham's entries about his own official announcement day might look like. The joke evidently went over the heads of the *Today* show's research team.

"Well, I mean, that is absurd," Graham said, who added that he hadn't even recorded the previous day's entries yet.[28]

The gaffe did nothing to slow down the requests to see the notebooks, with each reporter feeling the need to out-clever the last in mocking Graham. Even ABC News' online tipsheet, "The Note," agreed that the notebook-bashing was getting stupid.

"We cannot figure out to save our lives why Graham is not being taken more seriously as a formidable candidate by the Gang of 500,"[29] ABC's

---

[28]NBC News Transcripts, "Senator Bob Graham discusses why he wants to be the US president and what he would do if he won," May 7, 2003.
[29]The term popularized by ABC News' "The Note," perhaps the *insidest* of the inside-the-Beltway chronicles, to describe the Washington-to-New York political reporters, columnists, TV personalities, and associated hangers-on who like to think their interest level makes or breaks a presidential candidate.

writers opined the day of his official announcement. "No one has a hold on this nomination by a long shot; and, with all due respect, the field Graham formally joins today arguably has less combined charisma than the cast of 'The Beltway Boys.' We think it is pretty clear that Bob Graham is being underestimated in this deal."[30]

Not that this made even the slightest bit of difference to anyone.

"The questions must be posed," *New York Times* reporter Carl Hulse opined solemnly in a June 4 article. "Are American voters ready for a president who could all but moonlight as a stenographer? Is his habit a disqualifying eccentricity?"[31]

A disqualifying eccentricity?

During Graham's first appearance on Tim Russert's *Meet the Press* as a presidential candidate (he appeared on the show a half-dozen times following September 11 because of his Senate responsibilities), Russert flashed up on his screen a snippet from his notebook of September 17, 2002:

6:50 Awake at 3 ST TH (181)

6:50–7:00 Apply scalp medication

7:00–7:40 Kitchen—brew coffee—prepare and drink breakfast (soy, skim milk, OJ, peach, banana, blueberries)

—read Post

—dress in gray suit

"This has been called neurotic, obsessive, bizarre," Russert declared, and then demanded to know: "How would you explain to the American people why you keep such minute detail of what you do every day?"

Farther down in his article, Hulse stated: "His note-taking has been a topic of conversation for years in Florida, where some consider it endearing."[32] And finally, Hulse was able to find a psychology professor to clinch the obvious diagnosis:

---

[30]Mark Halperin, Marc Ambinder, David Chalian, and Brooke Brower, "We've Never Had a President Named Bob," ABCNews.com, May 6, 2003.

[31]Carl Hulse, "One Senator's Life, Minute by Minute," *New York Times*, June 4, 2003.

[32]Left unstated, presumably, is the corollary: Only yahoos from backwoods provinces like Florida could possibly see such a thing as endearing.

"'I think it is a bit compulsive,' said the psychologist, Aubrey Immelman, a professor at St. John's University in Collegeville, Minnesota. 'It almost has a pacifier element to it, a security blanket. It suggests to me someone who has a lot of uncertainty and needs to create a structure.'"[33]

Another college professor, University of Virginia's Larry Sabato, went even further, calling Graham "obsessive-compulsive." Sabato, who is possibly the most-quoted political pundit in America, nonetheless is not a psychologist.[34] That did not stop him from letting loose anyway: "There is no way they can explain this as normal. If they are going to explain this, they have to say why he has this abnormality and why it doesn't matter," Sabato told the *St. Petersburg Times*. "Americans want their president to be a real president, they want to relate to that person. Can anyone relate to this?"[35]

W hoa. Obsessive-compulsive. Neurotic, obsessive, bizarre. Disqualifying eccentricity.

Okay, how about a more basic question about Graham's note-taking: What does it possibly matter?

Yes, it's a quirk. But as quirks go, surely this is a benign one. Both Thomas Jefferson and George Washington were note-takers every bit as detail-obsessed as Graham. Should they have been disqualified as too eccentric? It's not as if Graham spends hours and hours on his logs. At most, perhaps twenty or twenty-five minutes is given to recording his daily routine. It doesn't intrude on his family life or peace of mind.[36] So whom does it harm?

Surely, there are a lot worse habits to have than writing down every little thing that happens to you. Indeed, in a country where millions of men keep careful track of the batting averages and slugging percentages of the players on "their" fantasy baseball teams, where millions more add up their

---

[33]Carl Hulse, "One Senator's Life, Minute by Minute," *New York Times*, June 4, 2003.

[34]Here is probably as good a place as any to rat out the dirty little secret of quoting political scientists in articles. All too often, these learned observers know what they know from reading the newspapers. It's a nice little racket: reporters quote pundits who get their information from other reporters. This nonsense continues because (1) reporters are lazy, and (2) editors insist that reporters quote *somebody* in their articles. Editors, like nature, abhor a vacuum.

[35]Bill Adair, "Dress in Gray Suit, Discuss CIA, Mingle," *St. Petersburg Times*, February 23, 2003

[36]One of the symptoms, by the way, of actual "obsessive-compulsive" disorder.

daily caloric intake from their Slim Fasts, the media pursuit of Graham's notebooks began to appear more bizarre than the notebooks themselves.[37]

Most of the punditocracy's fulminations, of course, featured that crutch of the journalist straining to evade the dictum that is supposed to keep him out of his own story: the passive voice. In both the Russert case and the *New York Times* article, the passive voice rules. *Questions must be posed. This has been called.* Posed by whom? Called by whom? Pundits and political writers, naturally.

Seriously: Is the *New York Times* suggesting that the notebooks and their content could actually constitute "a disqualifying eccentricity"?

What about a grown man traveling everywhere with his favorite pillow, like the current president? Isn't that a tad odd? Is that a disqualifying eccentricity? The previous president thought it neat to receive fellatio in the Oval Office from an intern. Surely *that* was a disqualifying eccentricity— or was it? Polls toward the end of his second term suggested he might have won a third term had the Constitution permitted it.

More disturbingly, there's a touch of downright meanness to the notebook jokes. Something that smacks of the playground bully and his toadies making fun of the kid with glasses.

Even Russert, probably the most respected political interviewer on television, picked on Graham for noting what he ate for breakfast and what he wore the morning of September 17, 2002. All of that accounted for thirty-two words in his notebook that day. Another fifty-five words fell into that same sort of category, with most of those coming at the end of the day when he had dinner and got ready for bed.

What Russert did not tell his audience was that there were another 552 words written that day—notes about Iraq, Cuba, a number of environmental projects in Florida, a prescription drug briefing, a vote on the Senate floor, and a poll about his higher-education petition drive in Florida. There is a "to do" list that includes finding out about the Afghan heroin supply and its possible effects on Colombian drug trafficking, meeting with Paul Wolfowitz, writing a note to the widow of former Florida governor

---

[37]A modest standard for notebook-bashing: Anyone who watches *Survivor* or any of its inane sequels is disqualified from ridiculing Graham's notebooks—or anything else on this planet, for that matter.

LeRoy Collins, and getting Texas senator Phil Gramm to cosponsor an amendment of his.

Is it "neurotic, obsessive, bizarre" to have kept track of those things?

Here, for the record, is the entire notebook entry for September 17, 2002, as transcribed by *St. Petersburg Times* reporter Bill Adair:[38]

> 6:50 Awake at 3 ST TH (181)
> 6:50–7:00 Apply scalp medication
> 7:00–7:40 Kitchen—brew coffee—prepare and drink breakfast (soy, skim milk, OJ, peach, banana, blueberries)
> —read Post
> —dress in gray suit
> 8:00 Al Cumming—have not received CIA answers to Iraq Qs
> 8:15–8:20 Walk to HSOB
> 8:20 Hart SOB 524
> —transfer dictation to Beth Powers
> 8:25–9:00 Priorities review w Bryant Hall, Buddy Menn, Paul Anderson, John Provenzano
> 9:00–10:05 Hart SOB 219—conference room
> —briefing on Iraq, Cuba, DHS with Al Cumming, Bob Filippone, Lorenzo
> 10:05 Dirksen SOB 226
> —mingle
> 10:15 International Drug Caucus hearing on Andean Regional Initiative
> 12:10–12:20 Walk, elevator, subway to Capitol w Buddy Menn—discuss EEF, Florida Gov's race
> 12:20–1:10 Capitol S-104
> 12:20–12:35 Review status of Apalachicola River + Forest, Miami Circle, Virginia Key beach w Amanda Wood, Kasey Gillette, Zev Simpser

---

[38]Bill Adair, "Excerpts from a Bob Graham Notebook," *St. Petersburg Times*, February 23, 2003.

12:35–1:00 Briefing on prescription drugs w Lisa Layman, Bryant Hall

1:00–1:10 Caroline Berver, Bryant Hall re Haitian detainees

1:10–2:15 Capitol S-211 (LBJ Room)

—Demo caucus luncheon (salmon)

—topics discussed: state of US economy—DHS—Iraq

2:15–2:25 Walk to HSOB w Senator Jay Rockefeller—discuss JIC hearing on 9.19.02

2:25 Hart SOB 219

—mingle

2:35–4:35 SSCI closed hearing on Iraq

—witness: DCI George Tenet

4:55 conference room

4:55–5:00 Paul Anderson—re JIC opening statement

5:00–5:35 George Tenet

(at 5:10) MC Goss & Pelosi; Senator Shelby; Stan Moskowitz

—re: WH cooperation

5:25–5:35 Walk, elevator, subway to Capitol

5:35–5:40 Senate chamber

—vote aye on closure on DHS

—talk w Senator Miller re prescription drugs

5:40–6:30 Capitol H405

—5:40 John Provenzano will bring dry cleaning, reading materials to 3 ST TH

—5:45 Buddy Shorstein—LVM

—5:50 Geoff Garin—w/CB at H

—5:55–6:30 JIC Leadership: Senator Shelby, MC Goss, Pelosi, Eleanor Hill

—review 9.18.02 format, schedule

—6:30 cloakroom—no votes

6:30–6:45 Walk, elevator, subway to Florida House via HSOB

6:45–7:40 at Florida House—attend reception

—mingle

—receive [award from Cuban-American group]

—intro MC Ike Skelton

7:40–7:45 Walk to 3 ST TH w John Provenzano

—7:40 Paul Kelly (asst sec of state)—Deputy Secretary Armitage will appear 9.19? or Wolfowitz

7:45 3 St TH kitchen

—drink supper—see 9.17.02 7:00 A.M.

—read news clips

8:30 Buddy Shorstein re: Governor's race; EEF

8:40–8:50—3 St TH bedroom, bathroom

—change to blue shorts

—apply scalp medication

8:50–10:50 3 ST TH office

8:50–9:00—update notebook

9:00–10:50 review staff memos, miscellaneous dictation

9:30 Geoff Garin—EEF poll

9:45 Adele—OK w ML

10:50–11:15 3 St TH bedroom, bathroom

—shower + dress for sleep

—read Post

11:20 Asleep at 3 St TH

[Start of "To Do" list]

Drug Caucus 10:15 A

Followup

—Don Evans, secretary of commerce, place for implementation of Andean Trade Pact

—schedule night with SouthCom

Heroin

—has there been a reduction of Afghan supply?

—if so, effect on Colombia?

—to date, FARC ELN have been primarily involved with coke— concern that heroin profits will be irresistible

AUC

is fracturing

still heavily engaged drug trafficking

SouthCom—wait and see
EEF
knowledge of EEF
15% is a lot of fair amount
19% some
65% not much at all

["To Do" lists for his staffers]

Bob Filippone
o Secure e-mail w request for information re Iraq
Mark Block
Paul Anderson
o Jim Lehrer NewsHour—video of 9.18.02 show
Buddy Menn
o Colonel Ted Pusey
o Office projects
—format for presentation
—topics

Adele

Things to do 9.17.02

o JIC
—Dick Clark re Islam presentation
—International intelligence collaboration
—Interpol
—Paul Wolfowitz re 9.19.02 panel FBI Director Bob Mueller
—agents behind screen
—Newt Gingrich
—Pat Moynihan
o EEF
—Joan Ruffier
—collaborative campaign

—Carol Shields

o Prescription drugs

o Medicare

—3 item package with reimbursement of providers bill

—Senator Phil Gramm—co-sponsor—secure memo on amendment

o "Night of the Hunter" rec by JRM

o Mrs. LeRoy Collins—broken hand

o Undersecretary of DOD for int'l

—Senator Warner

—call General Scowcroft

—Senator Lugar—solicit his support—concern for DHS

o Senator Blanche Lincoln

—Suzanne—Margarita Party

o Senator Kennedy per AFT $4.5 b ed approps

Despite the national press's fascination with his notebooks, Graham in the summer of 2003 continued to use them. Even when Russert asked on his program whether he would keep them in the White House should he become president, Graham answered: "I would assume so. . . . I did it for eight years as governor of Florida. I've done it in the U.S. Senate. It's been a valuable part of my effort to be disciplined and to be responsive to the people by assuring that I have it written down what they expect, and that I can check off that that request was responded to."

Graham said later that he cannot understand why the notebooks, as use-ful to him and as harmless to others as he believes they are, are of such fas-cination to the Gang of 500. "I can't answer that question," he said at the Concord, New Hampshire, belt and holster factory where he rolled out his economic plan. "I have been doing this so long. . . . They are part of my daily discipline. I can't really give an explanation as to how they have at-tracted so much attention."

Then he brightened at what he perceived as a rare, friendly inquisitor on the notebooks topic: "If you want to report those journalists to the

Columbia Journalism School for possible sanctions, you would be doing America a great favor."

At a street fair in Concord that evening celebrating the coming car racing weekend, Graham had out a small yellow notebook as he greeted passersby—favorite Graham small-talk words: "Okay!" "Good!"—in front of his campaign's new, NASCAR pickup truck. To each new potential supporter, Graham offered his notebook and pen and asked if they wouldn't mind jotting down their names, phone numbers, mailing addresses, and e-mail addresses.

After two hours, he had several pages' worth—eighteen names, to be exact. "And I got five cards, too," Graham said.

And with a *Washington Post* reporter who Graham knew would be writing a potentially influential article about his campaign, Graham did not hesitate to stop the conversation in midstream as the United Airlines jet at the Manchester, New Hampshire, airport backed away from the gate. Out came the notebook, down went the departure time—to the hundredth of a second.

"Airplanes now have a tendency to pull out a little earlier than they are scheduled to go," Graham reported to the reporter. "We're leaving almost two minutes before we're scheduled."[39]

In terms of quirkiness, of course, there's more to Bob Graham than just the notebooks. There are also the ties.

From his first run for the governorship until the spring of 2003, when he began campaigning for the presidency, Graham wore ties with the exact same pattern—the diagonal rows of Floridas on a contrasting background. They were polyester, cost about $15, and came from a men's store in downtown Tallahassee called Nic's Toggery. The ties have exasperated some—in 1990, Graham pal Jimmy Buffett jumped up with a pair of scissors and snipped off the bottom of one and tossed it out into a crowd of young Graham supporters—but Graham didn't care. He told everyone that the ties

---

[39]Manuel Roig-Franzia, "Changed by Terror, a Nice Guy Converted," *Washington Post*, July 27, 2003

were emblematic of his commitment to serve Florida. Adele didn't buy it. Her theory: Bob was cheap and didn't like to shop.[40]

In 1997, Graham had a scare when he heard a rumor that Nic's would no longer carry his tie. "I'm heartsick about it, and trying to stock up on supplies," Graham said. "All my ties are Florida ties. I've not bought a tie other than a Florida tie since 1977."[41]

It turned out that news of the Florida tie's demise was somewhat exaggerated. Nic's would continue to carry the tie, but in only two color combinations—burgundy with little white Floridas, or navy with little white Floridas—whereas before, all manner of different colors had been available. So it was probably good that Graham stocked up when he did, after all.

With the stretching of horizons that came with the presidential race, however, came the realization that the Florida tie was just not going to cut it when begging for votes in Iowa or New Hampshire. The Florida ties had to go, replaced instead with more traditional neckwear—presenting Graham with fashion quandaries he had avoided for a quarter-century.

"Well, you do have more decisions to make," said Graham on a June Thursday in 2003 on which he wore a pale yellow silk creation decorated with maps of regions of the country—New England, the Southeast, and so forth. "With the Florida tie, it was color, only. Now, it's design, color, appropriateness for audience, et cetera."

Adele, for one, has waited decades for the change. "I'm so glad he's finally wearing silk."[42]

Given Graham's "serious" side, like when he answers a question about Medicare or foreign policy, it comes as a surprise to many that he can also be, well, such a goofball.

The first time he unveiled the new, updated campaign song on the presidential trail, in Iowa at a candidates' forum, the audience at first sat

---

[40]Mike Ollove, "The Turning Point," *Miami Herald*, December 9, 1984.
[41]Diane Hirth, "Necktie Rumor Gets Graham All Choked Up," *Fort Lauderdale Sun-Sentinel*, April 15, 1997.
[42]Brian E. Crowley, "Graham Shakes Off Campaign Cobwebs," April 20, 2003.

in stunned silence, then slowly began laughing and finally roared with enthusiasm.

To those who know him, the corny songs and the quirks are part of his core personality. How else, for instance, to explain his long friendship with Key West-by-way-of-Alabama singer Jimmy Buffett? The two have performed together at the Tallahassee Capitol Press Corps Skits during his governorship and occasionally sing together at Buffett's campaign appearances for Graham.

Graham said the relationship began in 1980, when daughter Suzanne, then thirteen, wanted to attend a Buffett concert at Florida State University. Graham took her and afterward went backstage to tell Buffett how much he enjoyed the show and in particular the song "Growing Older But Not Up."[43]

"I told him how much I enjoyed the song that has the line, 'sometimes I feel like an old manatee going south when the water gets colder.'"[44]

At the time, Graham was pushing for protection for the dwindling manatees, and he asked Buffett if he would join him as a cofounder of the Save the Manatee Club. Buffett accepted, and the two have been close since.

This has led to some awkward moments. There was Graham's appearance in Buffett's video of his song "Who's the Blonde Stranger?" in 1985, in which Graham has a cameo as a flower-shirted bar patron. Three years later, the video became a source of consternation for Michael Dukakis's campaign as they studied Graham as a potential vice-presidential nominee. But more generally there are the questions about what straight-laced Graham, the guy who brags about having signed into law a fifteen-year-minimum prison sentence for drug smuggling, is doing hanging around with Buffett, whose songs kind of glorify that lifestyle.[45]

---

[43]University of Florida Oral History Project, Tape P, November 11, 1995.

[44]From the 1981 classic *Coconut Telegraph*, the song actually goes: *Sometimes I see me as an old manatee / Heading south as the waters grow colder / He tries to steer clear of the hum drum so near / It cuts prop scars deep in his shoulders.*

[45]"A Pirate Looks at 40" from the album *A1A* goes: *I've done a bit of smugglin' / I've run my share of grass / I made enough money to buy Miami but I pissed it away so fast.* And how about "Mañana" from *Son of a Son of a Sailor: But women and water are in short supply / There's not enough dope for us all to get high / I hear it gets better, that's what they say / As soon as we sail on to Cane Garden Bay.* (This is not meant as a criticism. After all, the tune ends: *And I hope Anita Bryant never ever does one of my songs.*)

Graham answers that in a rather imaginative way. Raising money to run for the Senate in 1986, he told a Little Rock columnist:

"Some of the Capitol reporters in Tallahassee have actually suggested there's something wrong with my being friends with a man whose lyrics have sometimes been associated with drug smuggling. My response has been that if you listen carefully to the words of those songs, they decry and lament the lifestyle of those who engage in that sort of thing."[46]

Okay. Sure.

The oddness of this friendship became clear anew during the difficult summer of 2003, when Graham, who had never had any trouble raising money as a Senate candidate, struggled to stay solvent in the presidential derby.

One bright hope had been a promise from Buffett to hold a series of fundraising concerts, the biggest of which was to have been a mid-summer event in Tallahassee. Figure 15,000 attendees, netting a hundred dollars a pop, and Graham's money guys were pinching themselves: $1.5 million! In a single evening!

And then Buffett's people were told: Oh, by the way, every ticket buyer would have to disclose name, address, and occupation, as per federal campaign finance rules. The no-can-do message was relayed to Graham's campaign. Typical Buffett fans, it turns out, were going to be none too eager to fill out a form so the government could learn who they were and where to find them. So much for the $1.5 million.

Still and all, that Graham's big celebrity friend is Jimmy Buffett says something. Both men take their business seriously, but not necessarily themselves. Buffett has rarely gotten much respect in the music world, because his songs aren't about angst and gloom; notwithstanding this, his enduring popularity and business savvy have made him one of the wealthiest entertainers in history. Graham, likewise, has never gotten much respect outside of Florida, because he isn't flashy and telegenic; notwithstanding this, his enduring popularity and political savvy will no doubt put him very near the top of Florida's, well, noteworthy leaders in the history books.

Regardless of what anybody thinks of his notebooks.

---

[46]John Brummet, *Arkansas Democrat-Gazette*, June 13, 1986.

Los Hermanos Bush

On May 6, 2003, at a little after noon, delayed first by open-heart surgery, then out of deference to a war he had opposed, Bob Graham climbed a stage in downtown Miami Lakes and formally announced that he was entering the Democratic race for the right to challenge George W. Bush for the presidency of the United States.

The setting of the announcement was imbued with meaning. Forty-one years earlier, there had also been a makeshift platform and a sound system. Except there had been no surrounding town, just barren cow pasture. Only a tent protected the guests from the blazing sun as they listened to the Graham brothers announce their "New Town." Philip Graham, who two summers previously had helped forge the Kennedy–Johnson ticket, was his witty and urbane self. Bob, barely out of law school, had been studying for the bar.

Four decades later, Bob Graham talked about his family, and the town his family built, and the dairy he grew up on. In twenty-six minutes and 1,800 words, Graham explained why he was running. It was mainly about Bush:

The Bush Administration has reneged on America's promise and jeopardized our future. . . .

Instead of pursuing the most imminent and real threats to our future—terrorism—this Bush administration chose to settle old scores....

It is painfully clear the President has no economic policy other than tax cuts for the very wealthy....

He has talked the language of diversity and opportunity—but walked away from doing anything to promote them....

They have divided our nation between the few at the top whom they serve and the many who are left to fend for themselves with the moral equivalent of duct tape.

Those were the reasons Graham cited time after time when explaining why he ran: disgust with President Bush's policies on tax cuts, the economy, budget deficits, the environment—and finally, after September 11, his fixation with Iraq at the expense of pursuing the terrorists who actually *had* attacked America.

Friends and confidantes say this is as they anticipated it—Graham's growing frustration with George W. Bush, and the feeling that he could do better. They also suggest it was a matter of time, and the dwindling supply thereof: Graham, who had long thought he might someday run for president, no longer had an endless number of somedays.

November 9, 2003, marked his sixty-seventh birthday, meaning had he succeeded, he would have become—Ronald Reagan aside—the oldest man elected president. In 2008, he will be seventy-two, and in 2012, seventy-six. Obviously, the age question does not improve with time.

Just as important as what Graham said on May 6 was what was left unsaid: that he is from Florida. That he has won five statewide elections over the past quarter-century, receiving, on average, 61 percent of the vote.

In the six Florida elections contested by the various Bush men—father and both sons—they have averaged 52 percent of the vote. Only one showing even approached Graham's *average*: that of George H. W. Bush, who received 60.9 percent of the Florida vote in 1988 against Michael Dukakis.

In case anyone missed the implications, Graham spelled it out, literally, in subsequent campaign appearances: "I am from Florida. F-L-O-R-I-D-A," Graham would say as a prelude to his best applause line. "I will win Florida, and I won't need the United States Supreme Court to cast the last votes."

It was primarily for this reason that the moment Graham ended his bid for the presidency, his name was instantly "in play" for the vice presidency.

Of course, any discussion of the 2004 election must turn to the 2000 election in Florida. State Republican strategists complained that hard-core Democrats three years later were still upset about what happened, and they were right.[1] To activist Democrats, the Bush presidency is accidental at best, conceived by conspiracy at worst.

Curiously, during the thirty-six-day aftermath, one prominent voice that was not particularly loud was Bob Graham's. The attack-dog stuff was left to more aggressive types like Congressmen Peter Deutsch and Robert Wexler, while Graham pursued a more low-key approach.

It is important to remember here that Graham, unlike many of the punditocracy, actually believed Gore had a strong chance of winning the state.

The conventional wisdom was that, at the end, a state that had been putting Republicans into local and state offices would "come home" to support the brother of the popular governor. Graham, in an interview with his University of Florida biographer two weeks before the election,[2] declared that the conventional wisdom was wrong.

"I do not accept the premise that this is a Republican state. I would describe it as it is being called in October of 2000. It is a battleground state."[3]

Graham, in fact, believed that the Gore campaign should have considered the entire South, not just Florida, as an important battleground. "I think one of the several mistakes that Gore made during the campaign was they conceded the South as a region too early. I urged them, particularly in Georgia and in North Carolina, to be competitive there."[4]

The advantage of keeping Georgia in play is that the Atlanta media set the tone for coverage all over the region, so campaigning and advertising

---

[1] Republicans, however, must of all people appreciate the power of fermented anger. It was anger, even *hatred*, of Bill Clinton among a cadre of hard-core Republicans that sustained eight years of anti-Clinton activism and lawsuits.
[2] An interview, it should be noted, that Graham had no reason to believe would be reviewed by anyone until years later, if at all.
[3] University of Florida Oral History Project, Tapes U–V, October 24, 2000.
[4] University of Florida Oral History Project, Tapes W–X, January 26, 2001.

there produces benefits in neighboring states, including Florida. In the end, the decision was made to essentially abandon the South, with the exception of Florida, Graham said. In hindsight, a win in any one of the other southern states—say, Gore's home state of Tennessee, or Clinton's home state of Arkansas—would have made Florida irrelevant.

B ut at 7 P.M. on election night, Florida was very much relevant, particularly with Gore looking strong in places like Pennsylvania. It was clear that a Gore win in Florida would pretty much give him the election.

Graham was live on MSNBC with Brian Williams when the networks called Florida for Gore. On TV, Graham pumped his fist and gave the hints of a grin. "Congratulations, vice president Gore, soon to be president."[5]

Inside, Graham knew something was amiss. "I was both happy but somewhat mystified, because I thought it was awfully early to be calling the state," Graham recalled later.[6]

In the days and weeks to come, the Gore team settled on a strategy to ask for hand counts in those counties where it believed he would pick up the most votes. It was a strategy Graham opposed, pushing instead a plan backed by lawyer and Miami Lakes neighbor Aaron Podhurst to challenge the Palm Beach ballot as constitutionally deficient and demand a revote.

He compared the two approaches to the offensive styles of Ohio State's Woody Hayes—three yards and a cloud of dust—versus Florida's Steve Spurrier—a forty-yard pass to regain the lead. What Gore needed was the forty-yard pass: the 2,500 or so votes accidentally cast for Pat Buchanan in Palm Beach County, not six votes in this Dade precinct and eleven votes in that Broward precinct.[7]

"Bush had done a very effective job of saying that he was the president-

[5]MSNBC News Transcripts, "Decision 2000 Election Day special," November 7, 2000.
[6]University of Florida Oral History Project, Tapes W–X, January 26, 2001.
[7]A March 11, 2001, *Palm Beach Post* analysis also found that Gore likely lost some 8,238 "double-punched" (not counted at all) ballots in Palm Beach County: 5,330 voters punched the holes for Gore and Reform Party candidate Pat Buchanan (whose hole was just above Gore's) and 2,908 punched the holes for Gore and Socialist Party candidate David McReynolds (whose hole was just below Gore's). After subtracting similar "double-punched" ballots for Buchanan and Bush, Gore lost a net 6,607 "overvotes" in the county—more than twelve times the 537-vote official statewide margin.

elect and that Gore was the sore-loser man trying to contest that election, and over time the public was going to believe that characterization and it would make it increasingly difficult for Gore to continue to pursue what avenues were available to him. He needed to pick an avenue that would get him the number of votes he needed quickly," Graham said. "I was very frustrated at what I thought was a fully winnable vote-count process, not the strategy elected, but the one Podhurst was urging, and that they were not willing to pursue that. I think it was a big mistake."[8]

Ultimately, it came down to who wanted it more. And that was Bush and the Republicans.

"I think the basic thing in the post-vote ballot count—and I do not say this with a value tinge—the Republicans wanted to win more than the Democrats, and were prepared to do things to achieve that objective," Graham said. "For instance, it was just outrageous that they sent a group of political operatives from Washington to Miami, pretending or at least creating the impression that these were local citizens outraged at the fact that they could not observe counting. They clearly intended to intimidate the canvassing board and apparently were successful at that."[9]

But even after it was over and Bush was sworn in as the new president, Graham did not seem to harbor ill will toward him in particular or Republicans in general—even toward Katherine Harris, who he said made a serious mistake by not accepting the Palm Beach County hand count returns that came in shortly after her deadline but who, nevertheless, did not deserve the vilification she received in the press and *Saturday Night Live* and elsewhere.

Graham was almost philosophical about the election and the fact that it happened to have centered on his home state. "I do not think this is peculiar to Florida. The only thing that was peculiar is that we ended up with 537 votes out of 6 million separating the two presidential candidates, and therefore every vote and every imperfection was magnified."[10]

No, the ill will that Graham would show to the elder Bush brother in the

---

[8]University of Florida Oral History Project, Tapes W–X, January 26, 2001.
[9]*Ibid.*
[10]*Ibid.*

summer of 2003 was first presaged by the frustration and anger for the younger Bush brother that welled up in him in 2001 and 2002.

The issue for Graham then, as it so often is, was education.

A brief history: Florida's Board of Regents, charged with overseeing the state universities, came into being in 1965, one year before Graham ran for the Florida House of Representatives in 1966.

It came into being because the previous oversight board, the Board of Control, was not working. Each of Florida's universities wanted what the others had and it lacked, and the Board of Control didn't have the structure to manage the competing wants in a rational fashion. Would Florida, for example, really need a half-dozen different doctoral programs in early French literature?

The decades-old Board of Control was also unable to protect the schools from the legislature when such protection was necessary. Graham points to the Johns Committee, named after its founder, state senator, and, briefly, governor, Charley Johns. The group was a nasty little version of Senator Joe McCarthy's committee, going after "integrationists," then Communists, and finally homosexuals in the state colleges.

"For about ten years, it was a wrecking ball through the university system," Graham said.[11]

What was needed was a system that spoke with one voice for the universities as a group, with an institutional mission and memory that outlasted a governor's tenure (back then, a Florida governor could serve only a single, four-year term). And so, in a genuine act of reform came the Regents, modeled after the governing boards in other states. The Board of Regents would coordinate the schools' budgets and decide which programs would be offered at which institutions, in order to reduce duplication and waste. To help minimize political interference, regents would be appointed from certain geographic regions of the state, and terms were fixed at nine years. A governor therefore could appoint only some of a board in a first term—

---

[11]University of Florida Oral History Project, Tape Y, June 18, 2001.

governors were allowed a second term starting in 1966—and most of the board only by the latter half of the second term.

That was the creation of the Regents. Understanding the demise of the Regents means, regrettably, understanding Florida college football.

For decades, Florida State University had an inferiority complex about the one thing that Florida colleges *have* excelled at. This is understandable—until 1947, Florida State was a women's college (Florida was men only), which, given traditional gender roles, made fielding a competitive football program a bit tough.

Finally there came a time in the late 1980s and early 1990s when the statehouse came to be run by an actual Florida State Seminole, a wide receiver named T. K. Wetherell, who took it upon himself to right the most egregious wrong vis-à-vis the two schools' respective amenities—the quality of their football stadiums.

The Florida Gators played in "the Swamp," the nickname for Ben Hill Griffin Stadium. It was huge, a monument to football excess, which was scheduled for yet another upgrade. The poor Seminoles, meanwhile, were forced to play in Doak Campbell Stadium, which at the time wasn't even fully enclosed. Behind the south end zone were high-school-style bleachers. Wetherell decided that this injustice could not stand. By the time he finished his terms as house appropriations chairman and then speaker, Wetherell had diverted money from the universities construction fund—$40 million worth, with another $70 million coming from booster donations—to rebuild the stadium as a monument to himself.

To satisfy the requirement that actual classrooms be built with school construction money, the eight-story façade around the football field is filled with classrooms—classrooms arranged in an odd, oval-shaped perimeter, but classrooms nonetheless.[12]

---

[12]Wetherell, who later became president of FSU, had a gift for playing it fast and loose with the public's money. As budget chairman, he built up dozens of goodwill chits, transferring money from his particular hometown pork-barrel project, or "turkey," in Tallahassee parlance, to that of his fellow house members' turkeys. What a swell guy, they all thought, to give up money for Daytona's own Silver Beach dune restoration to fund these other worthwhile projects all over the state. Sure, he was a swell guy, except for one little thing: There *is* no Silver Beach. It is a street in Daytona. There are no dunes for miles around. Wetherell invented it out of whole cloth as a parking spot in the budget for his little slush fund.

This was seen as quite a coup by all the aspiring presiding officers. Suddenly, all the normal goodies that a speaker or a president could bring home—an auditorium, a courthouse, a road—were made passé. A *football* stadium! Now, *that* was setting the bar.

Six years later, a subsequent Florida State alumnus who became house speaker was determined to meet the challenge. John Thrasher took over the house as part of the first all-Republican statehouse, along with senate president Toni Jennings and Governor Jeb Bush, in 1999.

Now what could Thrasher—who was never a college football player but who had served as a lobbyist for the Florida Medical Association[13]—do to rival Wetherell's accomplishment? What remaining things of value did the University of Florida have that Florida State did not? . . .

Hey, how about a medical school? Now, *there* was a turkey that kept on giving! Medical schools cost hundreds of millions of dollars to build and then at least many tens of millions to operate, year after year after year. Thrasher's turkey would put Wetherell's to shame.

There was one slight problem. There simply was no need for a new medical school—a premise backed up by an exhaustive Board of Regents study. The Regents made it clear that they would not back down to Thrasher. So, for help, he turned to his buddy, Governor Jeb Bush.

It was at a restaurant in Orlando, in the autumn of 1999, that Florida's meddlesome Board of Regents was done away with.[14] Thrasher and Bush, enjoying a nice meal, chatting about education and universities and . . . say, Thrasher suggested, wouldn't Florida's higher education be better run if, instead of this unwieldy statewide board, the schools were each run by a local board of trustees?

Thrasher sketched out his scheme on a napkin: ten universities, ten

---

[13]Thrasher actually admitted to the State Commission on Ethics that he had lobbied for the FMA even after his election to the house in 1992. Despite this stain on his record, he handily won election as house speaker and later was made chairman of FSU's board of trustees. This is *Florida*, remember.

[14]Gary Fineout, "Higher Education in Turmoil," *Sarasota Herald-Tribune*, February 4, 2001.

boards of trustees, all answering to a Board of Education appointed by Bush that would deal with governance issues with only the broadest of brushstrokes. Jeb Bush eagerly bought into the concept. It sounded like a great way to "devolve" authority from "Mount Tallahassee" down to the local level—one of his campaign themes.

With Bush's blessing, Thrasher was able to ram his higher education reorganization plan through the legislature, thereby eliminating the Board of Regents. He also pushed through a bill creating a medical school at Florida State. Naturally, the black caucus and Hispanic caucus were ready to go ballistic if Thrasher was the only one to benefit from this. And so it came to be that to keep the peace, Florida now has two unnecessary new law schools in addition to its unnecessary new medical school.

Former Board of Regents spokesman Keith Goldschmidt probably put it best, in the waning days of his employment: "The Board of Regents determined there was no need for additional medical and law schools. But the legislature decided there was a need for those schools and there was no need for the Regents."

In the years since, some of the inherent drawbacks of local control of state colleges have become evident. Essentially, each local board decided it was running Harvard, and started doling out commensurate presidential salaries. Florida university presidents began seeing $50,000 and $100,000 raises—outraging parents and students whose tuitions had been rising steadily and faculty members whose salaries had not. The foundation of one school, middle-tiered Florida Atlantic University, even decided to buy its outgoing president a red Corvette.

The change in the university structure also had one other significant effect: It pissed off Bob Graham.

Up until that point, Graham had kept a low profile relative to the Bush brothers. In 1998, Graham had campaigned with Jeb's opponent, Buddy MacKay, sharing his friendship with Jimmy Buffett at several rallies (*"Some people claim that there's a wo-man to blame, but I know / It's all Jeb Bush's fault."*). But he got along well with Jeb after the election.

Ditto when it came to George W. When Graham was not chosen by

Gore as his running mate, he put in the obligatory campaign appearances expected of a senior senator of the opposition party, but it was nothing terribly dramatic. No one had ever accused Graham of behaving in a particularly partisan way, and with good reason.

All that changed with Jeb Bush's elimination of the Regents.

Graham tried the nice way first. He spoke with the governor, explaining why he thought a central board was not only a good idea but necessary for the long-term health of the university system. He talked to key state lawmakers. None of it did a bit of good. With little debate, Bush and his cronies rammed through "education reorganization" and did exactly as they pleased.

That, the attitude of *how* it was done, was as maddening to Graham as *what* was done, longtime aide Charlie Reed said. "He also knew that the only reason Bush did away with them was that he could," said Reed, whom Graham appointed as the State University System chancellor in 1985.

Graham realized that if anybody had the political muscle to challenge Bush, he did, and created a political action committee called "Education Excellence for Florida" to raise money and gather citizen petitions to put a referendum undoing Bush's action on the November 2002 ballot. Each school would be allowed to maintain its local board of trustees—which the campus-level administrators liked—but above those would be a new, overarching board to manage the system as a whole. In its first fifteen months, Graham's network quickly raised $1.1 million for the effort, more than enough to gather the 488,722 signatures needed for ballot approval.[15]

Graham, who rarely loses his cool in public, did so about this issue. At a January 15, 2002, meeting of the state's newspaper editors in Tallahassee, Graham raised his voice and even uttered, for him, the rare epithet "damned" in describing what Bush and the legislature had done. "In 2000, the Board of Regents issued some of their judgments, which the legislature didn't like. They didn't like the judgment about the medical school here at FSU, didn't like the judgment about law schools at FAMU and FIU," Graham said. "The legislature did two things. First, it rejected all of those recom-

---

[15]It ultimately raised $1.8 million, including $175,000 in loans from Graham's political committees and a $10,000 loan from Graham personally.

mendations. Second, it lined the Board of Regents up against the wall and machine-gunned them."[16]

The effort, technically known as Amendment 11, commonly became referred to as the Graham Amendment, and Jeb Bush lashed out against it loud and often. His supporters quickly formed their own political committee, the "Floridians for Education Reform," to raise money to defeat it. The university presidents were whipped into line (at that point, they essentially reported directly to Bush's Board of Education) and leaned on to make the necessary public pronouncements against the proposal, and the battle was on.

"They were furious, absolutely furious, that he would dare question their ability to do whatever they want," said Graham daughter Gwen Logan.

Graham and his longtime pals traveled the state and met with editorial boards, pushing the amendment. The governor and his buddies did the same, opposing it. In the end, it wasn't even close. Amendment 11 passed overwhelmingly, 61 percent–39 percent.[17] Bush, in contrast, won reelection by a thirteen-point margin over Democrat Bill McBride.

For Florida Democrats, who got skunked in the statewide races that year, the victories of the Graham Amendment and an amendment to reduce class size in public schools were the only bright spots from November. Okay, Democrats could argue, they did not have a great candidate against Jeb, and he got beat. But their *ideas* were better, obviously. The voters said they would trust Jeb Bush with four more years—but they had some specific instructions for him to follow.

Many Democrats also cheered Amendment 11 because it showed that in a *mano a mano* match-up between their champion, Graham, and the Republicans' champion, Jeb Bush, Graham had won handily.

In fairness to Bush, he wasn't really trying his hardest against Graham, instead pouring the bulk of his energy and outrage against Amendment 9, the class-size amendment. That one was pushed by the longtime thorn in

---

[16]Bill Cotterell, "Florida Governor, Senator Debate State Education Plan," *Tallahassee Democrat,* January 16, 2002.

[17]Coincidentally, the margin is identical to Graham's average margin of victories over his five statewide elections.

Jeb Bush's side, then state senator, now congressman Kendrick Meek,[18] and supported largely by parents fed up with budget cuts and class-size increases in the public schools. Bush railed long and hard against the amendment, arguing that its massive implementation costs would force tax increases.[19] His public campaign against the class-size amendment, in fact, at times seemed to exceed his efforts against Bill McBride.

The result was that the Graham Amendment did not get the heavy artillery aimed against it that was used on the class-size amendment. Bush's anti–Amendment 11 group wound up raising a total of $192,000, which in Florida is barely enough for a single day's worth of television ads around the state. And since it sounded like a common-sense reform based on the ballot summary, it passed.

"I'm glad the people of Florida, by better than a twenty-one-point spread, voted to restore a central board," Graham said of his victory, but then acknowledged that Bush, as governor, still held the cards. It is Bush, not Graham or his supporters, who appointed the members of that new board, which by mid-2003 had done little to actually take on the responsibilities given to it by the amendment. "I'm disappointed that the incumbent governor," said Graham, "has essentially ignored the wishes of the people, and this is, of course, not the first time that that has happened. But either in court, or with the election of the next governor, the people's will shall be implemented."

Graham also denies that Amendment 11 had anything to do with his run for president, saying that the latter was based completely on "national" factors. Still, what would a Graham presidential candidacy have looked like if, instead of winning Amendment 11, Graham had lost? One of Graham's major selling points was that he could carry Florida in a national election. How would he have sold that claim if he hadn't been able to win approval

---

[18]Meek was the instigator of the sit-in in Bush's office in January 2000 to protest his undoing of affirmative-action programs. Meek also organized a protest march that two months later brought 10,000 blacks to Tallahassee, and is credited with the voter registration drive that increased black voter turnout to record levels—which was what let Gore even come close to winning Florida. Had black turnout remained at the levels it had been in 1996 or 1992, Gore would have lost by 280,000 votes.
[19]It is a measure of voters' dissatisfaction with public education in Florida that it passed, Bush's attacks notwithstanding, albeit by a 52–48 margin.

for a reasonable-sounding constitutional amendment on which he'd invested so much political capital?

So give Graham the benefit of the doubt: His irritation with Jeb Bush over higher education in Florida and his decision to push Amendment 11 had nothing at all to do with his decision to challenge Jeb's brother. But a Graham presidential run would have lost all credibility had Graham's referendum been defeated.

In any event, it is clear that Graham's general irritation with *both* brothers was rising within a few months after George W. Bush took the oath of office.

Particularly on Graham's two signature issues, the environment and education, Graham was convinced as early as June 2001 that the Bush brothers would undo much of the progress of the past decades. George W. Bush's natural predilection, for example, was to allow oil drilling wherever possible, including the waters off Florida's tourist-friendly beaches and environmentally delicate estuaries, Graham said.

"This administration has defined its energy policy as being increased domestic production, a policy that I call the Drain America First policy. If you look around where there are places in America to drain by exploiting the oil and gas, the eastern Gulf of Mexico sort of stands out like a sore thumb of where there is a lot of potential and no drilling activity."[20]

He attributed the brothers' agreement not to permit drilling in the eastern Gulf of Mexico as a temporary concession to get them through their respective reelections.

"I think that means that probably as long as he is governor, there will not be a frontal attack, but I do not think we can depend upon the accident of sibling politics to protect us from what I think would be a major environmental and economic threat."[21]

Similarly, he slammed the Bush brothers' efforts to privatize the public schools using vouchers, but also saw the whole voucher issue as a distrac-

---

[20]University of Florida Oral History Project, Tape Y, June 18, 2001.
[21]University of Florida Oral History Project, Tapes U–V, October 24, 2000.

tion from the real problems schools are facing. "While we are debating vouchers, class sizes get bigger, the tidal wave of teacher retirements that are going to come in the next ten years goes unabated and unattended to, and we continue to fall behind other states in terms of technological enhancements in our schools."[22]

Graham said he was also upset by what he saw as the new president's cavalier attitude toward budget deficits that had taken the better part of three presidential terms to fix after Reagan created them in the early 1980s. Graham, again bucking the trend of timid congressional Democrats, voted against the first Bush tax cut of 2001 as well as the second round in 2003.

As he started his short-lived presidential campaign, those votes gave him the intellectual and moral authority to rail against them on the campaign trail, but it's a position that Graham has been thinking about for a while, as part of a political outlook that sees elderly voters "coming home" in greater numbers to the Democrats.

"Today, older Americans are among the best off of Americans. In the 1970s and 1980s, the Republicans did a very good job of latching on to the issue of security and creating in the minds of many older voters the idea that their security was threatened by government and excessive government taxes and that they, older voters, should vote for Republicans who pledged, regardless of anything else, that they would not raise your taxes. So you had a series of Republican candidates for governor, for the legislature, Congress, who in the first sentence of their announcement said, 'And I commit not to vote to raise taxes,'" Graham explained to his University of Florida biographer.

"Today, the threat of raising taxes is much less meaningful. In fact, the question is how much tax is going to be given back rather than taxes being raised. Substituting for taxes as a threat to security is rising health care costs and particularly prescription drug costs. I believe that the older voter is going to identify again with the Democratic Party as the party that did something about that challenge to security, and it will help to bring at least a plurality, if not a majority, of the older voters back to the Democratic Party."[23]

---

[22]*Ibid.*
[23]University of Florida Oral History Project, Tape Y, June 18, 2001.

L ike just about every elected official in the country, Graham refrained
from criticizing President Bush or any of the intelligence agencies in
the months following the terrorist attacks. "Our focus right now ought to
be on supporting the intelligence, law enforcement, and military effort
against terrorism," Graham said on October 22, 2001. "There will be plenty
of time to decide how to proceed in determining what occurred before,
during, and after September 11. Now is not that time."[24]

It was not long afterward, though, that Graham began finding serious
flaws—and what he considered grave dangers—in Bush's handling of terrorism.

Instead of continuing the pursuit of al Qaeda, the Bush White House
decided instead to go after Saddam Hussein while the going was good. But
to do this, Graham charged, meant pulling troops and intelligence analysts
and spies out of Afghanistan—where Osama bin Laden was still likely hid-
ing out—to concentrate on Iraq.

During much of 2002, the thought of challenging Bush remained at the
back of Graham's mind. Adele Graham says he wanted to finish the Intelligence Committee report on the September 11 attacks before giving the
idea of a presidential run serious consideration. On November 5, the elections were over. The Senate had gone back to the Republicans. Amendment 11 had passed easily in Florida. On December 10, the Intelligence
Committee report was completed.

Graham began to make inquiries. What would it take to get into the
race? John Kerry and Howard Dean were already campaigning and raising
money. Joe Lieberman was a likely candidate, as were Richard Gephardt
and John Edwards. What consultants were available? How much would a
credible run need? Did he have enough time? Was it already too late?

On Friday, December 13, 2002, ABCNews.com's "The Note" carried the
following unattributed tidbit: "For those of you [who] think the Democratic nomination field is pretty set, what would you say if you heard that Sen-

---

[24]Larry Lipman, "Graham: Now Not Time to Probe Intelligence Flaws," *Palm Beach Post*, October 23,
2001.

ator Bob Graham of Florida had initiated some 'serious discussions' with people about whether he might put together a strong 2004 presidential campaign?"

The *St. Petersburg Times* reported on "The Note" report on December 14. A number of other papers carried the story the following week. The *Miami Herald* cited unnamed insiders who said a Graham bid was "unlikely."

On Monday, December 23, Graham appeared on WRHB, Radio Carnivale, Miami's largest Haitian radio station, as one of the morning talk-show hosts. It was his 385th "workday." He had taken calls from listeners, explained his views on Haitian immigration—all of it punctuated with a high-pitched *"Wheeeeeeeeee!"* sound effect to reward positive remarks—when the conversation turned toward how Graham believed the country was headed in the wrong direction. The host of the program kept egging Graham on: Then why don't you run? Why don't you run?

Finally, Graham said he would seriously consider it, thus becoming the first presidential candidate in history to announce an intention to get into the race on Haitian-American radio. From the study of their Miami Lakes town house, Adele listened as the host responded with the sound effect: *"Wheeeeeeeeee!"*

The Graham for President campaign was behind the eight ball from day one. There were many reasons, including Graham's rustiness on the trail as well as, possibly, some lingering fatigue from the heart surgery he underwent in January that cost him six weeks of campaigning time.[25]

There was also the almost uniform sneer he received from the national press. This he should have expected. With five serious candidates already in the running, the political press corps already had its requisite drama—the favorites of the Democratic "base" versus the pragmatic centrists versus the dark horse. All Graham was doing by jumping in was creating more

---

[25]Graham had known for years that the aortic valve in his heart was deteriorating and would eventually need replacement. It was during the intensive physical examination he underwent prior to formally getting in the race that it was realized the valve had reached a point where it needed surgery sooner rather than later.

work: yet another campaign profile to be done, plus a trip down to Miami at an inconvenient time of year. A jaunt in January would have been a welcome change from the slush of New York and Washington. But a trip in May? What was the benefit to that? The weather was already nice up north, and already unpleasantly steamy in Miami Lakes.

And so when Graham set up his platform to announce his candidacy, the national media grudgingly came down to cover it. The tone of the write-ups was predictable—droll and supercilious.

By midsummer, the Graham for President campaign included two dozen staffers in a corner suite of the three-story Main Street building occupied by the Graham Companies and the corporate offices of Don Shula's Steak Houses. Field offices had been established in New Hampshire, Iowa, South Carolina, and Oklahoma, with finance directors on board in New York, California, New Hampshire, and Iowa.

Still, there was little if any movement in the first big tests of Iowa and New Hampshire. Polls in both states showed Graham at about one percent, and the Graham campaign started focusing on states where his moderate record and message—"I'm from the electable wing of the Democratic Party"—might have more appeal, like South Carolina, Oklahoma and Virginia.

Certainly, Graham's innate caution, which served him well as a governor and a lawmaker, didn't necessarily help him make his case among Democratic primary voters. They wanted red meat, and Graham was more likely to give them medium to well-done, with the fat carefully trimmed away.

Watch how four candidates attacked President Bush in the summer of 2003 over the use of bad intelligence regarding Iraq's attempts to get uranium ore.[26] Bear in mind that this had been Graham's signature issue for the previous months—that Bush was dishonest, indeed "Nixonian," in his dealings with the American people.

Here is John Kerry, saying precisely that: "The problem is not just the wrong direction in which George Bush has led us, it's that he has misled us time and time again."

---

[26]Foxnews.com, "Dems Switch Gears, Attack President Rather Than Each Other," July 14, 2003.

Richard Gephardt brought it back to a Missouri local hero: "Here's the president of the United States saying 'Wasn't my fault, it's somebody else's fault. It's [CIA Director] George Tenet's fault, it's the CIA's fault.' Well, you know we had a president from Missouri called Harry Truman, and he had a sign on his desk that says, 'The buck stops here.' I think Bush needs to get that sign back on his desk."

Howard Dean managed to invoke the specter of Nixon: "We need to know what he knew and when did he know it."

And this is how Graham, who owned the issue, put it: "The President knew, or had every opportunity to know, that this information was false. Therefore, it was very inappropriate and deceitful to include that in a State of the Union speech."

Graham was more precise, more accurate, more logical—but far less rousing.

Longtime friend and Senate Democratic colleague Jay Rockefeller said Graham's reluctance to oversimplify his thoughts was a predictable barrier in a crowded Democratic field that had "nine people running, nobody listening."

Snappy sound bites that often state a viewpoint with more force and less nuance are simply not Graham's style, Rockefeller said. "Every instinct within him rebels against the need to spout off."

As to Graham's decision to drop out, that added more evidence to Rockefeller's suspicion that America's grueling process of selecting a president is imperfect at best. "Is there a relationship between who catches on and who ought to catch on? I'm not convinced there is."

Despite the negative articles, the difficulty raising money, the lack of respect from the Gang of 500, Graham still managed to have fun on the presidential campaign trail. Frequently, he would burst out with his new, improved campaign song with its national-election-friendly modifications. Other times, he would show his ability to match wits with and best smart-aleck reporters.

After the obligatory appearance at a Politics and Eggs breakfast in Bedford, New Hampshire, a local ABC affiliate reporter started ribbing Graham about the tradition of signing wooden eggs as mementos for audience members. Graham affably told him that it was important to start the signature at the pointy side, as it was much easier to finish with a flourish on the fat end than the pointy end. The reporter persisted, and Graham gave it right back to him, grabbing the microphone away and turning the tables on the interview:

> GRAHAM: Are you an expert in signing eggs?
>
> REPORTER: *(flustered)* I am not. Bacon, though, I have signed some strips of bacon.
>
> GRAHAM: What did you learn from signing strips of bacon? What would you say are some of the special challenges?
>
> REPORTER: I'd say that anyone who's running for president should not sign bacon. An egg, a wooden egg, is a, you know, a lot easier. Plastic bacon, perhaps.
>
> GRAHAM: What about asparagus? Or broccoli?
>
> REPORTER: Broccoli's bad. I mean, I guess Democrats might like broccoli. I know Republicans don't. *(more flustered)* Is this one of your workdays, here?
>
> GRAHAM: This is Channel Nine, where we bring you *all* the news.

The more confident Graham got, the more he brought out the dry wit that has won over audiences in Florida for a quarter-century. Asked a question about global warming by an environmentalist, Graham was able to turn it into a plug for his home state's tourism bureau.

"Florida is a very flat, low state," he told the Politics and Eggs audience. "And even a modest increase in sea levels as a result of the change in the composition of the glaciers above the Arctic would have a dramatic effect on Florida. In fact, I would encourage everyone here, as a means of assuring themselves that during their lifetime they could experience Florida as it is, to go quickly."

The more he campaigned, the better Graham got at converting his main themes into the snappy sound bites that would get better play on the evening news. For instance, this was how he originally started out presenting his concern about increasing federal deficits:

"We have not had a tradition of one group of Americans avoiding their financial responsibilities by off-loading onto their children and grandchildren. I am afraid that we may be on the verge of doing so."

Then he would go into the birth years of his father, himself, his eldest daughter, and his youngest grandchild to demonstrate the exponential increase in the per-capita national debt over the last generation. In 1885, every American's share of the national debt was $33. By 1936, the year Graham was born, the figure was $264. By 1963, the amount was $1,634. But by 2000, the figure was $20,163. "You have probably read the stories in the paper over the last few days that 2003 will be the largest deficit in the history of America—$455 billion. That's a $455 billion deficit on a total federal expenditure of approximately $2 trillion, so we're running close to 25 percent red ink."[27]

After some time on the trail, Graham managed to boil even that issue down to a TV-friendly nugget. After days of the above explanation, Graham debuted this two-liner before a small group of supporters at a Des Moines coffeehouse:

"If you're in a hole the first thing you do is to stop digging. We're in a hole but it looks like what George W. is doing is asking for more shovels."[28]

Certainly one advantage for the other Democrats to having Graham on the campaign trail was his daily attacks on President Bush for his handling of the wars on terrorism and Iraq. Graham, both because he had chaired the Senate Intelligence Committee and because he had, unlike the other Senators running for president, voted against the war with Iraq, had the credibility to criticize Bush. Doing so paved the way for the others. With Graham hammering Bush for ignoring "Osama bin Forgotten," the other Democrats could say such things, too.

In mid-July 2003, in the wake of the Niger uranium flap, Graham pointed out that President Bush's veracity problem made President Clinton's seem almost inconsequential.

---

[27]Graham, at the end of his talk, said he had done the initial math hastily in his head and offered his New Hampshire audience this footnote: "I would correct it to 23 percent."

[28]Amy Lorentzen, "Graham Pushes Economic Plan," Associated Press, July 19, 2003.

"If you look at the standard for impeachment that was set by the Republican House of Representatives for President Clinton, if that's the new standard, then I believe that the actions of President Bush are a more serious transgression of presidential power," Graham said. "If the president knew or should have known that important parts of his argument for going to war with Iraq were unfounded, that is a very serious transgression by the president of the United States of America. It is a transgression that not only reduces his credibility, it reduces the credibility of the United States of America in the world."

The charge, once again, broke new ground for the Democratic candidates.

As National Public Radio's Bob Edwards observed in July 2003: "All the Democratic presidential candidates have been getting bolder in their attacks on President Bush's handling of the war against Iraq, but one has led the way. Florida senator Bob Graham was the last candidate to get into the race, but the former chairman of the Intelligence Committee was the first and the most aggressive in his criticism of the President. He accuses the President of mishandling the war on terrorism, manipulating intelligence about Iraq, and covering up Bush administration failures before September 11."[29]

The many times in the past when Graham has *not* run for higher office, he and his family have denied there was any disappointment or even that he has any long-range goals.

"I believe, too—and Bob does very strongly—that you should not spend the time right now planning for something down the road. That you need to do what you are doing right now and enjoy it," Adele Graham told the *Palm Beach Post* in 1992—after 1978 governor, class cohort Bill Clinton, locked up the Democratic presidential nomination.[30]

"He thinks everything works out as it should. It doesn't do any good to wonder about what might have been," daughter Gwen Logan said.

---

[29]Mara Liasson, "Senator Bob Graham Campaigning for President," NPR's *Morning Edition*, July 28, 2003.
[30]Larry Lipman, "Graham: White House a 'Great Opportunity,'" *Palm Beach Post*, May 16, 1992.

Graham's family appeared to have a realistic idea of a presidential run. It is so big, and so unwieldy—and success so dependent on so many circumstances beyond their control—that it seemed to be implicitly understood that even their best efforts might not, in the end, prove enough.

Adele Graham, his wife of almost forty-five years, knew the uncertainties well—the risk that months and months of work, of keeping absurd schedules and rarely seeing each other or the grandchildren, of incurring the wrath of the Bush Brothers' political machine, could ultimately go for naught.

"We understand that," she said of all the downsides, but added that not to have run would ultimately have been worse. "I think he's been thinking about running for president, off and on, for a number of years. . . . Not to try, and not to give it your all, would be such a disappointment."

If nothing else, Graham's run for the presidency finally answered his critics who have for so long railed against him for not having risked enough or accomplished enough.

It has been a somewhat unfair critique—akin to chiding a solid laboratory researcher for not yet having come up with the cure for cancer. A presidential run is always a risky thing. At the end of it is only one winner, and the road along the way is littered with losers. Losers who are quickly reminded that the country takes a dim view of their kind, and that there was little nobility to unsuccessfully fighting the good fight.

The carpers also forget that Graham already took an enormous gamble a quarter-century ago when, at age forty-one, he spent about a third of his net worth on his longest-shot bid for governor. For an entire year, he slogged through, despite nonexistent poll numbers and support. How many of Graham's critics have spent one of every three dollars to their name, and a full year of their life, on something as improbable?

Such, though, have been the expectations.

It's as if after finally finding someone as decent and as smart as Graham in Florida politics, there could be no satisfaction until he had reached for the pinnacle, even if it was beyond his grasp.

Separate from this is the question of Graham's legacy, and this is a lot simpler.

For this is a guy who, for going on four decades, has hung around in government because he thought it was important. By Florida's dismal standards for elected officials, certainly, Graham's record is remarkable.

So many Florida politicians get into the game as a way to boost their outside businesses. To have one come along like Graham, who has knowingly and purposefully *forgone* many millions of dollars over the years to serve in public office, is both astonishing and refreshing. For that is easily today's value of the shares in the family business Graham cashed in twenty-five years ago to finance his governor's campaign, not to mention the money he could have made actively working at Miami Lakes rather than remaining in office.

From the actual accomplishments of his tenure—the massive funding boosts for education,[31] the new environmental programs, the Everglades restoration project—to the manner in which he got them done, with a genuine belief in Florida's open meetings and public records laws that other officials so frequently flout, Graham has won the respect and admiration of most of the journalists who have covered him and the voters who continue to reelect him.

Most telling in this regard is the Republican Party's two decades of frustration in dealing with him.

Republicans, time after time, have tried to psych themselves up to the idea that they can finally beat Graham because Floridians like Graham but do not seem to know why. Republicans view this as continuing goodwill built from his days as governor, buttressed maybe by the workdays, but something that nonetheless can be overcome.

But Republicans have been only half right about this. It is true that much of Graham's support is based on his being a nice guy who has been around forever. But a key part of that, the part that Republicans willfully ignore, is that Floridians seem to trust him to do the right thing and to do right by Florida.

---

[31]Which, alas, wound up being transitory. In subsequent administrations, education got smaller increases and, during two recessions, actually saw reductions.

No, he never had the ability to articulate an overarching vision for his leadership, and, yes, some of his habits are a bit odd, and it's true that not all Floridians have agreed with all of his positions on the issues. Still, particularly given the state's tradition of inept and self-aggrandizing elected leaders, the real question is whether Floridians are better off or worse off that Bob Graham entered politics.

On this one, the answer is easy: The populace could have done—and over the years, *has* done—a lot worse. Floridians were lucky to have him.

Appendix A

WE'VE GOT A FRIEND IN BOB GRAHAM

We've got a friend in Bob Graham,
That's what everybody's sayin'
All the way from Key West town to Tampa Bay.
From good ol' Pensacola, Jacksonville, down to Daytona,
Bob Graham is what Florida needs today!

Bob Graham is a cracker,
Be a Graham Cracker Backer!
Vote the man who will make Florida work again!

Appendix B

LIFE UNDER THE MICROSCOPE

By Bob Graham

This essay originally appeared April 17, 2003, in Bill Adair's campaign journal on the St. Petersburg Times' *Web log. It is the result of presidential candidate Graham's irritation with the traveling Florida press corps, who were not taking advantage of his suggested leads for their articles.* Times *reporter Adair told Graham that if he thought he could do better, Adair would lend him his laptop computer on the flights from San Francisco back to Boston. This is what Graham wrote:*

Always pushing, always present, the political reporter uses his special access to degrade, manipulate and attempt to humiliate the earnest candidate, striving to serve his fellow citizens. My hope is to take you where the bacterium lies naked for observation, analysis and, ultimately, evisceration.

This is the campaign from the candidate's end of the microscope.

Observation One:

As the squirmy virus would attest, it is no fun laying out on a cold glass surface where even your most gracious acts of kindness are misconstrued. When unexpectedly met at the airport by a stretch limousine, was the offer to the reporters to join in the ride to downtown seen as attentive hospitality? No way. It was yet another opportunity to harass the candidate with dull questions, which had previously been turned away with humor and goodwill. It was another opportunity to snidely comment about the luxury of the limousine while avariciously taking advantage of its offerings, from the tangible wet bar to the escapism into the exaggerated memories of high school proms. As the interrogators, failing to accept the truthful and, if I do say so myself, rather elegant answers to their questions, the probing went on:

Q. Are you going to run for re-election?

A. No, you eternal pessimist, I am going to be the President of the United States of America (and you are not).

Q. Don't you think you started the campaign too late?

A. Too late? With my intellect, wit, presence, and charm, it is the affection of the crowd, not the time on the calendar, which counts (you are just mad because you missed a few weeks of using your rich corporation's credit card).

Observation Two:

In the eighteenth-floor condominium overlooking downtown Los Angeles, an overflow of adulative, potentially high-finance supporters listened in rapt attention to the candidate. Their interest and level of commitment was indicated by their numerous and effusive rounds of applause, as well as the star status accorded to the candidate. But was this the way in which the scene was written for the reporters' diminishing handful of readers? No way. The most minor verbal slips were given elephantine scale: OK, so the reportee could not articulate a response to the question of what would you do about the national deficit; his mind is clearly on issues of greater importance (How can I get away from these guys tonight?). The one or two guests who had a discouraging word were elevated to be representative of the totality of the adoring audience: Why was he wearing the U.S. Flag tie? I came to see the handsome Florida tie (picky, picky, picky).

Observation Three:

Does a transcontinental air flight, with its distance from an intruding telephone and the respect of other passengers for privacy, afford an unusual opportunity to get serious public policy work accomplished? No way? Like Tom Sawyer's friends and the whitewashed fence, this candidate has become the newest columnist for the *St. Petersburg Times*. While the high-profile, luxuriously paid reporter rests and takes advantage of the airline's amenities, the candidate is subjected to a request to write the soon-to-be-slumbering journalist's column. While the opportunity to provide readers with a valuable insight into the soft underbelly of political journalism is appealing, the loss of the insights which would have been produced for the public good (what would I do about the deficit?) is temporarily lost as the reporter seeks only his personal pleasures.

And as the bacterium turns over to accept its fate, so does the candidate.

At least that is the way I would have written it. Sleep on, Bill.

Appendix C

THE "BLOOD ON YOUR HANDS" SPEECH

Remarks to the United States Senate regarding an amendment to the resolution authorizing use of military force against Iraq. Delivered October 9, 2002, largely extemporaneously, with notes but without a formal text. Graham's amendment would have given President George W. Bush the authority to attack terrorist training camps in other nations besides Iraq. After Graham's speech, and on a procedural motion by Arizona senator John McCain, Graham's amendment was defeated on a roll-call vote. The Senate the following day, October 10, voted to give President Bush the authority to attack Iraq. Graham voted against that resolution.

Mr. President,[1] I appreciate the thoughtful remarks of the senator from Connecticut and the senator from Arizona. The senator from Arizona concluded with the hope that we may soon be working together on expanding our capacity to reach those who threaten us here at home. I only hope that we will not have

---

[1] When used in the direct-address form, "President" in this speech refers to the president of the Senate. The presiding officer at the time of Graham's speech was Georgia Democrat Zell Miller. In the third-person usage, it refers to President George W. Bush.

another 3,025 Americans unnecessarily exposed to the risks that I see if we do not supplement this resolution with the immediate authority of the president to use force against these organizations which have access to weapons of mass destruction, which have killed Americans, and which have substantial numbers of operatives inside the United States of America at this hour. I would defy anybody to say that Iraq meets *those* standards.

We're not talking about a threat ninety days from now. We're not talking about a threat that may come a year from now if nuclear material is made available. *I'm* talking about a threat that can happen this *afternoon!*

Let us trace the history of what Congress did. The president asked for this authority on September 12, 2001. We denied it.

Now, when I went to law school, you read the legislative history to try to arrive at legislative intent. It seems to me that that says, just as a first-year-law legislative interpretation, that we probably didn't mean to give the president authority beyond that which is specifically provided. And therefore, the president of the United States, in my judgment, does *not have* the authority today to use force against Hezbollah and these other groups.

But even beyond the legalisms, let's talk about the pragmatics. The president of the United States in his State of the Union Address, January 29, said our first priority was terrorism—our *first* priority. And do you know what the first priority of the first priority was? The *training camps!* And *why* did he say that? Because those who were responsible had said if there was one major mistake we made in the 1990s, it was allowing al Qaeda's training camps to be a sanctuary where every year thousands—*thousands!*—of young people were converted into hardened assassins.

Well, Mr. President, if that's the criticism that we're going to have, because in the 1990s we allowed that to go on month after month, year after year, what is going to be our excuse *today*—when similar training camps are in operation in Iran, Syria, Syrian-controlled areas of Lebanon! And we are not going to give the president of the United States the authority to use force against those camps! It is inconceivable to me. The very fact that the president, recognizing this, has not acted against those camps is, in my judgment, the strongest verification that *he* doesn't think he has the authority to do so.

Mr. President, I believe that it is not in our national interest to leave this question ambiguous. We want to deter groups like Hezbollah from continuing to aid—to provide aid, comfort, and support to their operatives who are placed in the United States. Until we reach the point that we can domestically, through law-enforcement means and domestic intelligence, locate and eradicate those operatives who are in this country, we must pursue as aggressively as possible the second track, which is to cut off their support system.

I cannot believe that we are saying that we are not prepared today to make an unambiguous—we don't want to have the Hezbollah going to their lawyers and asking the question "What is the legislative interpretation of what the Congress did on September the 18, 2001? Does it put us under the gun or not?" *I* don't want them to have that question in their minds. I want them to know, in the clearest method that we can write in English, and that it can be interpreted in all the languages that these people speak, that we mean they are under the gun, and they are under the gun *now*.

Now, why? There has been a lot of discussion about urgency. Why do we need to do things now? Why can't we wait sixty days?

Let me tell you why I don't think we can afford to wait. We are taking an action by authorizing the president to take action against Saddam Hussein—and I will stand first in line to say he is an evil person. But we, by taking that action, according to our own intelligence reports—and, I will tell you, friends, and I would encourage you to read the classified intelligence reports, which are much sharper than what is available in declassified form—we are going to be *increasing* the threat level against the people of the United States. I think we have a moral and legal obligation to, at the same time, be taking what reasonable steps we can to confront that increased vulnerability.

If you don't like what I'm suggesting, if you don't think we ought to give the president the authority to use force against groups like Hezbollah, what *do* you think we ought to do? Or do you disagree with the premise that we're going to be increasing the threat level inside the United States? And if you disagree with that premise, what is the basis upon which your disagreement is predicated?

If you reject that, and think that the American people are not going to be at additional threat, then, frankly, my friends—to use a blunt term—the blood's going to be on *your* hands. I think we *are* going to be at substantially greater threat. I think there are some things we ought to be doing now. We certainly should be escalating the FBI and intelligence and other forces' efforts to root out the terrorists who are among us. But we also ought to be attacking the terrorists where they live, because it is on the offensive—not the defensive—in my judgment, that we are going to eventually win this war on terror.

So, my friends, as I said earlier, I am not optimistic about the adoption of this. I recognize there were backroom deals made; this is what people have come together, locked down on, and said: We are locking down on the principle that we have *one* evil, Saddam Hussein. He is an enormous, gargantuan force, and that's who we're going to go after.

That, frankly, is an erroneous reading of the world. There are many evils out there, a number of which are substantially more competent, particularly in their ability to attack Americans here at home, than Iraq is likely to be in the foreseeable future.

But we are going to say: We're going to ignore those and we are going to allow them to continue to fester among us. I do not wish to be part of that decision. I am concerned—I am concerned by those who see only one evil, who feel that we must all commit ourselves to the arrangement that has been made by a few to that view of the world. I urge my colleagues to open their eyes to the much larger array of lethal, more violent foes who are prepared today to assault us here at home.

Mr. President, I said in my closing remarks that I was concerned and saddened. I am saddened because I know that my colleagues would not knowingly place U.S. lives in unnecessary peril. As assured as I have ever been of anything in my life, the peril here in America caused by the action that we are about to take could be substantially reduced by giving to the president of the United States the additional power to send the strongest possible message, and, if necessary, the force to eradicate those who are evil and who have placed evildoers among us, and who are prepared to awaken those evildoers to attack.

The responsibility is ours.

Thank you, Mr. President.

Bibliography

As is the case with most contemporary politicians, the vast majority of what has been written about Bob Graham is contained within many thousands of newspaper, magazine, and wire-service articles dating back to his years in the Florida legislature in the late 1960s and 1970s. Taken as a whole, they provide the nuts-and-bolts framework of Graham's public life, from what he said on a given day, to why he vetoed a particular bill, to the social and economic context to his actions. All praise to the front-line journalists. As Philip Graham once said, they really are writing the first draft of history (as ludicrous as that might at times appear).

Among the stacks of articles, these bring Graham and those closest to him to life in the reader's mind:

Adair, Bill. "Dress in Gray Suit, Discuss CIA, Mingle," *St. Petersburg Times*, February 23, 2003.

———. "In Race for Senate, a Battle of Opposites," *St. Petersburg Times*, October 12, 1998.

Bridges, Tyler. "Strategy Changed Him from Shy Policy Wonk to Popular Politician," *Miami Herald*, April 27, 2003.

Cerabino, Frank. "Country Boy to 'Workday' Politician," *Palm Beach Post*, May 4, 2003.

———. "Graham Goes from Governor to Senator," *Palm Beach Post*, May 4, 2003.

Dahl, David. "Graham: Mr. Inside on the Outside," *St. Petersburg Times*, October 13, 1991.

Groer, Anne. "Teflon Bob," *Orlando Sentinel*, January 8, 1995.

Grunwald, Michael. "Running Scared," *Washington Post*, May 4, 2003.

Ollove, Mike. "The Turning Point," *Miami Herald*, December 9, 1984.

Peterson, Bill. "The Kingmaker of the 30-Second Spot: Robert Squier, Political Image-Maker on a Winning Streak," *Washington Post*, November 27, 1979.

Poppe, David. "Man in the Middle," *Florida Trend*, June 1996.

Silva, Mark, and Tamara Lytle. "He Has Been Long Shot Before," *Orlando Sentinel*, April 20, 2003.

———. "The Making of Bob Graham," *Orlando Sentinel*, April 20, 2003.

There are not many books that mention Graham or his family. Here, though, are six:

Graham, Bob. *Workdays*, Banyan Books, Miami, 1978.

Graham, Katharine. *Personal History*, Alfred A. Knopf, New York, 1997.

Halberstam, David. *The Powers That Be*, Alfred A. Knopf, New York, 1979.

Morris, Allen. *The Florida Handbook*, Peninsular Publishing Co., Tallahassee, 1971, 1973, 1975, 1981, 1987.

White, Theodore H. *The Making of the President, 1964*, Atheneum, New York, 1965.

Von Drehle, David. *Among the Lowest of the Dead*, Times Books, New York, 1995.

Bob Graham's campaign book, *Workdays*, provides some telling insights into the man. Even the minutiae that fill sections of it, of course, say something about its author. Allen Morris's handbooks provide terrific primers on Florida politics through the years, and include lengthy sections detailing the state's history. White's book includes an appendix written by Philip Graham to set down, for the record, his role in persuading the Kennedy brothers to choose Johnson at the

1960 convention in Los Angeles. And finally, the masterfully done Von Drehle book: Sections of this work recount and explain in vivid detail Governor Graham's role in reinstituting the American death penalty. However, the book is so well done, and so compelling, that it ought to be read for its own sake.

Finally, the single best resource on Bob Graham: the thirty hours of audiotapes compiled by University of Florida historian Samuel Proctor. Professor Proctor, who taught Graham as an undergraduate, persuaded Graham to participate in his oral history project of famous Floridians after Governor Graham became Senator Graham and left Tallahassee for Washington. Most of Proctor's subjects put their lives on tape in about six hours. Graham has already quintupled that standard. The tapes, A through Y, were recorded between February 13, 1989, and June 18, 2001.

Index

About the Author

Shirish V. Dáte has covered Florida politics for a decade for the *Orlando Sentinel*, the Associated Press, and the *Palm Beach Post*. The author of the novels *Final Orbit, Black Sunshine, Deep Water, Smokeout,* and *Speedweek,* he lives in Tallahassee with his wife and their two sons. For more information on Dáte, go to his website at svdate.com.